The Rise of China-U.S. International Cooperation in Higher Education

Spotlight on China

VOLUME 5

The titles published in this series are listed at *brill.com/spot*

The Rise of China-U.S. International Cooperation in Higher Education

Views from the Field

Edited by

Christopher J. Johnstone and Li Li Ji

BRILL

SENSE

LEIDEN | BOSTON

All chapters in this book have undergone peer review.

Library of Congress Cataloging-in-Publication Data

Names: Johnstone, Christopher J., editor. | Ji, Li-Li, editor.
Title: The rise of China-US international cooperation in higher education :
  views from the field / edited by Christopher J. Johnstone and Li Li Ji.
Other titles: Rise of China-United States international cooperation in higher
  education
Description: Leiden, The Netherlands ; Boston, MA : Brill Sense, 2018. |
  Series: Spotlight on china ; Volume 5 | Includes bibliographical
  references.
Identifiers: LCCN 2018007035 (print) | LCCN 2018011268 (ebook) | ISBN
  9789004368361 (E-book) | ISBN 9789004368354 (hardback : alk. paper) | ISBN
  9789004368347 (pbk. : alk. paper)
Subjects: LCSH: Educational exchanges--United States. | Educational
  exchanges--China. | Education, Higher--International cooperation. | United
  States--Relations--China. | China--Relations--United States.
Classification: LCC LB2376.3.C6 (ebook) | LCC LB2376.3.C6 R57 2018 (print) |
  DDC 378.1/04--dc23
LC record available at https://lccn.loc.gov/2018007035

Typeface for the Latin, Greek, and Cyrillic scripts: "Brill". See and download: brill.com/brill-typeface.

ISSN 2542-9655
ISBN 978-90-04-36834-7 (paperback)
ISBN 978-90-04-36835-4 (hardback)
ISBN 978-90-04-36836-1 (e-book)

Contents

Acknowledgements

This book would not have been possible without the editorial support of Laura Seithers and Yilin Wei. It was a joy to work with these scholars toward the development of this book.

CHAPTER 1

The Rise of Sino-U.S. International Partnerships in Higher Education: An Introduction

Christopher J. Johnstone

This book provides a unique focus in the *Spotlight on China* book series published by Brill | Sense. In the following chapters, authors (scholars, leaders, and practitioners) will describe the theoretical and practical implications of partnerships between higher education institutions in the U.S. and China. Over the past several decades, thousands of institutional collaborative agreements have been signed between Chinese and U.S. higher education institutions. The results are far-reaching. Student mobility between the two nations is at an all-time high, collaborative research is emerging, and international branch campuses can be found in both China and the U.S.

This book seeks to take stock of these historic events through the voices of those engaged in process. Our book starts, however, with a theoretical exploration. In the next chapter, Rui Yang of Hong Kong University provides readers with an overview of China's soft power approach through higher education. Following Yang's overview, Katherine Punteney and Yilin Wei provide an overview of the dynamics shaping internationalization of higher education in both China and the U.S. Chapter 4 provides a starting point for the scholar-practitioner contributions to this book. These contributions begin with Anthony Ogden and Huajing Xiu Maske's descriptions of how Confucius Institutes have been used to leverage international exchange at the University of Kentucky. In Chapter 5 Deane Neubauer and Joanne Taira (University of Hawai'i) chronicle the development of a multi-national research partnership founded at their university. Anne D'Angelo and Lili Dong then explore collaboration through the lens of Business Education. In their chapter "Internationalization 2.0 and Counting," the authors describe a collaborative between the University of Minnesota and Lingnan University at Sun Yat-sen University. Chapter 7 (authored by Mary Schlarb, Shufang Strause, and Lu-Chung Dennis Weng) describes creative collaboration in areas of teacher education between the State University of New York (Cortland) and Capital Normal University (Beijing), Qufu Normal University (Qufu), and Tamkang University (Taipei City, Taiwan). The next chapter is a submission

© KONINKLIJKE BRILL NV, LEIDEN, 2018 | DOI 10.1163/9789004368361_001

by Yu Lizhong, Chancellor of New York University (NYU) Shanghai. Lizhong's chapter provides an overview of the history and rationale for the NYU campus with translation from Jia-Ling Lin. Chapter 9 features another high ranking official – Chi Jian (President of Beijing Sport University) and Li Li Ji (University of Minnesota and co-editor of this volume). The team describe the China Champion program, which supports former Chinese Olympians in further education in the United States.

The next two chapters focus specifically on student mobility as an aspect of internationalization and international partnerships. In their chapter "Sino-Global Higher Education Partnerships: Student Mobility Programs," Jing Tian, Jiansheng Ma, and Juan Cai describe Beijing Normal University's efforts to enhance two-way mobility of students. Finally, Merritt Huang (American Councils for International Education) provides an overview of acculturative and mental health considerations for international students, based on her experience in the field and recent literature on the topic.

The final chapter provides a critical overview of the book and a look forward. This book is designed primarily for international education administrators and practitioners who may benefit from the conclusions drawn across multiple case examples. At the same time, scholars may be interested in emergent trends in the partnerships described. All partnerships have elements of soft power and diplomacy, all feature reflections on cross-cultural collaboration, and all provide models of how practitioners have envisioned and orchestrated international partnerships. We hope you find this volume useful in your work.

About the Author

Christopher Johnstone is an Assistant Professor in the Department of Organizational Leadership, Policy, and Development. His research areas include internationalization of higher education and inclusive education in schools and universities. He serves as the coordinator of his department's Leadership in International and Intercultural Education PhD program and has written on international education topics such as international student integration, institutional culture as it relates to internationalization, and international partnerships. Prior to his faculty role, Johnstone served as Director of International Initiatives and Relations at the University of Minnesota's College of Education and Human Development.

CHAPTER 2

China's Soft Power Projection through Higher Education: A Preliminary Assessment

Rui Yang

Abstract

Power comes in many guises. Coined by Nye in 1990, the concept of soft power is now widely invoked in foreign policy debates. A country's soft power rests on various resources including its culture, political values and foreign policies. As higher education continues to go global, colleges and universities contribute more and more significantly to cultural diplomacy. China is rich in soft power resources. China has been projecting its soft power via higher education for decades. In line with rising Chinese power, great efforts have been made by the government to use higher education as a vector of soft power. Both scale and intensity have been expanded significantly over recent years to match its increasing wealth from conventional education aid to international students and overseas visibility of Chinese higher education institutions. Yet, China remains deficit in soft power. Its approach to soft power and public diplomacy in and through higher education has been far less effective than expected. This chapter first introduces the latest policy context in China to set the stage. It then assesses China's exercise of higher education for soft power in education aid, overseas students, offshore affiliates of Chinese universities, and global engagement of university operation. It ends with some theoretical interrogation of the notion of soft power.

1 Introduction

The term of soft power was first forged by the Harvard University political scientist Joseph S. Nye (1990), who borrowed what Peter Bachrach and Morton Baratz called the "second face of power" much earlier, in relation to a country's power of attraction and persuasion as distinct from the "hard" power of force or coercion. Stemming also from the attractiveness of a nation's culture, ideals and policies and resembling Carr's (1954) "power over opinion" and Lukes'

(1974) "third dimension of power," it is usually defined as culture, education, and diplomacy, providing the capacity to persuade other nations to willingly adopt the same goals (Nye, 2004). The term is now widely used in International Relations. International higher education has been strongly attracted to the concept of soft power. According to Knight (2015), many academics would consider soft power as a fundamental premise of international education engagement, as demonstrated by some popular programs in higher education such as the Fulbright Program, British Council activities, German Academic Exchange initiatives, and Erasmus Mundus projects.

Although without systematically addressing the issue, Hopf (2013) notes the role of educational soft power. He claims that "education, and especially universities and graduate schools attracting foreign students are one of the most important institutions of hegemonic reproduction" (p. 330). Indeed, international education exchange and cooperation falls squarely under the rubric of soft power, and winning hearts and minds still composes an important part of the international higher education equation. Governmental tensions ebb and flow but connections between higher education institutions are a steadying and civilizing influence. University activities such as enrolled international students, foreign scholars in-residence, and academic exchange, may reinforce official foreign policy goals. The millions of people who have studied in other countries constitute a remarkable reservoir of goodwill for those host countries. Many of the former students eventually wind up in positions where they can affect policy outcomes that are important to their host countries.

The concept of soft power has been a fundamental part of military thinking in China for over 2000 years. Ancient China distinguished kingly and hegemonist ways of ruling, focusing respectively on soft and hard power. Sun Tzu's (2005) *Art of War* elegantly stated in the 5th century BC that "To fight and conquer in all your battles is not supreme excellence; supreme excellence consists in breaking the enemy's resistance without fighting." With such long and rich legacy, it is not at all surprising to see Nye's notion of soft power has fast become popular in China. The Chinese governments at different levels have indeed applied the concept in a variety of domains from politics and culture to the development of cities, regions and enterprises. Generations of Chinese leaders have adopted stratagems and long-term planning. These stratagems formed a part of statecraft which looked to an integrated strategy to win victories without striking a blow.

China poses to take more active actions to match its own increasing wealth with greater soft power especially when the U.S. power wanes on a variety of fronts (Dawson, 2010). With the Chinese power assuming increasing global significance, soft power exercise has been placed highly on the central government's agenda. China has demonstrated its great ambition to become a global cultural power, and has spared no efforts in implementing such policies. 'Soft power' has become a popular concept in Chinese political discourse, frequently appearing in government documents, academic discussions and the mainstream media. China's enthusiasm for it is now deeply embedded in its political, social and cultural spheres (Chen, 2016). Chinese language, culture and education are significant in China's quest for soft power. Due to its growing role in economic, social and cultural development, as well as in knowledge and scientific innovation, one important area is the realm of higher education. Soft power becomes an opportune concept for many China observers to analyze the rise of China.

However, China remains deficit in soft power compared with its hard power. According to the Center for Modernization Research based at the Chinese Academy of Sciences (2015), China is ranked substantially lower in its cultural influences compared with other global economic powers. Often prioritizing a more hardball approach, China has been weak at cultivating its soft power. According to Portland Communications, which uses data to rank the top 30 countries in terms of soft power, China comes in last, viewed as the worst of the world's major countries at harnessing soft power. China's lack of soft power skills is seen as the reason (Sawahel, 2016). This is also evident in higher education. In comparison with its contribution to hard power, China's higher education lags far behind its counterparts in developed countries in its contribution to soft power. Calls are increasingly sonorous for China's universities to enrich and advance their soft power to serve the rejuvenation of the Chinese nation (Li, 2009).

While higher education plays a growing and significant role in leveraging soft power and cultural diplomacy, the notion of soft power has not been well incorporated in the literature on higher education as an analytical framework. Wojciuk, Michalek, and Stormowska (2015) even claim that the educational dimension of soft power has been least developed both in the literature and in the existing indexes. Employing the concept of soft power, this chapter examines the public diplomacy dimension of China's higher education in a global landscape. After an introduction to the policy context to set the stage, it selects a few major areas of China's exercise of higher education for soft power including education aid, overseas students, offshore affiliates of Chinese universities, and global engagement of university operation. It ends with some theoretical interrogation of the notion of soft power.

2   The Policy Context

To better understand China's soft power projection through higher education, it is necessary to note the policy context. During 1982–1983, the Chinese government gradually gave up its previous focus on "The Three Worlds" during the 1970s by Mao Zedong (dividing international relations into three politico-economic worlds: the first world of superpowers, the second world of lesser powers and the third world of exploited nations), and pursued "independent foreign policy of peace." China needed a peaceful international environment to achieve modernization. Since the late 1970s, the Chinese leadership realized its legitimacy relied mainly on improving its own people's living standards and their political performances. After the Tiananmen Square Incident in 1989, Deng Xiaoping made a series of remarks on international situations and China's foreign policy within the circle of high officials. One doctrine was to "keep a low profile while trying to accomplish something." The policy was that China should work hard to develop its economy rather than seeking international leadership and that it should make a difference in international affairs as permitted by its capabilities (Wang, 2014).

For years, Chinese foreign policy followed the first half of Deng's formulation closely, avoiding getting deeply involved in or taking a strong position on international issues outside the immediate national interests of China (Wang & French, 2013). With economic strength comes political clout around the globe. As China's influence on global affairs grows, its actions to safeguard its interests increasingly affect the interests of the international community as a whole (Eisenman et al., 2007). Chinese policy makers and analysts began to rethink the virtue and value of keeping a low profile. The shift in China's conduct of foreign policy from "keeping a low profile" to "trying to accomplish something" started moderately in late 2003 when the then Chinese administration led by Hu Jingtao and Wen Jiabao put forward "peaceful rise," which changed into "peaceful development" in the next year when China established a new Public Diplomacy Division. No matter if it was "rise" or "development," and despite the peaceful intention, this gave much weight to soft power, in line with hard power.

The term soft power first appeared officially in the government report at the 17th National Congress of the Communist Party in October 2007 by the then President Hu Jintao who stated that China must enhance its cultural soft power and argued that China needed to invest more heavily in a soft power strategy. Five years later, the term was used twice in Hu's (2012) keynote report during the opening ceremony of the 18th National Congress. He elaborated on it and reclaimed its significance: "The country's cultural soft power should be improved significantly" in chapter III and "To complete the building of a moderately prosperous society in all respects and achieve the great renewal of the Chinese nation, we must create a new surge in promoting socialist culture and bring about its great development and enrichment, increase China's cultural soft power, and enable culture to guide social trends, educate the people, serve society, and boost development" in chapter VI.

With his ambitious Chinese Dream, the term has also been embraced by China's current President Xi Jinping. On 30 December 2013 he presided over a conference on how to enhance China's national cultural soft power within current policy frameworks. In his speech entitled "Elevate Soft Power, Realize the Chinese Dream," he remarked that

> To strengthen China's soft power, the country needs to build its capacity in international communication, construct a communication system, better use the new media and increase the creativity, appeal and credibility of China's publicity. The stories of China should be well told, voices of China well spread, and characteristics of China well explained.
>
> We should strive to spread the values of contemporary China, namely the values of socialism with Chinese characteristics, and strive to increase China's international discourse power. (Xi, 2014)

As a national policy framework of the current leadership, Chinese Dream has since been heavily popularized in political circles and the mass media. Xi subsequently delivered a significant speech at the headquarters of UNESCO in Paris in March 2014, asserting that "the realization of Chinese dream is the development of material civilization and spiritual civilization" and "with the peoples of the world together," China wants to "create a colorful civilization for mankind and provide the correct spiritual guidance and strong motivation." As China emerges as a global power, its range of national interests expands, and soft power has become an important component of the Chinese Dream, promising a fully integrated national revival. Both political leaders and academic elites are strategically aware of soft power leverage and resources (Chen, 2016). The government has advanced public diplomacy in its recent white papers (Jin & Tang, 2009).

The concept of soft power has found a receptive audience and its advocacy has been given a boost in China. Contending that China's soft power must be strengthened to match its economic power and political status on the world stage, Chinese policy elites have put in place specific initiatives to expand China's soft power and increase its legitimacy as an emerging superpower. Embarking on numerous initiatives, with billions of dollars committed to "soft" initiatives, the government has made great efforts to wield its soft power. The investments appear in various forms from high-profile aid programs for Africa and Latin America to substantial schemes to push academics to publish internationally. One can easily identify strategies and policy tools Beijing has consciously used to boost its soft power (Kurlantzick, 2006). Its desire for national revival includes returning to the position China had before a rising

Europe began to eclipse it in the 18th century (Jain & Groot, 2006), with all the cultural influence that implies.

3   Education Aid

William Easterly (1997) once called international aid "The White Man's Burden," claiming that the West's efforts to aid the rest had done much ill and little good. This is not only incorrect, but also culturally arrogant. Donors of international aid to education are not only limited to Western societies. China is one of the world's most experienced providers of foreign assistance, with an aid program dating back to 1950 (Reilly, 2013). With an international reputation in education aid, China's increasing role as a donor has been reflected in its international education discourse (Nordveit, 2009). At a conference organized by UNESCO in Beijing in 2005, a high official from USAID spoke highly of China's contribution to international aid to education as a great emerging force (Wu, 2005).

The Chinese government attaches much importance to aid to education in other developing countries. Two of the eight cooperation measures put forwarded by China's then Premier Wen Jiabao at the Fourth Ministerial Conference of the Forum on China-Africa Cooperation in November 2009 were educational aid (Xinhua News Agency, 2009). China has recently strengthened its aid to education in other developing countries, helping them build over 100 rural primary schools, increasing government scholarships and the number of teachers who come to receive training in China, dispatching more Chinese teachers abroad to help build up academic disciplines, and enhancing cooperation with other developing countries in vocational, technical and distance education.

According to China's Foreign Aid White Paper (Information Office of the State Council, 2011), education aid from China has helped recipient countries train a large number of qualified personnel in the fields of education, management, and science and technology, and rendered intellectual support for their social and economic development. By 2009, China had helped other developing countries build more than 130 schools, dispatched nearly 10,000 Chinese teachers to other developing countries, and trained more than 10,000 principals and teachers for them. For example, education has become an important sector of Chinese developmental aid in Africa, responsible for approximately 10 per cent of total aid projects. The aid is targeted mainly at educational infrastructure development (construction of schools, libraries, and museums), scholarships, and training programs (e.g., in engineering). It improves perception of China in Africa (Wojciuk et al., 2015).

China's educational aid has been based on its principle of non-intervention into the domestic politics of the recipient countries. China's remarkable success in educational development as a developing nation has offered its aid strong discursive support for other developing countries to borrow the Chinese experience. China also attempts to tackle some lingering bottleneck issues in educational development in the poorest countries through its aid programs. The programs in Africa pay close attention to fostering the local community's capacity to recover and further develop education, target specifically at indigenization of African education, and train local professionals. The central purpose is to find a path to independent development of African education that suits local social and economic demands. Specific measures include shifting from providing to training teachers, from comprehensive to functional elimination of illiteracy, and from simply increasing school enrolment rate to avoiding drop outs and school repeats. Many informal educational programs have been set up to better meet local needs (Wu, 2013).

As a rising global power, China tries to play down the influence of political differences in its foreign aid to education, and attempts to treat all recipient nations on an equal footing. Stressing mutual benefits and close collaboration with recipients, its education aid has been expanding in scale, becomes more systematically planned and integrated with its overall international aid programs. The effectiveness of aid programs has been placed highly on the agenda. In line with China's policy-making generally, its education aid is featured by top-down agenda-setting, careful planning, efficient implementation and strict supervision. China tends to be selective in choosing its targets to provide aid, with particular focus on the least developed nations. The programs have generally achieved their intended goals. China's education aid without political conditions has been perceived as a positive force to promote educational development in developing countries, such as those in Africa.

However, in comparison with the U.S. education aid programs, for example, those aided by the Chinese serve China's global positioning much less strategically. A closer scrutiny of China's international aid to education reveals the aid received by various countries is highly unequal, depending to a great extent on the relations between donors and recipients. Most of China's international aid to education is spent on building schools, providing teaching equipment and materials, dispatching Chinese teachers abroad, training teachers and interns from other developing countries and offering government scholarships to students from other developing countries to study in China. Problems of China's programs are often related to the quick expansion of the aid and development sector, leading to absence of a professional aid and coordination structure, ad-hoc replies to demands, and unstructured aid that does not always correspond to the needs of the recipient (Nordveit, 2011; King, 2010).

Moreover, China's foreign aid to education has long focused too much on higher and vocational education, with certain neglect of basic education. For least developed countries, higher and vocational education only covers a small proportion of the population. In some African countries, for instance, less than 1 percent of the age cohort could receive higher education. As for approaches, China's aid has been mainly via educational training, construction of educational basic infrastructure, provision of government scholarships, donations of teaching and learning equipment, dispatching teachers, and establishment of research programs in universities to help the recipients with local human development. China's practices have demonstrated a pragmatic mindset which, together with the shortage of knowledge of the human deprivation of local communities, has affected China's more integrated policy making and implementation.

It appears that China has become aware of such issues and has attempted to address them. China now includes basic education and medical and health work into its list of aid priorities. The central focus has been turned to human development and strengthening the self-development capacity of local communities. However, the majority of China's foreign aid to education remains confined to hardware such as construction of school buildings, only taking consideration of some software such as teacher training. Such strategies have shown their inappropriateness for systematic and integrated planning of China's foreign aid to education.

China has not been able to avoid criticism. To some, China uses its foreign aid to secure access to strategic natural resources (LaFraniere & Grobler, 2009). According to Reilly (2013), China has repeatedly used its foreign aid programs to advance broader strategic and economic objectives internationally including securing access to strategic natural resources. Some even claim that China's aid has interrupted the due economic development and social stability in the recipient countries (Giry, 2004). To others, however, China is creating its own approach to international aid to education, with distinct logics, practices and foci. The Chinese media use a proverb from Lao-Tzu to describe China's logic of educational assistance for Africa: 'Give a man a fish and you feed him for a day; teach him how to fish and you feed him for a lifetime' (Yuan, 2011).

The difference of China's aid modality from the Western is on the basis of an assumption of the 'normality' of the Western framework or logic of aid. This is often inappropriate as Chinese aid is not about doing stand-alone projects or directly financing in order to reduce transaction costs, nor about giving more or less ownership to recipient countries, or whether they should intervene into the recipient countries' governance issues. China's aim is pragmatic to create a win-win situation. Unlike Western 'aid' from the beginning, the Chinese approach is a blended model of aid, investment, trade, and technology as levers for development, and embeds education into the wider and more complex political economic context.

China has thus distinguished itself by a discourse based on notions of "win-win" friendship and non-interference. A major feature of China's role is a member from the South working as a partner of South-South cooperation. This distinguishes China's educational aid approaches from those of the traditional donors. However, as both China's domestic and international situations change, China will run the risk of being perceived as an aid donor rather than in its preferred role of being seen as a large developing country involved, to the best of its ability, in South-South cooperation with other developing countries (King, 2013). The challenge for China is to work out ways to maintain its distinction from the discourse and practices of the traditional donors. With marked contrasts between its engagement with developed and developing societies, China needs to figure out how to coordinate the two aspects both theoretically and in practice.

4   Overseas Students

Hosting overseas students is another main area through which China is proactively promoting its soft power. Chinese leaders recognize the effectiveness of international education exchange in China's public diplomacy. Former Premier Li Peng, for example, is reported to say that foreign student work is an integral part of diplomacy, and must serve the general foreign policy (Li, 2009). Another example is the Studying in China Scheme promulgated in September 2010 by the Ministry of Education to strengthen international exchanges between China and other countries, advance the internationalization of China's education system, and enhance China's attractiveness to international students. According to the scheme, the government plans to recruit 500,000 international students to study in China by 2020. Among them, 150,000 students will be degree-seeking students. If materialized, China will become the largest international education hub in Asia. Ultimately, the goal is to develop Chinese soft power and promote the Chinese concept of Harmonious World to the outside world (Ding, 2014).

Over the past decade, a growing number of overseas students come to study in China. China has fast developed into an important study-abroad destination in its own right. According to China Scholarship Council, the number of overseas students in China rose from a modest base of 1,900 in 1978 to 110,844 in 2004 and 265,090 in 2010. A total of 397,635 students from 182 countries/regions studied in China in 2015 (Project Atlas-China, 2016). This was enough to place China as the third-largest global study destination, with a roughly eight percent share of the world's five million internationally mobile students

(OECD, 2016), and leaving it well on track to reach a national target to entice 500,000 students from overseas by 2020. However, China still compares poorly with the USA and the UK which hosted 974,926 and 493,570 international students in 2014 respectively and were 2.6 and 1.3 times of the population of international students in China. This is also a huge deficit in comparison with the 1.26 million Chinese students studying abroad in 2015. To boost overseas student numbers in China, the central government issued a policy in 2014 to pay equal attention to study abroad and study in China.

In today's scholarly world, China is not yet at the central position in many fields. In order to attract overseas students to study in China, extra efforts have to be made and great investment committed. This is exactly what China has been doing. According to China's Foreign Aid White Paper (Information Office of the State Council, 2011), China had funded 70,627 students from 119 developing countries to study in China by 2009. In 2009 alone, China extended scholarships to 11,185 foreign students who studied in China. The number of scholarships offered by Chinese government has also increased dramatically. In 2008, the government not only increased living stipends for undergraduate and postgraduate scholarship holders, but also increased 3,000 more scholarships consecutively for three years till 2010. Holders of Chinese government scholarships reached 25,700 in 2010 and 40,600 in 2015, accounting respectively for 9.69 percent and 10.21 percent of China's total population of overseas students.

Africa has been attached high symbolic value by the Chinese government. China actively recruits African university students offering them scholarships in order to increase soft power. By 2003, half of African students studying overseas were in China. By fostering future African leaders such as President Malatu Teshome of Ethiopia, China hopes to improve its image in Africa and to strengthen its economic, scientific and technological cooperation with Africa. Most recently, ASEAN countries have also been placed highly on the agenda (Yang, 2012). Both the scale and the amount of scholarships are expected to increase in the years to come as China's Belt and Road Initiative takes more effect. Many provincial and local governments have joined the action with an aim to pull young talents from overseas to study at the higher institutions in their jurisdictions and to strengthen the links between their localities with the countries and regions where the students come from. Meanwhile, more and more Chinese big companies have offered their support. Yet, it is important to note that the expansion of Chinese scholarship programs does not keep pace with the surging foreign interest in studying in China. By the first decade of the 21st century, 9 out of 10 overseas students were fee-paying (Haugen, 2013).

Chinese scholarship program has been hailed by some commentators as an effective approach to development, in sharp contrast to the recruitment of international students by the West that encouraged human capital flight from

Africa (Brautigam, 2009). However, some earlier studies on the experience of scholarship participants found mostly negative results: few students were satisfied with their experience in China, and the Chinese international education programs were unsuccessful in most respects (Chen, 1965). Nowadays, respondents are generally satisfied with their experience in China and believe that the scholarship program plays a positive role in promoting the development of positive, long-term, friendly relationships between China and their home countries. According to Dong and Chapman (2008), the Chinese Government Scholarship Program has been successful in spreading goodwill and strengthening China's soft power.

Overseas students in China come mainly from developing countries, with 60.4 percent from Asia. China has been particularly keen to attract students from its neighbors. The efforts have paid off. According to the Center for China and Globalization (2016), China is particularly attractive to students from neighboring countries. Of the 397,635 students studying in Chinese universities in 2015, top 15 senders were South Korea (66,675; 16.8%), the United States (21,975; 5.5%), Thailand (19,976; 5.0%), India (16,694; 4.2%), Russia (16,197; 4.1%), Pakistan (15,654; 3.9%), Japan (14,085; 3.5%), Kazakhstan (13,198; 3.3%), Indonesia (12,694; 3.2%), France (10,436; 2.6%), Vietnam (10,031; 2.5%), Germany (7,536; 1.89%), Mongolia (7,478; 1.88%), Laos (6,918; 1.74%), and Malaysia (6,650; 1.67%). According to the Ministry of Education (2016), a total of 184,799 overseas students were studying for academic degrees, accounting for 46.47 percent of the total number of overseas students. Compared with the same period of last year, this figure increased 12.41percent, with a rise of 20,405 in number. The year 2015 witnessed an increase of 13.47 percent in the number of Master's (39,205) and Doctoral (14,365) students from overseas.

5   Offshore Affiliates of Chinese Universities

Since the 19th century, China has long prioritized learning from the West. Recent signs, however, show China's global reaching out, indicating a new stage of its internationalization of higher education (Yang, 2014). Establishing offshore affiliates of Chinese universities is part of such deliberate and ambitious strategies. The latest example is the Global Innovation Exchange in Seattle which is jointly constructed by Tsinghua University and the University of Washington. It is designed to open in the fall of 2017 to host the second year of a dual degree program offering a Master's degree in technology innovation to approximately 30 students. Playing to both Tsinghua's strengths in business and computer science as well as the campus's location in Seattle, it plans to offer other programs and enroll 3,000 students by 2025. Reporting for University World News, Rachel Brown (2015) calls this another step in China's soft power.

While it is the first physical presence of Chinese universities in the United States, it is not China's first attempt of such sort to expand China's global educational footprint. Before it came into being, a few affiliates of other Chinese universities had already been established in various countries, including a campus of Soochow University in Laos, a branch of Xiamen University under construction in Malaysia and a joint lab sponsored by Zhejiang University and Imperial College London in London. One of China's earliest soft power strategies is to launch Confucius Institutes at universities outside its borders 12 years ago (Yang, 2010). Patterned after the British Council, Goethe Institute or Alliance Française, they were initiated by the Office of Chinese Language Council International (Hanban), as a pillar of China's wider policy (Chen, 2016). They are government-sponsored centers to promote Chinese language and culture abroad and are complementary with other programs (Wojciuk et al., 2015). Their operation relies on joint efforts by Chinese and overseas partners and personnel from various social sectors.

To date, 511 Confucius Institutes have been established in 140 countries and regions. In 2016, the Confucius Institutes around the world, with a team of 46,000 Chinese and overseas full-time and part-time teachers, enrolled 2.1 million students, hosted cultural events of various types, and received a total of 13 million participants (Confucius Institute Headquarters, 2016). They have become a "bridge builder" for exchanges and mutual learning between Chinese and other civilizations as well as a pivotal window for the world to know China and for China to strengthen its friendship and cooperation with other nations. According to Madam Liu Yandong (2016), Vice Premier of the State Council and Chairwoman of the Council of the Confucius Institute Headquarters, they are making steady progress to continuously enhance the education quality, expand service capabilities and improve operation mechanisms, thus injecting new vitality into their sustainable development.

Confucius Institutes target overseas universities and colleges. As a public diplomacy strategy, they are built on the close cultural and language bonds between overseas Chinese and their motherland. They have already made significant headway in entering higher education institutions in many parts of the world. However, initial efforts to spread aspects of the Chinese education system globally have met with resistance. Certain Confucius Institutes have triggered controversies surrounding academic freedom. In addition, because the Confucius Institutes are state-sponsored, "political concerns have been raised over the presence of a Chinese government-backed institution on Western university campuses" (Starr, 2009). In a similar way, controversies could also arise at China's other outposts overseas. Considering China's strong commitment to expanding soft power through education, collaborations between Chinese and overseas universities on a global appear poised to spread.

6   Global Engagement in University Operation

Globalization has put the international dimension of universities on steroids, and has entailed a complex set of boundary-breaking. Higher education leaders around the globe are seeking new social orders and institutional rules in developing and sustaining partnerships that move across cultural and national borders. Both traditional and new higher education providers adapt international cooperation as a strategy to build up the capacity and competency of their institutions to seek resources internationally for staff and student development and to cope with the ever-changing global trends and agendas (Abbott, 2006). Within this context, domains of daily university operation assume increasing soft power functions. Chinese universities now reach out globally with heavy investments. China's use of international exchange and cooperation in higher education as an exercise of soft power is unprecedented and has gone far beyond the zone of traditional theories.

Decades of reforms have seen much integration between Chinese higher education and the international community. This indicates a change in the frame of reference in China's higher education policy; a fervent embrace of international norms, especially in the top layer of universities. Chinese universities once competed between themselves without looking out at their international peers. Starting from the last decade China's top universities have been embracing a larger international sense of themselves. Chinese major universities would be able to exert strong influence on their peers in other countries. Their regular international engagement assumes increasing soft power implications. This is even more the case after China issued the *Outline of China's National Plan for Medium and Long-term Education Reform and Development* (2010–2020) which made clear that the government sees higher education as a key element of its public diplomacy and soft power.

According to the White Paper on China's Peaceful Development released in 2011, China not only accepts multiculturalism, but also actively advocates for it. Soft power thus assumes an important role. One effective approach to projecting soft power is through international exchanges and collaboration in higher education in various shapes and forms. Indeed, educational opening-up has constituted a vital part of China's reform and opening-up policies. In 2016, China put forward *Several Opinions on Better Work on Educational Opening-up in the New Period* to further promote the quality and level of China's educational opening-up to the world. The policy would have three kinds of consequences: more assistance provided for Chinese students studying abroad and overseas students studying in China so as to cultivate outstanding talents of various types for China and the world, better international cooperation in education, and upgraded educational exchanges as a national strategy through the platform of cultural and people-to-people exchanges.

Another factor is the changing role of Chinese higher education in the global system. China's leading universities have become the partners of choice for so many of the world's most distinguished universities. Chinese science has come into its own in a way that few believed would be possible. China's international ranking in terms of the number of scientific essays published increased from 38th in 1979, to 23rd in 1982, to 15th in 1989, and 5th in 2003. In the 1970s, China ranked 34th in the number of scientific articles cited internationally. In 2015, of the countries that produced the world's top research, China came the second, after the United States only (Phillips, 2016). With an understanding of their growing international impact, Chinese universities answer the nation's call to initiate new programs specifically aiming at soft power leverage. Two latest examples are the Schwarzman College and Yenching Academy affiliated respectively to Tsinghua University and Peking University. Based on the institutional prestige, the two programs expect to identify, recruit, and train future world leaders.

Since the early 2000s, led by national policies and facilitated by resources from local governments, China's higher education sector has become increasingly active on a global scale to actively promote China's soft power. First, Chinese higher education institutions often take the initiative to host international conferences and forums as a major part of and an effective platform for their internationalization. This is evident at national, provincial/municipal and institutions levels, usually with strong support and great expectations from governments. For instance, Shenzhen municipal government invested massively in August 2011 to host the 26th World University Games together with the World University Presidents Forum. Similarly, for nearly a decade, there have been annual China-ASEAN exhibitions, always with forums of various sorts, with local higher education institutions playing central roles (Yang, 2012). Such activities pave the way for further networking, exchange and collaboration in higher education.

Secondly, China's higher education authorities and institutions have signed various agreements initially mainly with former communist nations and later with European and North American countries. By the first decade of this century, China had higher education exchange agreements with nearly 50 countries. For instance, from January 2007 when China signed the free trade agreements with ASEAN to July 2011, China had signed educational exchange agreements with Singapore, Malaysia, Vietnam, Brunei, Myanmar, Laos, Cambodia and Philippines, and mutual recognition in academic higher education qualifications with Malaysia and Thailand. On 25 November in the same year, China signed the Asia Pacific Recognition Convention on the Recognition of Qualifications in Higher Education in Japan. China now has established 2,469 joint programs in higher education with over 700 overseas higher institutions and signed agreements with 44 countries/regions on mutual recognition of academic qualifications. Such engagement is closely linked with and will lead to further collaboration and exchange in various domains of university business.

7   Concluding Observations

According to Shambaugh (2013), "China is in the community of nations but is in many ways not really part of the community; it is formally involved, but it is not normatively integrated (p. 7) ... We witness a large and growing number of China's cultural activities abroad – but very little influence on global cultural trends, minimal soft power, and a mixed-to-poor international image in public opinion polls" (p. 207). Although Shanbaugh here is commenting from a Western perspective to observe what and how China has been doing in its quest for soft power, it is clear that China's soft power efforts have encountered obstacles. To conclude this chapter, I have two observations to make:

First, a fundamental flaw in China's soft power efforts is the lack of coordination in various aspects and on different levels. At this moment, although rich in soft power resources, China has not developed coordinated, consistent, coherent and comprehensive soft-power strategies. Both the Ministry of Education and individual institutions are short of a clear understanding of the strategic role played by higher education and its institutions in the projection and enhancement of soft power. A related issue is the often over-dominant role of China's central government in the exercise. As Martin Davidson, the Chief Executive of the British Council, recently points out, the paradox of soft power is that the greater the government involvement is, the weaker the soft power is (Sharma, 2013).

The lack of coordination takes various forms and shapes: between different levels of governments, between various sectors, and between the state and higher education institutions. Even within an institution, various departments often lack concerted efforts. Although the central government usually has strong intensions, institutions have their own priorities and considerations. More coordination is also badly needed between the engagement with developed countries and those with developing countries. As it is now there have been great imbalances between the two. An equally prominent issue is international engagement in the humanities and social sciences. Such disciplines have long been neglected within higher education and in the wider community in China's century-long catch-up with the West, mainly in science and technology. However, they have their uniquely significant role in a new age of bring China to the world (Yang & Xie, 2015).

Second, China's soft power liabilities alert us to the limitations of the concept of soft power. Since Nye coined the term, the theory of soft power has been widely used without sufficient interrogation. The framework is often treated too mechanically and statically. As Zhang (2013) argues, whether a power resource is soft or hard depends on the perceptions and feelings of various actors in specific situations. The same power resource could be soft power in one situation and hard power in another. It could also have different effects depending on its targets, approaches and acceptance. The effect changes according to situations. Moreover, potentiality rather than actuality is an important aspect of the concept (Lukes, 2007). The divide into soft and hard is over-simplistic, arbitrary, sometimes self-contradictory, and does not always reflect the reality. The utility of soft power as an analytic concept needs to be interrogated on both ontological and methodological grounds. It is a chaotic conception, encompassing different mechanisms that operate through discrete pathways (Hall, 2010).

Although I have employed it as a useful concept in the above discussions of a major aspect of Chinese higher education, I believe it does not fully capture the essence of China's higher education development and implications. Set in an inexplicit yet powerful context of conflicting national self-interests, the notion is a Western construction, with deep roots in modern history featured by conflicts. As demonstrated by the word "power," its central focus is on conflicts. It is little surprising that the concept is a close relative of clash of civilizations (Iriye, 1997). The notion likely leads to a view of China's rising soft power as a zero-sum game (Ramani, 2005). China is a civilization state. Its global engagement in higher education functions as more than a soft power. The cultural mission of Chinese modern higher education is to combine Chinese and Western elements to bring together the aspects of both philosophical heritages. Such a notion provides us with a much more meaningful perspective to assess China's higher education development than Wende and Zhu's (2016) suggestion that China could become either a follower or a leader in global higher education, for instance.

References

Abbott, M. (2006). Competition and reform of the New Zealand tertiary education sector. *Journal of Education Policy, 21*(3), 367–387.

Brautigam, D. (2009). *The dragon's gift: The real story of China in Africa.* Oxford: Oxford University Press.

Brown, R. (2015 , November 28). The next step in soft power. *University World News.* Retrieved November 8, 2016, from http://www.universityworldnews.com/article.php?story=20151112155923897

Carr, E. (1954). *The twenty years' crisis*. New York, NY: Macmillan.

Center for China and Globalization. (2016). *Blue books of global talent: Annual report on the development of Chinese students studying abroad (2016) No. 5*. Beijing: Social Science Academic Press.

Center for Modernization Research. (2015). *China modernization report: Cultural modernization*. Beijing: Chinese Academy of Sciences.

Chen, Q. (2016). China's soft power policies and strategies: The cultural activist state. *Special Issue 'Cultural Economies and Cultural Activism', 1*, 1–13. Retrieved May 2, 2017, from https://www2.warwick.ac.uk/fac/soc/law/elj/lgd/2016–1/chen_finalfinal.pdf

Chen, T. (1965). Government encouragement and control of international education in communist China. In S. Fraser (Ed.), *Governmental policy and international education* (pp. 111–133). New York, NY: John Wiley & Sons, Inc.

Confucius Institute Headquarters. (2016). *The 11th Confucius institute conference successfully closes*. Retrieved January 30, 2017, from http://english.hanban.org/article/2016–12/14/content_668294.htm

Dawson, K. C. (2010, April 23). Confucius institutes enhance China's international image. *China Daily*. Retrieved September 14, 2010, from http://www.chinadaily.com.cn/china/2010–04/23/content_9766116.htm

Ding, S. (2014). *Chinese soft power and public diplomacy: An analysis of China's new diaspora engagement policies in the Xi era* (EAI Fellow Program Working Paper Series No. 43). Retrieved December 9, 2013, from http://www.eai.or.kr/data/bbs/eng_report/201404011627122.pdf

Dong, L., & Chapman, D. W. (2008). The Chinese government scholarship program: An effective form of foreign assistance? *International Review of Education, 54*(2), 155–173.

Easterly, W. (1997). *The White man's burden: Why the West's efforts to aid the rest have done so much ill and so little good*. Oxford: Oxford University Press.

Eisenman, J., Heginbotham, E., & Mitchell, D. (2007). *China and the developing world*. New York, NY: M.E. Sharpe.

Giry, S. (2004). China's Africa strategy. *The New Republic, 231*(20), 19–23.

Hall, T. (2010). An unclear attraction: A critical examination of soft power as an analytical category. *The Chinese Journal of International Politics, 3*(2), 189–211.

Haugen, H. Ø. (2013). China's recruitment of African university students: Policy efficacy and unintended outcomes. *Globalization, Societies and Education, 11*(3), 315–334.

Hopf, T. (2013). Common-sense constructivism and hegemony in world politics. *International Organization, 67*(3), 317–354.

Hu, J. T. (2012). *Report to the eighteenth national congress of the communist party of China*. Retrieved November 24, 2012, from http://en.people.cn/90785/8024777.html

Information Office of the State Council. (2011). *China's foreign aid*. Retrieved December 1, 2013, from http://english.gov.cn/official/2011–04/21/content_1849913.htm

Iriye, A. (1997). *Cultural internationalism and world order*. Baltimore, MD: John Hopkins University Press.

Jain, P., & Groot, G. (2006, May 17). Beijing's 'soft power' offensive. *Asia Times*. Retrieved from http://www.atimes.com/atimes/China/HE17 Ado1.html

Jin, Z. K., & Tang, N. N. (2009). Culture and public diplomacy: A new diplomatic channel in modern China. *Teaching and Research, 8*, 33–38.

King, K. (2010). *China's cooperation in education and training with Kenya: A different model?* Oxford: Pergamon.

King, K. (2013). *China's aid and soft power in Africa: The case of education and training.* Rochester, NY: James Currey.

Knight, J. (2015). Moving from soft power to knowledge diplomacy. *International Higher Education, 80*, 8–9.

Kurlantzick, J. (2006). China's charm: Implications of Chinese soft power. *Policy Brief, 47*, 1–8.

LaFraniere, S., & Grobler, J. (2009, September 22). Uneasy engagement: China spreads aid in Africa, with a catch. *The New York Times*. Retrieved April 18, 2017, from http://www.nytimes.com/2009/09/22/world/africa/22namibia.html?pagewanted=all&_r=0

Li, M. J. (Ed.). (2009). *Soft power: China's emerging strategy in international politics.* Lanham, MD: Lexington Books.

Liu, Y. D. (2016, December 16). *Working together to open up new prospects for the development of Confucius institutes.* Retrieved January 30, 2017, from http://english.hanban.org/article/2016–12/16/content_668477.htm

Lukes, S. (1974). *Power: A radical view*. New York, NY: Macmillan.

Lukes, S. (2007). Power and the battle for hearts and minds: On the bluntness of soft power. In F. Berenskoetter & M. J. Williams (Eds.), *Power in world politics* (pp. 83–97). New York, NY: Routledge.

Ministry of Education. (2016). *Statistics on overseas students in China in 2015.* Retrieved January 31, 2017, from http://www.moe.edu.cn/jyb_xwfb/gzdt_gzdt/s5987/201604/t20160414_238263.html

Nordtveit, B. H. (2009). Western and Chinese development discourses: Education, growth and sustainability. *International Journal of Educational Development, 29*(2), 157–165.

Nordtveit, B. H. (2011). An emerging donor in education and development: A case study of China in Cameroon. *International Journal of Educational Development, 31*(2), 99–108.

Nye, J. S. (1990). *Bound to lead: The changing nature of American power*. New York, NY: Basic Books.

Nye, J. S. (2004). *Soft power: The means to success in world politics*. New York, NY: Public Affairs.

OECD. (2016). *Education at a glance: OECD indicators*. Paris: OECD Publishing.

Phillips, N. (2016). *US tops global research performance: Nature index, 20 April.* Retrieved January 30, 2017, from http://www.natureindex.com/news-blog/us-tops-global-research-performance

Project Atlas-China. (2016). *International students in China.* Retrieved January 31, 2017, from http://www.iie.org/Services/Project-Atlas/China/International-Students-In-China#.WJACVFN96Ul

Ramani, S. (2005, June 10). Interview: Joseph Nye. *The Diplomat.* Retrieved from http://thediplomat.com/2015/06/interview-joseph-nye/

Reilly, J. (2013). China and Japan in Myanmar: Aid, natural resources and influence. *Asian Studies Review, 37*(2), 141–157.

Sawahel, W. (2016, February 1). Seeking soft power, China expands activities in Arab higher education. *Al-Fanar News & Opinion about Higher Education.* Retrieved November 8, 2016, from http://www.al-fanarmedia.org/2016/02/seeking-soft-power-china-expands-activities-in-arab-higer/

Shambaugh, D. (2013). *China goes global: The partial power.* New York, NY: Oxford University Press.

Sharma, Y. (2013 , March 8). Higher education as soft power in the age of autonomy. *University World News.* Retrieved November 8, 2016, from http://www.universityworldnews.com/article.php?story=20130308145531673

Starr, D. (2009). Chinese language education in Europe: The Confucius institutes. *European Journal of Education, 44*(1), 65–82.

Sun, T. (2005). *The art of war* (S. B. Griffith, Trans.). London: Watkins.

Van der Wende, M. C., & Zhu, J. B. (2016). *China: A follower or leader in global higher education?* (Research & Occasional Paper Series No. CSHE.1.16). Berkeley, CA: Center for Studies in Higher Education, University of California.

Wang, H. Y. (2014). *From "taoguang yanghui" to "yousuo zuowei:" China's engagement in financial miniliteralism.* Waterloo: Center for International Governance Innovation.

Wang, H. Y., & French, E. (2013). China's participation in global governance from a comparative perspective. *Asia Policy, 15*(1), 89–114.

Wojciuk, A., Michalek, M., & Stormowska, M. (2015). Education as a source and tool of soft power in international relations. *European Political Science, 14*(3), 298–317.

Wu, J. (2005, November 29). US official: China is becoming an emerging force in international aid to education. *Xinhuanet.* Retrieved December 15, 2013, from http://news.xinhuanet.com/edu/2005-11/29/content_3852818.htm

Wu, X. R. (2013). A comparative study of Chinese and American basic education aid strategies to Africa. *Contemporary Educational Research, 13*, 34–36. (In Chinese)

Xi, J. P. (2014, January 1). Elevate soft power, realize the Chinese dream. *People's Daily* (Overseas ed.). Retrieved January 20, 2017, from http://paper.people.com.cn/rmrbhwb/html/2014-01/01/content_1369744.htm

Xinhua News Agency. (2009, November 9). *China comes to help Africa with aid and whole heart: China premier.* Retrieved December 18, 2013, from http://www.focac.org/eng/ltda/dsjbzjhy/t625624.htm

Yang, R. (2010). Soft power and higher education: An examination of China's Confucius institutes. *Globalization, Societies and Education, 8*(2), 233–243.

Yang, R. (2012). Internationalization, regionalization and soft power: China's relations with ASEAN member countries in higher education. *Frontiers of Education in China, 7*(4), 486–507.

Yang, R. (2014). China's strategy for the internationalization of higher education: An overview. *Frontiers of Education in China, 9*(2), 151–162.

Yang, R., & Xie, M. (2015). Leaning toward the centers: International networking at China's five C9 league universities. *Frontiers of Education in China, 10*(1), 66–90.

Yuan, T. T. (2011). *China's aid modalities of human resource development in Africa and an exploration in Tanzania: Differences and recognitions.* Paper presented at the Development Studies Association-European Association of Development Research and Training Institutes Annual Conference, York.

Zhang, C. (2013). A dynamic approach to the analysis of soft power in international relations. *Journal of China and International Relations, 1*(2), 60–70.

About the Author

Rui Yang is Professor and Associate Dean in the Faculty of Education at The University of Hong Kong. With nearly three decades of academic career in China, Australia and Hong Kong, he has an international reputation among scholars in English and Chinese languages in the fields of comparative and international education and Chinese higher education. With an impressive track record on research at the interface of Chinese and Western traditions in education, he is frequently called on to deploy his cross-cultural knowledge and expertise globally. He has an extensive list of publications, research projects, invited keynote lectures in international conferences, leadership in professional associations, and membership in editorial boards of scholarly journals. Bridging the theoretical thrust of comparative education and the applied nature of international education, his research interests include education policy, cross-cultural studies in education, international higher education, educational development in Chinese societies, and global politics in educational research.

CHAPTER 3

Dynamics of Internationalization in U.S. and Chinese Higher Education

Katherine Punteney and Yilin Wei

Abstract

The United States and Chinese higher education systems are undertaking internationalization within a context of rapid global change. Those changes include the massification and commodification of education, emphasis on developing students' global competency, and the publication of international rankings of institutions. Examining student mobility, curriculum internationalization, research collaboration, and international partnerships, this chapter compares and contrasts U.S. and Chinese internationalization contexts, policies, and priorities. Areas of partnerships between the two nations are introduced, such as student and scholar mobility, joint degrees, branch campuses, language learning, and cultural exchange. For the partnerships to be successful, proponents must find ways to work within both cultural and political contexts, conforming to the realities and requirements of both systems.

1 Introduction

The internationalization of higher education is of growing international importance and the United States and China play key global roles in all facets, including student mobility, curriculum internationalization, research collaboration, and international partnerships. Worldwide, the higher education landscape is shifting and national education systems, as well as individual institutions, are adapting and reacting to these changes. The global changes include neoliberalism, the massification and commodification of education, increasing emphasis on developing graduates' global competency to prepare them to take their places in a globally connected workforce, and the development and publication of international higher education rankings which are, in part, compelling emphasis on both research and internationalization as universities strive for global recognition.

© KONINKLIJKE BRILL NV, LEIDEN, 2018 | DOI 10.1163/9789004368361_003

Despite sharing some elements of common context, internationalization efforts in China and the U.S. have manifested quite differently. In the U.S., the national government is relatively less involved whereas the Chinese government has a much more active role in education policy and oversight, along with more involvement in the work of individual institutions. Both China and the U.S. actively send university students and receive them from other nations. Notably, the U.S. is the world's number one receiver of international students and China is the number one sender (Macready & Tucker, 2011).

Regional partnerships play a much greater role in Chinese internationalization than they do in the U.S. In particular, China has engaged heavily with Association of Southeast Asian (ASEAN) countries and sponsors many transnational education programs. Chinese internationalization has emphasized English language learning and encouraged the introduction of Chinese language and culture to the rest of the world. In the U.S., there is greater emphasis on student mobility and the development of international partnerships. Curriculum internationalization focuses on preparing graduates to engage in the global workforce, while learning world languages gets little attention in the U.S. colleges and universities, despite the existence of multiple U.S. government sponsored language programs. These and other differences are highlighted in this chapter.

As part of their efforts to internationalize, U.S. and Chinese institutions have embarked on many collaborative initiatives aiming to benefit the students and institutions in both countries. These partnerships are extensive and continually growing in number. They include collaborations such as student and scholar exchange, joint degrees, branch campuses, research collaborations, and cross-cultural programming. Challenges include differing values related to education, communication and logistical barriers, and the disparate role of government in higher education in the two nations. For partnerships to be a success, and to contribute to internationalization, they must be designed to benefit all of the partners, and substantial time needs to be invested in communication, logistics, and relationship-building.

Introducing internationalization in U.S. and Chinese contexts, this chapter examines the role of government, the emphases of internationalization efforts, U.S.-Chinese partnerships, and the challenges to partnerships given the different political, economic, and cultural contexts for internationalization in each nation. This chapter is organized in five sections: (1) An introduction to the literature on the internationalization of higher education; (2) An introduction to global education policy; (3) Discussion of internationalization trends and characteristics in the U.S.; (4) Discussion of internationalization trends and characteristics in China; and (5) Examination of partnerships trends between the U.S. and China and the accompanying benefits and challenges.

2   Internationalization of Higher Education

Although the exact meaning of internationalization is contested (Hudzik, 2015; Knight, 2004), the most commonly accepted definition, arguably, is that internationalization is "the process of integrating an international, intercultural or global dimension into the purpose, functions or delivery of post-secondary education" (Knight, 2004, p. 11). This definition emphasizes that internationalization is happening both within and beyond higher education institutions in a wide range of sectors including nonprofits, government, and public and private universities. Further, the definition emphasizes internationalization as a strategic process with a focus on intercultural or global competency-related outcomes.

    Within universities, activities of internationalization typically include internationalizing the curriculum, recruiting international students, sending students abroad, supporting faculty international research and collaboration, and partnerships between universities. Other aspects of internationalization may include establishment of branch campuses, using technology for international engagement, community outreach, and international development projects (Hudzik, 2015). Though Knight's 2004 definition emphasizes that internationalization is a process that applies to all aspects of an institution's work, the internationalization of student services, for example career counseling, receives less attention in the internationalization literature (Punteney, 2012). While much of the assessment of internationalization focuses on measuring outputs, such as the number of students studying abroad, leaders in the field remind us that internationalization is not just the activities, but also the processes, of achieving more internationalized institutions and developing global competency in graduates (Knight, 2004; Hudzik, 2015).

    In an international survey of universities, the International Association of Universities (IAU) found that 87% of higher education institutions include reference to internationalization in their mission statements and 78% of institutions reported that emphasis on internationalization has been increasing (Egron-Polak & Hudson, 2010). Rationales for internationalization are wide-ranging and include academic, economic, political and socio-cultural motivations (Knight, 2004). In the IAU survey, the most frequently offered reason for internationalization was to improve student preparedness for a globalized world, while other common institutional goals included enhancing the reputation of the institution, strengthening research and knowledge production, and internationalizing the curriculum (Egron-Polok & Hudson, 2010).

Internationalization of the curriculum is typically a key component of comprehensive internationalization. It can be conducted at the course, department, or institution level through a structured cycle of (1) reflection and self-evaluation; (2) imagining what is possible; (3) developing plans and priorities; (4) taking action; and (5) evaluating the results and then beginning the cycle again (Leask, 2015). Betty Leask's "Questionnaire on Internationalization of the Curriculum" is a commonly used tool for beginning the process of structured reflection (see Leask, 2015 for two versions of the questionnaire). The process of internationalization of a higher education institution follows a similar format of structured reflection, planning, action, accountability, and assessment in a cyclical process. Increasingly, institutions are trying to formalize this process (Ergron-Polok, 2010).

3   Global Policy Context

The conceptualization of the role of higher education has changed in the past 50 years in a shift towards neoliberalism. Where there was once an unquestioned belief that the purpose of higher education was to serve the well-being of society, higher education is now thought to serve the primary goal of maximizing the economic competitiveness of individuals and nations. While education policy was previously focused on promoting national values, socialism in the case of China and democracy in the case of the U.S., now the strongest policy focus is on economic competitiveness. To achieve this goal, the minimization of government influence in economic markets is widely believed to be desirable and essential (Olssen & Peters, 2005). Scott (2016) describes three ways in which this shift towards neoliberalism manifests itself in higher education: (1) public funding for education has dwindled because the ideal of public funding of services is at odds with the current belief in the value of free markets, (2) globalization has created increased opportunities for intercultural and international education while also erecting barriers particularly in the form of immigration controls, and (3) changes in communication technology and norms have increased capacity for higher education to offer educational programs remotely or in non-traditional ways, while also allowing for greater individual access to information production and consumption.

Ziguras and McBurnie (2015) argue that there are three ideologies which shape national government policies related to the internationalization of higher education. The first is a commitment to free trade in general, and in the education sector in particular. The second is a desire to avoid the negative consequences of global academic mobility, including brain drain, increasing inequity, and potential exploitation of students. The third is a commitment to playing an active role in regulating mobility for purposes of economic and social development. These motivations affect government policy in varied ways. In some cases, they lead to a policy commitment that there should not be trade barriers in education. In other cases, they lead to developing programs to develop a nation's workforce with global skills such as language and technology skills. In developing government policy to support (or hinder) internationalization, governments may engage in lawmaking, funding, promotion, monitoring, or creation of international education initiatives. Policy analysts generally agree that there is a link between the higher education sector of a nation and its economic competitiveness. As economies grow in prosperity, they typically shift more towards a knowledge economy, which necessitates the development of advanced expertise among college graduates, which in turn prompts further economic growth, in a virtuous cycle (Jain, 2015; Lim, 2015).

3.1   *Internationalization and Rankings*
Rankings of higher education institutions have gained increasing importance over the last decade as institutions compete for reputation and prestige. Global rankings were first issued by the Shanghai Jiao Tong University Institute of Higher Education in 2003 and Times Higher Education (THE) in 2004 (Marginson, 2010). The QS World University Rankings were launched in 2010, breaking away from a prior partnership with THE. Universities play an essential role in the global knowledge economy that encompasses intellectual property, industrial know-how, and knowledge and research that is freely circulated (Marginson, 2010). Based on the internationalization rationale related to global competitiveness and scientific and technological achievement, the higher education rankings emphasize research output without regard to quality of instruction (Marginson, 2010). Such rankings give greatest weight to research awards and publication in top journals. Leading journals are typically published in English, giving an advantage to universities in English speaking societies and reinforcing the power and prestige that the institutions already have. Further, rankings compare all institutions to each other, without categories, ignoring the diversity of missions of institutions worldwide (Marginson, 2010; Lim, 2015). Rankings pressure may result in institutions developing policies and programs in contradiction to their missions, and a gradual convergence of institution types into the research university model. Despite the criticisms, rankings have strongly affected higher education policies and programs as governments and institutions seek to compete on the global scale to gain the reputation of world-class universities.

3.2   *Commodification of Higher Education*
Higher education is being increasingly commodified. Rather than being considered a public good that governments support in order to develop a

highly skilled and well-educated citizenry, education is being looked at with an entrepreneurial lens, and policy makers and administrators are seeking ways in which education can generate revenue. With a need for new sources of revenue, institutions seek to enroll students from outside national boundaries, both for existing and new programs. This can manifest in increased recruitment and enrollment of international students, twinning programs, branch campuses, online degrees, and many other configurations (Knight, 2008). The General Agreement of Trade in Services (GATS) has facilitated these changes by encouraging national governments to limit barriers to trade in education (Knight, 2008). Certain countries, including the U.S., United Kingdom, and Australia are predominantly "receiving" nations, welcoming many international students. Other countries such as India and South Korea are predominantly "sending" nations in that many of their young adults go abroad for study while comparatively few international arrive. China and Japan are both sending and receiving countries, sending many students abroad, while also enrolling an increasing number of international students themselves, particularly from among their Asia-Pacific neighbors (Macready & Tucker, 2011).

3.3   *Massification of Higher Education*
Another impactful global trend is the massification of education. Many nations are engaged in the process of higher education massification, the pervasive access of the general population, rather than just the elites, to higher education. Between 1995 and 2011, the worldwide gross tertiary enrollment rate (the percentage of the world population, in the relevant age group, who are enrolled in higher education) increased from 15% to 30% (Marginson, 2015a). Based on population growth and rates of higher education massification, by 2020, it is predicted that more than half of the world's students enrolled in higher education will be from China, India, the U.S., and Brazil (Mahbubani & Chye, 2015), forcing expansion of these education systems.

4   Internationalization Dimensions in the U.S.

Internationalization in the U.S. is driven much less directly by government policy than in the rest of the world. In the U.S., the public higher education system is managed through the states rather than national government, and there is a large private education sector with little government oversight. Therefore, the economic and political goals of the national government, which might in many countries shape education policy, play a lesser role in the United States (Green, 2010). In fact, in a global survey, North American universities named the lack of internationalization as a top national policy priority as one of the three primary external barriers to internationalization. No other world regions rated this concern among their top three (Egron-Polok & Hudson, 2010). The comparative lack of national concern in the U.S. for higher education internationalization is likely the result of the assignment of responsibility for education to the state governments in the highly decentralized U.S. system. The lack of a national internationalization policy may be reinforced by the complacency of a dominant economic power, used to having the most highly regarded higher education system in the world.

Though comparatively less involved in education than in many other countries, the U.S. federal government is still involved in international higher education in significant ways that promote internationalization. The U.S. government actively tries to attract international students to the U.S. through the Department of State's Education USA network of advising offices located around the world. In addition, the Department of Commerce's education section promotes international trade in education and offers support to institutions aiming to recruit international students. The U.S. government runs a range of citizen diplomacy programs which bring both students and professionals to the U.S., as well as sending U.S. citizens to other parts of the world (Macready & Tucker, 2011). Signature programs include the Fulbright Program, International Visitor Leadership Program, Humphrey Fellowships, and Boren Fellowship, among many others. More than 55,000 participants travel overseas through Department of State funded exchange each year (Bureau of Educational and Cultural Affairs, 2016).

The Department of State has launched an Office of U.S. Study Abroad within the Bureau of Educational and Cultural Affairs, tasked with promoting study abroad. In collaboration with the government and more than 600 partner institutions, the Institute of International Education is spearheading Generation Study Abroad which aims to double the number of U.S. students who study abroad by the end of the decade. Among the 600 partner organizations, $185 million has been pledged to support study abroad and 188 institutions and organizations have pledged to at least double the number of students they have who study abroad. Additionally, 84% of the partner organizations have committed to creating scholarships for underrepresented students to study abroad (Institute of International Education, 2015a). Many states and regional consortia have also been formed to recruit international students. Campaigns include *Destination Indiana* for the state of Indiana and *One Big Campus* for the Philadelphia area (Macready & Tucker, 2011).

Further, a survey of 1,020 U.S. institutions of higher education found that 32% of institutions refer to international or global education in their mission statements and 19% refer to some other aspects of internationalization. Among institutions, 35% said that internationalization is among the top five priorities in the institution's strategic plan (American Council on Education, 2012). Internationalization in the U.S. is not limited to institutions of higher education. Cross-border education and programs are increasingly run by private and publicly traded companies including Apollo Group, Kaplan, and DeVry, rather than by non-profit entities (Altbach & Knight, 2007). The U.S. pays the least attention to the global rankings, focusing instead on the *U.S. News and World Reports* rankings of U.S. colleges and universities, indicating a complacent assumption that the top U.S. institutions will remain at the top of the global rankings (Marginson, 2010). This lack of concern for rankings and global comparison leaves the U.S. susceptible to ultimately losing in the global race for superiority, and potentially losing its reputational domination in higher education.

4.1   *Student Mobility*

Student mobility into and out of the United States is at an all-time high. For the 2014/2015 academic year, the Institute of International Education (2016) reports that there were nearly 1,044,000 international students studying in U.S. colleges and universities. This is a 7% increase over the previous year and part of a 60-year trend in which international student enrollments in the U.S. increased almost every year. In the last decade, the number of undergraduate international students studying in the U.S. has just surpassed graduate students. The most common fields of study are Engineering (20.8%), Business and Management (19.2%),and Math and Computer Science (13.6%) (Institute of International Education, 2016). Using a different data set, U.S. Immigration and Customs Enforcement (2016) reports that there are 1,184,324 students with F and M visas studying in the United States, 200,861 J visa exchange visitors, and 157,014 spouses or children accompanying those above.

The U.S. is the most popular destination for the world's internationally mobile students seeking a degree outside their home country. While most of the world's students come to the U.S. for an entire degree, students from Europe are more likely to come on an exchange program for a semester or year (Institute of International Education, 2015b), primarily with the goal of cultural enrichment. Reasons that degree-seeking students are attracted to the U.S. include the large number of institutions and variety of programs, opportunity to learn or improve English language skills, the reputation of the higher education system for providing high quality study opportunities, the possibility to study a subject not available at home, the prospect of career opportunities in the U.S., or the expectation that a U.S. education will lead to better jobs or a higher salary in the home country (Macready & Tucker, 2011). A potential deterrent for both short-term and degree-seeking students is the high cost of tuition and living in the U.S. (Macready & Tucker, 2011).

The number of U.S. students studying abroad is also at an all-time high of more than 313,000 studying abroad for academic credit in 2014/2015 (Institute of International Education, 2016). Of the U.S. students who study abroad, the most represented majors are Science, Technology, Engineering and Math (23.9%), Business (20.1%), and Social Sciences (17.3%). The greatest number of U.S. students study abroad in the United Kingdom followed by Italy, Spain, France, and China (Institute of International Education, 2016). Whereas international students are most likely to come to the U.S. to complete a degree, the Institute of International Education (2016) reports that U.S. students are more likely to study abroad for a period of their studies, with a trend towards shorter programs. In fact, only 2.5% of U.S. students who study abroad do so for a year, while 34.3% study abroad for one semester or one or two quarters, and 63.1% participate in summer or shorter programs. Generally, these programs are considered a complement to a student's degrees at home, offering additional language or culture study. While the majority of U.S. students who study abroad do so for only a part of their degree, the Institute of International Education gathered data from 14 countries where U.S. students frequently study abroad. They found that 46,500 U.S. students were directly enrolled in full degree programs at universities in these countries (Belyavina & Bhandari, 2013).

Despite the increase in the number of U.S. students studying abroad, less than 10% of students who graduate with associate and bachelor's degrees in the U.S. have studied abroad. Students from minority groups are underrepresented in U.S. study abroad. Although these students make up almost 40% of all enrollments in U.S. higher education, they are less than 25% of the population of students who study abroad (Institute of International Education, 2015a). It is this minimal enrollment that prompted the initiative of Generation Study Abroad (discussed above) by those who believe in the power, importance, and urgency of developing the global competence of U.S. graduates.

4.2   Research

Since the 1940s, it has been U.S. government policy to engage in research and development in order to promote economic growth. Key principles include a commitment to develop talented scientists and to distribute scientific knowledge (Jain, 2015). To achieve this goal, the U.S. government set aside funding for research agencies such as the National Science Foundation and the National Institutes of Health. In addition, the U.S. government developed a system for collaboration between higher education, government, and industry in which basic research was done by universities and disseminated freely so that applied research and innovation would follow (Jain, 2015).

The U.S. and Europe dominated research output through the 1970s. Since that time, however, research output from outside the U.S. and Europe has boomed, with particular growth in Russia, India, China, and South Korea. In the early 1970s, 73% of research publications came from Group of 7 (G7) countries. Now, only about half are being produced by authors in G7 countries (Adams, Pendlebury, & Stembridge, 2013). Investment in research by businesses in the U.S. has remained static, while Chinese business investment in research increased between 2005 and 2010 (Adams et al., 2013). This global shift in research, and the correlations between research and economic growth, reinforces a U.S. policy emphasis on the need for global competitiveness.

In the U.S., as government funding for U.S. higher education has decreased, universities in the public sector in particular have had to develop alternative revenue streams. Increasingly, academic capitalism is developing, defined as "the involvement of colleges and faculty in market-like behaviors" (Rhoades & Slaughter, 2004, p. 37). One of the characteristics of academic capitalism is an emphasis on research as a revenue source through developing and licensing patents and developing partnerships with industry (Rhoades & Slaughter, 2004). This pursuit of revenue deviates from the historical expectation that universities freely distribute research findings for the betterment of society. Given the global nature of science, technology, and most contemporary issues (climate change, terrorism, poverty, etc.), international research collaborations often develop organically from the academic interests of the researchers themselves (Laughlin, 2008). With academic capitalism on the rise, however, more and more scientific research is being held as proprietary industry knowledge, rather than being shared freely among the international scientific community.

4.3   Curriculum

In a survey of U.S. colleges and universities, the American Council on Education (ACE) (2012) found that 51% of institutions reference internationalization or international education in their mission statement. For example, many institutions speak of preparing students to be effective global citizens or to be prepared for professional and civic lives in a globalized world. While this emphasis on internationalization has shown steady growth over time, there is still room for improvement in the amount of emphasis placed on internationalization in general, and more specifically, internationalization of the curriculum. The same ACE survey shows that:

- Only 26% of institutions have established international or global student learning outcomes for all students, while 29% have established global learning outcomes for students in some departments or programs.
- Only 26% of institutions provide funding for the internationalization of courses or programs while 55% of institutions report that they are engaged in initiatives to internationalize the undergraduate curriculum.

- Only 2% of institutions have a foreign language requirement for all undergraduates while 25% have foreign language requirements for some students, presumably in particular degree programs. The most common requirement is one year of language study.
- Only 28% of institutions require undergraduates to take a general education course that features global issues (such as global health, environment, etc.).
- Only 29% of institutions require undergraduates to take a general education course that features perspectives, issues, or events from areas outside the U.S. Of the institutions with these requirements, 56% require one course, while 27% require two courses, and 17% require three or more courses.

Despite the increase in number of universities focused on internationalization, the Modern Language Association of America found that enrollments in foreign languages declined 6.7% between 2009 and 2013 in a survey of U.S. colleges and universities. Although this decline is partially attributed to overall decreases in higher education enrollment, it is also notable that less than 10% of tertiary students nationwide take language courses other than English (Goldberg, Looney, & Lusin, 2015).

In addition to collecting data on internationalization at U.S. colleges and universities, the American Council on Education runs the ACE Internationalization Laboratory. This program provides structure and guidance to U.S. institutions working on internationalization. Operated in a cohort system, each institution forms a senior leadership team for internationalization and works through a guided, structured process of evaluation and planning, including discussing issues within the cohort and receiving site visits from ACE staff (American Council on Education, n.d.). One approach to internationalizing the curriculum is to use technology to connect individuals, classrooms, and faculty virtually. This facilitates intercultural interaction and collaboration without the physical movement of people across borders (American Council on Education, 2010; American Council on Education, 2016). Together with the State University of New York (SUNY) Collaborative Online International Learning (COIL) Center, ACE launched the Internationalization through Technology Awards program which supports and promotes the use of technology to enhance global learning while showcasing outstanding programs (American Council on Education, 2016).

An area of opportunity for internationalization of the curriculum is to encourage faculty to develop international experience, understanding, and collaborations. The benefits of developing the international and intercultural competence of the faculty have the potential to be widespread:

- The more knowledge faculty have about their disciplines in international context, the better prepared they will be to internationalize their own courses through incorporation of international topics, perspectives, and materials.

- With a trend in student mobility towards short-term programs, the result has been increased demand for short, faculty-led programs. The more faculty who can lead the programs and the diversity of majors offering such programs will likely increase the number of students who participate in study abroad.
- The more faculty know about other cultures, the better they will be able to support the international students in their courses and facilitate meaningful intercultural dialogue in the classroom.
- If faculty are engaged in international conferences or research, they are more likely to make the kinds of international connections that would enable them to make meaningful contributions to global challenges.
- As faculty have more international experience, they are more likely to develop relationships with colleagues with whom they can develop technology-supported connections between both of their classrooms.
- Faculty connections and international relationships are a common foundation for building successful joint and dual degrees (see below).

U.S. systems of faculty evaluation, including the hiring and tenure review processes, rarely place value on international research, collaboration, or experience. Within the structures of a system with intense pressure to publish, faculty typically have little incentive to invest their limited time and energy in expanding their international work or in internationalizing the curricula of the courses they teach. Institutions have done little to systematically develop these competencies in faculty, though when they do there is great potential for benefit (Brewer, 2015; Williams & Lee, 2015; Pysarchik & Hudzik, 2015).

As U.S. higher education culture as a whole has placed increasing emphasis on assessment, so, too, has international education. Increasingly, educators are being asked to measure and document the outcomes of internationalization. While this sometimes manifests in measuring the number of students engaged in a particular activity, such as study abroad, more often institutions are being asked to document student learning outcomes. Desired learning outcomes may include increased understanding of global systems, appreciation for the arts, intercultural communication skills, soft skills such as adaptability, and language skills. Assessing student learning at the program and institutional level requires careful articulation of the target learning goals and development of a way to measure and capture changes in student learning. In the U.S., the allocation of funding and resources is increasingly linked to demonstrating the effectiveness of internationalization efforts, particularly with regard to curriculum and academic programs (Hudzik, 2015).

4.4 *Partnerships*

Within the context of internationalization, partnerships can expand and strengthen internationalization efforts in research, curriculum, and student mobility. Discussed in previous sections are the potential for research collaborations, classroom to classroom connections, and student exchange. Increasingly, U.S. universities are engaging in international partnerships with other institutions or foreign governments in order to internationalize their institutions. In this section, two additional key areas for U.S. international partnerships are introduced: branch campuses and joint degrees.

The Cross-Border Education Research Team (2016) has identified 90 branch campuses around the world established by U.S. colleges and universities along with 10 that opened but are now closed. In many cases, these campuses were established with substantial investment of foreign governments, eager to expand and improve their higher education systems (e.g. Write, 2010). For the U.S. university, the motivation may be prestige, creation of international opportunities for home country students, and/or developing new revenue streams. Branch campuses have the potential to help internationalize the home university by facilitating student exchange, faculty exchange, and international collaborations. Often these campuses are established by top administrators which can cause rancor among the faculty, upset that resources are being directed away from the home campus, that the home campus mission is not being served, or that they as faculty were not involved in the decision-making (Altbach, 2013). In the host country, students are often attracted by the possibility of earning a prestigious U.S. degree without having to leave their families and home country. However, branch campuses may vary substantially in terms of the extent to which they deliver education of the same quality and style as the home institution, raising ethical concerns about the fair treatment of students (Altbach, 2013).

Joint and double degrees are another type of partnership that is proliferating. A 2011 Institute of International Education survey found that, among U.S. institutions who responded, 22% offered joint degrees (students earn one degree, awarded jointly by two institutions) and 82% offered double degrees (students earn a degree from each institution). Seventy-seven percent of these institutions established their first joint or double degree between 2001 and 2009, demonstrating the relative recency of this trend. The top country for U.S. partner institutions was China, followed by France, Turkey, Germany, and India (Obst, Kuder, & Banks, 2011). Goals of U.S. institutions in the establishment of joint and double degrees include preparing graduates for success in a global workforce, maintaining the U.S. competitive advantage in business, science, and technology, internationalizing the curriculum, creating a competitive advantage to attract prospective students, and the prestige of being globally engaged (Delisle, 2009; Obst et al., 2011).

Partnerships are very challenging as well as labor-intensive and many fail. Among the challenges are language barriers, varied cultural values around education, communication styles, needing to align the requirements of two education systems, and the extensive bureaucracy involved. Extensive time must be given to logistics, communication, and relationship building. Partnerships are typically most effective when built on an already existing and successful partnership, such as building a joint degree program with a partner with whom an institution already has a successful student exchange., Knowing this, the most common way that institutions find partner universities is by building on existing relationships, such as existing faculty connections (Obst et al., 2011; West, 2015).

5   Internationalization Dimensions in China

The internationalization of Chinese higher education can be traced back almost two centuries. In 1840, following the defeat of the Chinese Empire in the Opium Wars, China was introduced to the concept of modern Western education. Chinese higher education started in 1912, with one university and 94 professional staff. Chinese involvement in World War II against Japan slowed the development of higher education institutions until 1949. By 1949, there were only 205 colleges and universities with a total of 116,504 students. Beginning in 1949, Chinese higher education shifted its attention to the Soviet model. The Soviet model of higher education emphasized producing industrial workers to meet the needs of a socialist economy (Abrahamsen, 2012). Aiming to contribute to the public good and the prosperity of the nation, colleges and universities were highly specialized, offering a limited number of majors and subjects. Enrollments grew rapidly. In 1960, the system had its peak with almost one million students. Then, during the 10 years of the Cultural Revolution (1966–1976), many universities and colleges were shut down and the national entrance test (Gao kao) was officially banned. From 1966 to 1969, no new students were enrolled among the entire system (Li, 2010).

Reform and expansion of the Chinese higher education system began in 1977 and 1978 facilitated by the economic reforms of Deng Xiaoping. This period can be described as the pre-massification of Chinese higher education in terms of the number of universities and student enrollment. The Chinese government has implemented a market-oriented reform in the higher education system in the aspects of admission, tuition, international collaboration, and assisting the labor market (Li, 2010). However, Abrahamsen (2012), identifies two persistent obstacles to Chinese educational reform, "the old Soviet-borrowed concept as a means of producing workers for a socialist-style economy" (para. 9) and "social control as one crucial traditional role of Chinese education" (para. 11).

5.1   *Contemporary Policy Context*

The current development of Chinese higher education is closely associated with the ideologies of *knowledge economy* and *human capital,* following the global imperative to cultivate competitive manpower to ensure the prosperity of the national economy. Benefiting from the rapid growth of the Chinese economy, Chinese higher education has been driven to set up a solid technology base, influenced by western higher education systems (Ennew & Fujia, 2009). Thus, it has been experiencing a reform process with four dimensions: commercialization, decentralization, systematic expansion, and marketization and privatization (Wu & Zheng, 2008). Another contemporary trend of Chinese higher education is to build up "world-class universities." Specifically, "a research university with world-class capacity, often called a world-class research university, is regarded as a central part of any academic system and is imperative to developing a nation's competitiveness in the global knowledge economy" (Wang, Wang, & Liu, 2011, p. 33). The Chinese way to build a world-class research university features a top-down policy, with the majority of funding facilitated by the national government and directed towards a few elite institutions. The priority of the Chinese government towards higher education is the necessity of improving academic quality and producing graduates who have increased professional capacity (Huang, 2015). Moreover, in the light of western research universities and global university rankings, and even more, the nation's competitive characteristic, China has been forced to promote the idea of world-class research universities. Projects 211 and 985, which were implemented during the 1990s, are the most observable national reaction to the trend. Project 211 focuses on upgrading the teaching and research quality at 100 Chinese universities while Project 985 aims to advance a small group of Chinese universities to the level of world-class universities with international ranking and reputation (Xinyu, 2009). Those Universities are featured as institutions for "carrying social, cultural, ideological, political and economic responsibilities to the country" (Ma & Yue, 2015, p. 218).

5.2   *Cultural Influences in Chinese Higher Education*

Cultural beliefs and values shape institutions as well as policy making (Liu, 2012). In China, top government offices espouse collectivist cultural beliefs and values. Modern Chinese culture can be characterized by two parallel mainstream philosophies: Confucianism and Communism. Both philosophies promote the mindset that education is a societal duty with both private and public benefits (Liu, 2012). Confucianism has encouraged submission to social hierarchy in Chinese society for the purposes of "harmony and prosperity" (Chow, 1996). At the same time, Communism, which partially integrates Marxism, promotes the idea of civic engagement. These influences have been found to cause difficulties for individuals to accomplish their own self-achievement, and instead reinforces "meritocratic elitism" (Liu, 2012, p. 650). Under these conditions, Chinese culture has become "goal-oriented, emphasizing doing and results" (Liu, 2012, p. 650). At the same time, the neglect of a critical orientation has become one of the biggest issues in Chinese education. The most direct consequences may be that graduates lack critical thinking capabilities and many education leaders are more focused on short-term gains than concerned with long-term transformation of the education system and creating transformative educational outcomes for students.

The Chinese education system is shaped by a strong and detailed national policy agenda (Marginson, 2011). Decentralization, as an important approach of Chinese higher education's reform, has changed the dynamic among universities, local authorities, and private entities. However, most decisions in education are still made by the central power with a strict top-down structure. The investment in higher education in China has been closely associated with the national culture and history. For the public good, the higher education system promotes national development and political stability, especially in technology and among the social elite (Liu, 2012). With regard to individual gains, Chinese families are very eager to invest in education to build their children's social capital (Liu, 2012). Because expansion and investment in higher education in China is a shared goal for both collective and individual development, it is easy for the national government to take charge.

5.3   *Student Mobility*

In upper-middle-income countries like China, the main motivations for engaging in internationalization are the promotion of both in-bound and out-bound student mobility, as well as a desire to Westernize the curriculum (Ma & Yue, 2015). Student mobility in China can be examined by looking at three main trends: (1) the increasing outflow of Chinese students for foreign degrees; (2) the increasing inflow of international students to attend Chinese universities in China; and (3) the increasing return of foreign-trained Chinese students who may work or continue studying in Chinese universities (Pan, 2010). Between 1978 and 2013, 3,058,600 Chinese students studied overseas, which makes China the largest export country of international students in the world (Neubauer & Zhang, 2015). In 2013 alone, there were 413,900 Chinese students studying abroad (Ministry of Education of the People's Republic of China, 2013).

While student mobility was primarily supported and promoted by Chinese government initiatives in the past, now many middle-class students, supported by family funds, make the individual and family choice to study abroad in order to enhance their social capital (Fong, 2004; Fang, 2012;

Tsang, 2013). Before 2001, when China officially joined the World Trade Organization (WTO), financial aid provided by either the foreign institutions or local authorities was the only resource for most Chinese students if they wanted to study aboard. From 1996 to 2006, the largest increase of Chinese international students was in the range of self-funded students who benefited from the rapidly increasing Chinese economy. In 1998, there were 11,000 self-funded Chinese students studying abroad. In 2006, the number had increased to 121,000 (Pan, 2010). Self-funded students have full freedom to choose schools, majors, and degree plans. More importantly, they can also engage in the host country's job market, if there are opportunities. Thus, the option of enrolling in different disciplines in foreign universities has opened up a less politically-dependent condition than in the past. Even with these changes, the student motivation for studying abroad remains the same: becoming more competitive in the job search.

While many more Chinese students have the financial means to choose a foreign university, the rapid growth in the number of Chinese students choosing to earn degrees abroad is also heavily impacted by perceived weaknesses in the Chinese higher education system. In other words, the disparity in quality between the Chinese higher education and some Western countries' systems has been pushing the local students away. The perceived weaknesses of the Chinese higher education include the uneven development in different geographic regions in China, the traditional teaching methodologies (Yang, 2008), limited research resources, and the traditional educational structures in both recruitment and curriculum (Pan, 2010). Li (2010) mentions that, since 1994, the number of Chinese students in foreign graduate programs was one-third of those enrolled in Chinese graduate programs. In addition, in recruitment for both the Chinese job market as a whole, and for Chinese academic institutions specifically, foreign-trained Chinese graduates are often considered more highly qualified than most graduates educated in China.

Meanwhile, the international student inflow population is also increasing. In 2012, the total number of international students studying in China reached 328,330 (Kuroda, 2014). The initiative "Plan for Study in China," created by the Ministry of Education of the People's Republic of China (2010) indicates that by 2020, the population of international students in China should reach 500,000. The increase over the past 20 years has averaged 2.245% annually. The Chinese government is aiming to establish China as the country in Asia that attracts the largest population of international students (Kuroda, 2014). However, the diversity of majors in which international students enroll remains relatively limited. Most programs in which international students enroll focus on language, culture and business. Very few programs focus on science and technology, and those that do typically include Chinese language and culture courses, rather than scientific subjects only. In addition, international students in China are mostly enrolled in non-degree programs, other than those majoring in Chinese language (Kuroda, 2014).

The third trend of Chinese student mobility is the inflow of foreign-trained graduates. During the early 1990s, when most Chinese students studying abroad were government-funded, students were required to return to China as a condition of their scholarships. Now, most Chinese students who go abroad are self-funded and therefore have the choice to return or pursue other opportunities abroad. Their decisions are typically influenced by the flows of the global market (Pan, 2011). Between 1978 and late 2006, 1.067 billion Chinese international students left China to study abroad. Of those, only 275,000 students returned to work in China (Pan, 2010). In the last decade the number of the returnees has increased exponentially, based on an initiative undertaken by the nation to encourage the returnees to become entrepreneurs, government leaders, and university faculty members. By 2003, returned students established some 5,000 companies with a profit value of RMB$30 billion – mostly high-tech enterprises located in start-up business parks (CSCSE.EDU.CN, 2006, as cited in Pan, 2010).

China's growing economy and national emphasis on internationalization reinforces the national importance of attracting foreign-trained Chinese graduates to repatriate. Beginning in 1992, the national government announced three principles for overseas studies: "undertaking to support oversea studies, encouraging the returnees, and lifting restrictions on the students' coming and going" (Pan, 2010, p. 268). Later, the Chinese government prompted more programs to support Chinese universities to recruit young and highly achieving foreign-trained scholars, such as the Changjiang Project and Qianren Project in both science and social science disciplines (Yuan, 2011). The programs are intended to promote returnees who will stimulate advancement in business, industry, and education.

Furthermore, the national government also wants to take in foreign-trained students to invigorate economic and educational reforms in the policy arena (Pan, 2010). Culturally and politically, it has been a big step forward for the Chinese government to try to change their political leadership's views on foreign-trained students since the politically-charged 1989 student movement. Political tensions have cooled since the Tiananmen Square era, yet the government still seems unsure of the actual impact returnees may have because most returnees are located in the field of education, academic research, finance and foreign affairs (Pan, 2010). In general, governmental departments related to education, research, and finance in China have less influence in terms of passing legislation than other government branches. To this end, placing highly qualified returnees in those branches creates less tension in terms of possible potential political conflicts between the foreign trained officers and those trained in China.

5.4   Curriculum

In 2001, the Chinese Ministry of Education (MOE) issued regulations that "5–10% of all the undergraduate curriculum must be taught in English or bilingual, especially in biology, information technology, finance, and law" (Hu, 2007; Liu, 2001, as cited in Ma & Yue, 2015, p. 222). In the years since, language, especially English, has become the starting point of Chinese higher education's curriculum reform. Most universities in China have adapted bilingual education or even English only programs over the past decade (Yuan, 2011).

Another key aspect of the internationalization of the curriculum in China is a shift towards more Western teaching methods. The focus of teaching methodologies has transferred from teacher-oriented to student-oriented. With this change, the students' learning style has been shifted from individual study to collaborative study for students to support and motivate each other on and off campus (Mok, 2007).

5.5   Research

The U.S university model emphasis on a combination of teaching, research, and service has been implemented in China to replace the former Soviet model. Professors in all disciplines are encouraged to take part in more research within their own fields and preferably across borders. The competition for research support is intense. In response, the Chinese central government has already founded two national foundations, the National Natural Science Foundation and the National Social Science Foundation. Both foundations help the government to evaluate the best university programs in research and also provide funding for substantial financial support to scientists (Mohrman, 2008).

Altbach (2013) indicates that universities in developing countries will not be able to "attract and retain top academic talent," if the academic freedom is lacking (p. 44). In recent years, scholars in China have found that there is increasing academic freedom in conducting research, especially in the natural sciences. The key step forward to academic freedom is internal governance (Huang, 2015). Within elite national universities, there is some "governance autonomy" (Huang, 2015, p. 211) provided to support the international competition which requires massive scientific innovation. The Chinese way to achieve its innovation is completely different from other advanced nations. Its model relies heavily on private companies and government research institutes, instead of universities, although in recent years, China has increased its investment in university research. As a result of striving for innovation, the expansion of Chinese publications in science and engineering has become significant (Zhang, Patton, & Kenny, 2013). By 2008, the proportion of Science Citation Index citations (SCI) has increased to 30% of the number of citations by U.S. authors (Zhang, Patton, & Kenny, 2013). However, government support of academic freedom in the social sciences is still limited. Many research universities focus on the natural sciences to maximize financial support from state and local authorities and corporations (Mohrman, 2008). This condition may cause a deficit in social science knowledge nationwide, while China is still struggling with the ethics of economic development.

Another concern is that the emphasis on conducting research in Chinese higher education may shift the institutional mission. Higher education institutions have multiple responsibilities including providing social services, faculty development, teaching, and student advising. It has become a common situation, especially in the research universities, that faculty spend the majority of their time on research, instead of curriculum development and teaching. As institutions strive to become world-class research universities, they may shift resources away from their other responsibilities. There is also concern that reliance on western models will be harmful. For example, in terms of evaluating Chinese faculty performance in conducting research, the current publishing standards tend to mirror the international criteria set by the ranking agencies. But, it is important for Chinese universities to strengthen faculty ties with local and regional peers as well as focusing on international research collaborations (Lamont & Sun, 2012). Mok (2007) argues that if internationalization is considered an opportunity for intercultural understanding and exchanges, the research standards should be more supportive of preserving "national heritage and cultural traditions" (p. 447), instead of only promoting Western concepts.

Furthermore, preventing plagiarism by students and scholars has become a main theme of research activities in Chinese universities. Many methods of oversight have been implemented such as censorship of essays and selective examinations. However, the hierarchy of publishing in Chinese journals remains, which means that research and publishing are still primarily in the hands of professors and scholars. Students, including graduate students, are not actively encouraged to research and publish independently. Furthermore, institutions' mindsets of fully joining the team of world-class research universities is mostly about emulating Western structures and ranking criteria. There are two main concepts that have been ignored. First, "a culture of academic peer review" (Huang, 2015, p. 213) has yet to be implemented. Second, Chinese cultural and social perspectives have not been truly integrated into the research methodology (Mok, 2007). Thus, most of China's research output is not well suited or influential for domestic or international audiences.

5.6   *International Partnerships*

Like other regional and global higher education systems, Chinese universities are actively engaging with the international community (Yang, 2014). The most direct outcome of Chinese internationalization and the reform of the Chinese higher education system has been the establishment of international partnerships between Chinese and foreign universities in the areas of teaching and research. These partnerships create an expectation and a platform for Chinese institutions to improve their pedagogy, curriculum, and the international competence of their graduates. More importantly, by working with private funding partners, these international partnerships have contributed positively to the Chinese government's desire to massify higher education without additional public funding support (Ennew & Fujia, 2009).

One key international partnership category is transnational higher education. Chinese transnational higher education is defined as the cooperation of international institutions for delivering higher education services within the territory of China, mainly to Chinese citizens (Fang & Wang, 2014). Therefore, transnational higher education is in-between domestic and international models of higher education. It exists for the purposes of integrating and perpetuating foreign educational resources for mostly Chinese recipients. In 1995, there were only two programs which could provide foreign degrees in China. By 2004, the number of the transnational programs increased to 745, with 169 programs qualified by the Chinese government to offer students foreign degrees (Yang, 2008). By 2011, more than 600 foreign degree-granting programs were listed on the website of the Ministry of Education (Fang & Wang, 2014). The majority of the degrees are offered at the bachelor level (Fang, 2012).

5.7   *Programs*

The program models of transnational higher education in China are diverse. Many of the programs are focused on disciplines within science, technology, engineering, and math. Programs vary by institutional model, student recruitment methods, and whether or not enrolled students earn degrees. There are foreign degree programs in which degrees may be offered by independent foreign institutions or institutions that are affiliates of local schools in China, Chinese degree programs, double degree programs, and non-degree programs. Students of foreign degree programs and non-degree programs do not need to take the national university entrance exam or reach the score required by the government (Wang & Fang, 2014). Both dependent and independent foreign institutions in China are required to be sponsored by either a legal citizen or a cooperating Chinese institution (Feng, 2013).

5.8   *Evaluation*

To evaluate the effects of Chinese transnational higher education programs, gaining a comprehensive understanding of the "dynamics" among students, domestic partners and foreign partners is essential (Naidoo, 2009, p. 327). Wang and Fang (2014) present three circumstances affecting Chinese transnational higher education programs. First, while making decisions, students primarily judge the quality of a program based on the Chinese university's reputation. After graduation, if those students decide to study abroad, they generally choose another foreign university instead of the university that partnered with their transnational education program. Second, Chinese students generally think poorly of transnational higher education programs, but take advantage of them as a step to other more prestigious institutions because the entrance requirements of those programs, especially the standards of the Gaokao scores, are usually lower. Third, students have trouble finding information about transnational education programs because it is not easily accessible (Wang & Fang, 2014). Therefore, the rapid growth of transnational education in China can be considered premature growth that is developing more quickly in quantity than quality. Awareness of transnational higher education programs in China is generally low and when they are known, they often have a low reputation.

5.9   *Partnership with ASEAN Countries*

In recent years, China has become a regional leader in higher education development among Association of Southeast Asian Nations (ASEAN) countries (Brunei Darussalam, Cambodia, Indonesia, Laos, Malaysia, Myanmar, Philippines, Singapore, Thailand, and Vietnam). This has been achieved by investing both soft power and resources in less developed Chinese provinces, such as Yunan and Guangxi. One major difference between transnational and regional partnerships is that regional programs are intensively concentrated on vocational training and specific academic resources. Thus, most of them are technically-oriented, instead of broadly academically-oriented. In addition, universities and local authorities play the key roles in the facilitation of programs. China has been successful in attracting international students to these programs because of the economic and scientific success of the programs (Yang, 2012). It is worth mentioning that the regional partnerships are "quiet achievers" (Yang, 2012, p. 503) which go largely unnoticed in the world of higher education, yet have made great contributions to both China and ASEAN countries' higher education through innovation and development of graduates' marketable skills (Feng, 2013).

5.10   *Programs*

There are diverse structures for regional collaborations between China and ASEAN countries including University Mobility in Asia and the Pacific, the

Asia-Pacific Association for International Education, and the Asia Pacific Quality Network (Yang, 2012). Within these communities, different types of academic programs are facilitated. Different from the transnational higher education programs in China (in which most partners are from western countries), geographic proximity plays an important role in most programs with ASEAN countries. Three types of regional collaborations are described below:

1 *Programs across National Borders.* Guangxi and Yunan have enrolled the largest number of ASEAN students. From 2007 to 2008, the population of ASEAN students enrolled in Guangxi increased 33%, to 4,378 students. Meanwhile, in Yunan, from 2006 to 2007, the percentage of ASEAN students increased to 70% of the entire number of international students. In fact, student mobility moves in both directions. By early 2007, more than 600 Chinese students were studying in the transnational partnership programs with ASEAN countries at Chinese local universities and at the programs in their universities also (Yang, 2012).

2 *Institutional and Joint Programs.* Institutional exchange and collaboration are the most common strategies. However, the joint collaboration programs have become more "stable and diversified" due to their advantages of utilizing both countries' higher education resources and facilities (Yang, 2012, p. 499). Most importantly, the students who develop high proficiency with both cultures and languages have an advantage in the labor market (Yang, 2012).

3 *Training and Degree Programs.* Short-term training programs are increasingly an important part of regional collaboration focused on the development of both ASEAN countries and China's southeast region. The main foci of the programs are languages and vocational training. For instance, through China's Ministry of Agriculture, Guangxi Agricultural Vocational-Technical College has provided training for 37 groups of 715 Vietnamese technicians (Yang, 2012). More complex educational exchange programs are developing as student interest shifts from languages to specialized technical fields (Yang, 2012).

5.11   *Evaluation*

Through regional collaborations, the general quality of higher education in ASEAN countries has greatly improved. Collaborations are a productive way to raise ASEAN higher education voices in global dialogues, as well as their global leadership. In addition, a regional community of higher education has been created without regard for national borders. However, it is necessary to consider the role of non-state actors (universities, local labor markets, and private donors) in fostering regional community, based on the reality of the Chinese government's restrictions on education. The most important impact of the collaborations is that they have stabilized the regional order by enhancing the partnership among China's neighbors (Yang, 2012).

In terms of China's situation, other than gaining the same benefits as the ASEAN countries, it has been practicing its soft power through the regional partnerships. The Chinese government has implemented mostly their own strategic plans for educational partnerships in collaboration with the ASEAN countries, instead of using Western educational approaches. The government has offered extensive scholarship funding for ASEAN students (Yang, 2012). Although the regional partnerships are not as well publicized as transnational higher education initiatives, they have become an essential part of China's political movement to gain more international political and economic support in less-developed nations.

6   Partnership Trends in China-U.S. Collaborations

6.1   Government Initiatives

Aiming to promote Chinese language and culture, the Chinese government has established Confucius Institutes around the world, with more in the U.S. than in any other host nation. Confucius Institutes are the representatives of Chinese cultural diplomacy which provide Chinese language and culture education globally. Although Chinese cultural diplomacy mostly depends on "principles of independence, equality, mutual respect and noninterference" (Xinhua, 2002, art. ix, as cited in Kwan, 2013, p. 113), reinforcing cultural values and political loyalty is always the priority. According to Kwan (2013), "one of the most contentious issues associated with the Confucius Institute involves the fear of interference by the Chinese government into the autonomy of the host universities, especially in the funding formula and the operational structure" (p. 124). Most Confucius Institutes in the U.S. are located within U.S. universities. Establishment of the Confucius Institutes has been well received by U.S. institutions as it furthers their own internationalization agendas (Laughlin, 2008).

The U.S. Department of State has likewise emphasized relations with China in its public diplomacy initiatives, many of which are managed by the Bureau of Educational and Cultural Affairs. For example, Chinese is one of a select group of languages in the Presidential National Security Initiative that funds critical language study for high school and university students, as well as teachers. The Fulbright Program facilitates the movement of students and scholars between the U.S. and China through a variety of programs. The English Language Fellow Program sends well qualified teachers of English to Speakers of Other Languages (ESOL) to China and welcomes Humphrey Fellows to the U.S. for advanced professional development. Each of these initiatives aims to strengthen political, social, and cultural relations between the U.S. and China (Farrell, 2008).

Both the U.S. and Chinese governments are actively cooperating to promote international exchange and intercultural learning. For example, The U.S. Fulbright program for exchange between the two countries was renamed the U.S.-China Fulbright program in 2004 and is now equally funded by the two governments (Blumenthal & Xinyu, 2008). In 2009, U.S. President Barack Obama, in cooperation with Chinese leadership, announced the 100,000 Strong initiative which aimed to have 100,000 U.S. students study abroad in China. Coordinated by the U.S.- China Strong Foundation, this target has been reached and new programs have been initiated including 1 Million Strong, which seeks to have 1 million U.S. youth learning Mandarin by 2020 (U.S. China Strong, n.d.).

6.2   *Student Mobility*

In the era following the Chinese Communist Revolution, from the 1950s through the 1974/1975 academic year, no students were sent from China to study in the U.S. In the late 1970s, in the aftermath of the Cultural Revolution, China sought to rebuild its devastated higher education system, particularly in the area of science and technology. Deciding that sending bright students abroad was the fastest road to reinvigorating the education system and bringing the needed expertise home, Chinese representatives traveled to the U.S. Though formal relations did not yet exist between the countries, in 1978, representatives of both countries came to an 'unofficial' agreement to send 500 to 700 students and scholars from China to study in the U.S. and for the U.S. to send 50 students to study in China. Though both nations have seen record growth in their study abroad numbers in the decades that followed, this exchange imbalance has persisted (Blumenthal & Xinyu, 2008).

As relations between China and the U.S. warmed in the 1970s, the number of Chinese students coming to study in the U.S. increased dramatically, with China becoming the leading sender of international students in the U.S. at various points in the 80s, 90s, 2000s, and 2010s. In 2015–2016, there were 328,547 Chinese students in the U.S. (Institute of International Education, 2016). The Institute of International Education (2016) reports that for the past seven years, China has been the leading nation of origin for international students in the U.S., with 31.5% of the total international students. Among the Chinese students studying in the U.S., 41.3% are undergraduates, 37.5% are graduate students, 15.9% on optional practical training work authorization, and 5.3% classified as 'other.' Top fields of study for Chinese students in the U.S. are Business (24.3%), Engineering (18.6%), and Math and Computer

Science (14.1%) (Institute of International Education, 2016). U.S. government data (Immigration and Customs Enforcement, 2016) likewise shows China as the number one leading place of origin, sending more students to the U.S. than Australia, the Pacific Islands, Africa, North America, South America, and Europe combined. They report that they are 353,069 students from China studying in the U.S. as of March 2016, an increase of 7.9% over March 2015.

In contrast to the more than 300,000 Chinese students studying in the U.S., only 12,790 U.S. students studied in China in 2014–2015, a mere 4.5% of all U.S. students studying abroad. Unlike Chinese students who often study abroad for an entire degree program, U.S. students are likely to study abroad for less than a year, shortening the opportunity for U.S. students to learn about Chinese culture. In addition to study abroad, 829 U.S. students are reported to have done non-credit work, intern, or volunteering abroad in China in 2014–2015 (Institute of International Education, 2016).

6.3   *Partnerships*

Joint degree collaborations between the U.S. and China have increased since the late 1990s. Often building on successful exchange programs, these degrees are typically partnerships between top Chinese U.S. universities and U.S. institutions of varying levels of prestige (Laughlin, 2008). Growth in research partnerships between the U.S. and China has also proliferated. In some U.S. institutions, such as Yale, Arizona State University, and George Mason University, an institution-wide China coordinator has been selected to help coordinate and convene conversations around the diverse range of China-related research being conducted within the institution (Laughlin, 2008).

One example of a China-U.S. partnership is the Schwarzman Scholars. The program is a privately funded initiative launched in 2016. Founded by Stephen A. Schwarzman, the program will enroll up to 200 students per year in Schwarzman College, situated on the Tsinghua University campus in Beijing. All courses will be taught in English and enrolled students will receive full scholarships. The program plans to enroll 45% U.S. students, 20% Chinese students, and 35% from other countries. The program aims to develop future global leaders who have cross-cultural understanding, an understanding of Chinese culture, and a network of other up and coming global leaders (Schwarzman Scholars, n.d.; Stanley, 2016).

Another area of partnership is the establishment of branch campuses. Many U.S. institutions have established branch campuses in China including the Hopkins-Nanjing Center and the Missouri State University branch campus at Liaoning Normal University (Laughlin, 2008). In addition to partnerships between two institutions, or between an institution and a government, nonprofit associations can also play a role. For example, the Sino-American Cooperation on Higher Education and Professional Development program provides an opportunity for Chinese students to spend one or two years at a U.S. institution and earn a dual degree (two degrees – one from a Chinese university, and one from a U.S. university). This program is jointly administered by the American Association of State Colleges and Universities and the China Center for International Educational Exchange (West, 2015).

6.4   Cultural Challenges

Chinese and U.S. partnerships have the capacity to enhance internationalization in both nations, providing opportunities for students to develop their global competency through language learning and cultural exchange, as well as through student mobility programs. Partnerships can advance internationalization in both countries and further the goals of helping institutions to improve their teaching and research quality in order to be globally competitive and internationally ranked. These collaborations have the potential to advance the cultural, financial, academic, and political objectives of the two governments and higher education institutions. Yet, with the many opportunities and extensive growth in partnerships between the U.S. and China comes challenges.

One challenge is that the governments and people of China and the U.S. have different philosophies of education and differing educational methodologies. Though there is some convergence, teaching styles vary, and beliefs about student and teacher roles in education are quite different. The barrier between Chinese social and academic cultures and the Western template must be taken into consideration. The definitions of "knowledge" and "scholarship" are different in the Chinese and U.S. education systems. China and the U.S. have different legal regulations for copyright and intellectual property, as well as different beliefs about the conception of property. As Chinese institutions aim to emulate high ranking Western institutions, there is a contradiction within Chinese society itself. On one hand, academics and government leaders take Western knowledge to be legitimate knowledge, but at the same time believe in the importance of the Chinese social systems and traditional culture as the best guiding principles in Chinese people's lives (Yang, 2008). On the opposite side of the partnership, U.S. institutions may exhibit arrogance, often discounting other ways of knowing, and other ways of carrying out teaching, learning, and research that are different from that which is usual in Western countries (Majidi & Restoule, 2008). Within this context, for any academic partnership to be successful, it must address the underlying values of the educational endeavor and include extensive discussion of expectations around teaching methodology, testing, rules, and disciplinary procedures.

Gaining or maintaining a reputation as a world-class university is desirable for both U.S. and Chinese universities, although U.S. universities have begun the race for global reputation with a head start. This desire to be globally competitive has resulted in U.S. attention focused on excellence in internationalization measured by awards, reputation, and the enrollment of international students as a sign of the desirability of U.S. institutions. Meanwhile, Chinese attention has also focused on internationalization as a way to improve educational quality and with it, global reputation. In China, however, global rankings play a much stronger role than in the U.S., as a way of legitimizing success and global reputation. Srivastava et al. (2001) emphasize that it takes a long process to build a real reputation (as cited in Delgado-Marquez et al., 2013, p. 622), and the reputation is not always stable. In some Chinese higher education cases, internationalization may actually reduce reputation, if the institutions regard internationalization as existing only for the sake of better ranking status (Delgado-Marquez et al., 2013). However, the biggest contradiction in China may be that internationalization has become an official request, a policy issued from the top-down, instead of a process of institutional growth that benefits educational quality.

6.5   *Structural Challenges*

Beyond the cultural challenges, there are many legal, political, and structural challenges in partnerships between U.S. and Chinese institutions. In the U.S. education system, there is less centralization and more institutional autonomy. By contrast, the Chinese national government is much more involved in education strategy and oversight. This becomes highly relevant when U.S. institutions attempt to establish transnational education programs in China. When compared to other countries, the Chinese government is fairly restrictive in allowing such programs to be established. Research cooperation is one of the main purposes of many transnational programs in China. In recent years, China has become a leader in some research fields, especially in STEM. However, there are many state demands in governance by the central government, the local authorities, and state enterprises. Thus, bureaucratic interference in decision-making has become the most significant barrier to free academic debate within universities (Marginson, 2015b). In addition, because of the different regulations for copyrights and disparate ideas about property, allegations of corruption and plagiarism may arise and there may be differences in how the value of research is judged (Yang, 2016).

In order for Chinese-U.S. partnerships to be successful, it may be necessary for Chinese universities to gain academic autonomy. For example, Jamshidi, Arasteh, NavehEbrahim, Zeinabadi, and Rasmussen (2012) discuss the necessity for contemporary higher education and research around the globe to focus on serving the public good. According to Laughlin (2008), fighting against propaganda and undue government influence is necessary to establish a truly innovative environment. For U.S.-Chinese transnational education partnerships, the government assumes authority for approving the establishment of all programs. All programs must meet the national education requirements of both partners. However, because U.S. institutions enjoy more autonomy, they typically have more flexibility in the academic requirements and structures that they establish. Ultimately, to meet the academic requirements of both systems, any exchange agreement or joint degree must carefully articulate courses to meet the requirements and expectations of both systems (Laughlin, 2008).

Challenges continue after the initial approval of programs. Unfortunately, in China, while the government is highly involved in the establishment of programs, there is inconsistent willingness or capacity for the government to monitor quality after approval (Yang, 2008). Without ongoing government oversight, adopting a shared long-term strategic vision is a key step for foreign universities to establish a sustainable partnership in China (Feng, 2013). Feng (2013) argues that learning ways to cooperate and seeking to promote mutual benefits (instead of paying attention to government control) are two effective methods for success. It is not realistic to expect this to be an easy endeavor; education in China has historically maintained a hierarchy. No partnership program can bypass the established political norms to gain total academic freedom. Thus, cooperation among multiple partners can be mutual, but at the same time, there are always social and political parameters which require the foreign partner to adjust. Adjusting to national goals and government requirements so that the partnership programs can continue to have support from the state adds more burden on institutions.

Internationalization of partnerships is uneven in both the U.S. and China. More elite universities, often the top public research-focused universities, are more aggressively pursuing internationalization and international partnerships. Vocational, less-prestigious, and more rural institutions have been engaged in internationalization at a lesser level. While there have been many productive policies, research activities, and international partnerships undertaken by the Chinese government, Ma and Yue (2015) find that the higher the prestige of the university, the greater likelihood that they have developed international curricula and programs to support both their students and faculty in gaining more prestige in their fields. Further, because of China's special attention in the global knowledge market to mostly STEM fields, the opportunities that are provided within institutions are uneven, with STEM fields receiving more resources.

6.6   *Intercultural and Linguistic Challenges*

Developing the intercultural competence of graduates is a key motivation for internationalization in both the U.S. and China. Despite that, in both countries there is little evidence that the many efforts at internationalization, including student mobility and international partnerships, are effective. This lack of evidence may be attributed both to a lack of rigorous assessment and evaluation, as well as to the possibility that not all of the programs are well designed or supported. Ma and Yue's (2015) research found that although Chinese students' intercultural competence has improved, there are still obvious divisions among subjects and institutions of faculty and scholars' intercultural competence. Even more, students' intercultural competence mostly emerged from one-on-one individual interactions and media exposure, rather than from formal educational training. In addition, they found that in China, there has been no expectation from university administrations to enhance student and staff intercultural understandings and implement multiculturalism in the institutions. In the enactment of internationalization globally, the importance of social and cultural development does not hold as much importance as economic and political-based demands (Knight, 2004).

Many transnational programs of Chinese universities are taught in English or have adapted Western curricula so that they can prepare students better for the global market. Giving instructions in English leads to a Westernized classroom and cultural colonization. Therefore, "international transparency in the programs" is needed (Altbach, 2012, p. 9). U.S. students are likewise limited. Their relative lack of foreign language ability often restricts them from enrolling in host university courses, or maintains their linguistic privilege if the partnership program functions in English. The communication challenges are not only caused by language barriers, but also by the mutual understanding of different cultures and communication techniques. When students lack intercultural competence it not only affects students, but may also affect institutional structures. Enrolling international students necessitates additional administrative help and support for those students (Spencer-Oatey, 2013).

7   Conclusion

China and the U.S. are reacting to a common set of global provocations including neoliberalism, the massification and commodification of higher education, the increasing desire to produce globally competent graduates who can compete in the global workforce, and emphasis on research output prompted by systems of international rankings. Despite the shared global context, China and the U.S. have taken different approaches to the internationalization of higher education. These differing approaches reflect the variance in their national contexts, including the role of each national government in education policy and oversight, the economic differentials between countries, national culture and values, and the global reputation of the education systems, among many other influences.

Contemporary Chinese higher education is a young but quickly developing system. Prompted by the worldwide trends of globalization and internationalization in both economics and education system growth, Chinese higher education institutions are highly engaged in global work. Internationalization has brought a new concept of higher education to China in which academia not only benefits individuals and the nation, it also develops human capital and encourages international diversity. Internationalization offers Chinese higher education hope for improved quality of education and human development as it gains increased autonomy away from social control and political regulation.

In contrast, the U.S. is leading the trend of internationalization with its stable higher education system and strong will to develop global and intercultural competence among graduates. Academic quality is supported through a culture of academic freedom and rigorous peer review. International students and scholars seek opportunities in U.S. universities, bringing both financial revenue and intercultural perspectives. Joint degrees and other international partnerships are also proliferating. At the same time, there is room for improvement in more robust internationalization of the curriculum, including language education, and greater incentivization for faculty to internationalize their courses and research.

Sharing the common goal of internationalization, the U.S. and China have engaged in a wide range of public and private partnerships. These partnerships focus on student and scholar mobility, joint degrees, branch campuses, language learning, and cultural exchange. For the partnerships to be successful, they must find a way to work within both cultural and political contexts, conforming to the requirements of both systems. Extensive time and energy must be invested in communication, logistics, and articulating academic requirements. Partnerships that work best are established so that the partnerships are win-win, and so that both parties in the partnership have their voices heard. With these efforts, there is the potential for institutions in both nations to reap all of the best outcomes of internationalization for the betterment of their students and education systems.

References

Abrahamsen, E. (2012, July 3). A liberal arts education made in China. *New York Times*. Retrieved from http://latitude.blogs.nytimes.com/2012/07/03/a-liberal-arts-education-made-in-china/?_r=0

Adams, J., Pendlebury, D., & Stembridge, B. (2013). *Building BRICKS: Exploring the global research and innovation impact of Brazil, Russia, India, China, and South Korea*. Philadelphia, PA: Thomson Reuters.

Altbach, P. G. (2013). *The international imperative in higher education*. Rotterdam, The Netherlands: Sense Publishers.

Altbach, P. G., & Knight, J. (2007). The internationalization of higher education: Motivations and realities. *Journal of Studies in International Education, 11*(3–4), 290–305. doi:10.1177/1028315307303542

American Council on Education. (2010). *Bringing the world into the classroom: ACE award to recognize the innovative use of technology to promote internationalization*. Washington, DC: American Council on Education.

American Council on Education. (2012). *Mapping internationalization on U.S. campuses*. Washington, DC: American Council on Education.

American Council on Education. (2016). *Internationalization in action: Special edition: Connecting classrooms: Using online technology to deliver global learning*. Washington, DC: American Council on Education.

American Council on Education. (n.d.). *ACE internationalization laboratory*. Retrieved from http://www.acenet.edu/news-room/Pages/ACE-Internationalization-Laboratory.aspx

Belyavina, R., Li, J., & Bhandari, R. (2013). *New frontiers: U.S. students pursuing degrees abroad*. New York, NY: Institute of International Education.

Blumenthal, P., & Xinyu, Y. (2008). Introduction. In S. Laughlin (Ed.), *U.S.-China educational exchange: Perspectives on a growing partnership* (pp. xi–xv). New York, NY: Institute of International Education.

Bradford, A. (2012). Adopting English-taught degree programs. *International Higher Education, 69*, 8–10.

Brewer, E. (2015). Beloit College: Internationalization in the American Midwest. In J. K. Hudzik (Ed.), *Comprehensive internationalization: Institutional pathways to success* (pp. 135–143). New York, NY: Routledge.

Bureau of Educational and Cultural Affairs. (2016). *Facts and figures*. Retrieved from https://eca.state.gov/impact/facts-and-figures

Chow, K. W. (1996). *The rise of Confucian ritualism in late imperial China: Ethics, classics, and lineage discourse*. Stanford, CA: Stanford University Press.

Cross-Border Education Research Team. (2016, January 27). *C-BERT branch campus listing* [Data originally collected by K. Kinser & J. E. Lane]. Albany, NY: Author. Retrieved from http://globalhighered.org/branchcampuses.php

Delgado-Márquez, B. L., Escudero-Torres, M. A., & Hurtado-Torres, N. E. (2013). Being highly internationalised strengthens your reputation: An empirical investigation of top higher education institutions. *Higher Education, 66*(5), 619–633.

Delisle, P. (2009). Rationales and strategies behind double degrees: A transatlantic approach. In D. Obst & M. Kuder (Eds.), *Joint and double degree programs: An emerging model for transatlantic exchange* (pp. 19–27). New York, NY: Institute of International Education.

Egron-Polok, E., & Hudson, R. (2010). *Internationalization of higher education: Global trends, regional perspectives*. Paris: International Association of Universities.

Ennew, C. T., & Fujia, Y. (2009). Foreign universities in China: A case study. *European Journal of Education, 44*(1), 21–36.

Fang, W. (2012). The development of transnational higher education in China: A comparative study of research universities and teaching universities. *Journal of Studies in International Education, 16*(1), 5–23.

Fang, W., & Wang, S. (2014). Chinese students' choice of transnational higher education in a globalized higher education market: A case study of W university. *Journal of Studies in International Education, 18*(5), 475–494. doi:1028315314523989

Farrell, T. A. (2008). National policy goals: U.S. government activities supporting U.S.-China exchange. In S. Laughlin (Ed.), *U.S.-China educational exchange: Perspectives on a growing partnership* (pp. 25–33). New York, NY: Institute of International Education.

Feng, Y. (2013). University of Nottingham Ningbo China and Xi'an Jiaotong-Liverpool University: Globalization of higher education in China. *Higher Education, 65*(4), 471–485.

Fong, V. (2004). Filial nationalism among Chinese teenagers with global identities. *American Ethnologist, 31*(4), 631–648.

Goldberg, D., Looney, D., & Lusin, N. (2015). Enrollments in languages other than English in United States institutions of higher education, fall 2013. New York, NY: Modern Language Association of America.

Green, M. (2010). North America: Focus on Institutional internationalization in the USA. In E. Egron-Polok & R. Hudson (Eds.), *Internationalization of higher education: Global trends, regional perspectives* (pp. 191–198). Paris: International Association of Universities.

Hu, J. H. (2007). The progress of internationalization of curriculum in China's universities. *China Higher Education Research, 9*, 69–71.

Huang, F. (2015). Building the world-class research universities: A case study of China. *Higher Education, 70*(2), 203–215.

Hudzik, J. K. (2015). *Comprehensive internationalization: Institutional pathways to success*. New York, NY: Routledge.

Institute of International Education. (2015a). *Generation study abroad: Year one impact*. New York, NY: Institute of International Education.

Institute of International Education. (2015b). *Open doors.* New York, NY: Institute of International Education.

Institute of International Education. (2016). *Open doors.* New York, NY: Institute of International Education.

Jain, C. R. (2015). The knowledge economy and the transformational dynamics of education in Asia's emergent economic growth. In R. Bhandari & A. Lefébure (Eds.), *Asia: The next higher education superpower?* (pp. 39–56). New York, NY: Institute of International Education.

Jamshidi, L., Arasteh, H., NavehEbrahim, A., Zeinabadi, H., & Rasmussen, P. D. (2012). Developmental patterns of privatization in higher education: A comparative study. *Higher Education, 64*(6), 789–803.

Knight, J. (2004). Internationalization remodeled: Definition, approaches, and rationales. *Journal of Studies in International Education, 8*(1), 5–31.

Knight, J. (2008). *Higher education in turmoil: The changing world of internationalization.* Rotterdam, The Netherlands: Sense Publishers.

Kuroda, C. (2014). The new sphere of international student education in Chinese higher education: A focus on English-medium degree programs. *Journal of Studies in International Education, 18*(5), 445–462. doi:1028315313519824

Lamont, M., & Sun, A. (2012). How China's elite universities will have to change. *The Chronicle of Higher Education, 59*(16), A29.

Laughlin, S. (2008). Trends and models of academic exchange between China and the U.S. In S. Laughlin (Ed.), *U.S.-China educational exchange: Perspectives on a growing partnership* (pp. 1–23). New York, NY: Institute of International Education.

Leask, B. (2015). *Internationalizing the curriculum.* New York, NY: Routledge.

Li, Y. (2010). Quality assurance in Chinese higher education. *Research in Comparative and International Education, 5*(1), 58–76.

Lim, M. (2015). Global university rankings: Determining the distance between Asia and "superpower status" in higher education. In R. Bhandari & A. Lefébure (Eds.), *Asia: The next higher education superpower?* (pp. 23–38). New York, NY: Institute of International Education.

Liu, J. (2001, September 22). The MOE has taken 12 measures to strengthen undergraduate teaching. *China Education Daily*, p. 1.

Liu, J. (2012). Examining massification policies and their consequences for equality in Chinese higher education: A cultural perspective. *Higher Education, 64*(5), 647–660.

Ma, W., & Yue, Y. (2015). Internationalization for quality in Chinese research universities: Student perspectives. *Higher Education, 70*(2), 217–234.

Macready, C., & Tucker, C. (2011). *Who goes where and why: An overview and analysis of global educational mobility.* New York, NY: AIFS Foundation and Institute of International Education.

Madjidi, K., & Restoule, J. (2008). Comparative indigenous ways of knowing and learning. In K. Mundy, K. Bickmore, R. Hayhoe, M. Madden, & K. Madjidi (Eds.),

Comparative and international education: Issues for teachers (pp. 77–106). New York, NY: Teachers College Press.

Mahbubani, K., & Chye, T. E. (2015). Is Asia the next higher education superpower? In R. Bhandari & A. Lefébure (Eds.), *Asia: The next higher education superpower?* (pp. 1–22). New York, NY: Institute of International Education.

Marginson, S. (2010). Global comparisons and the university knowledge economy. In L. M. Portnoi, V. D. Rust, & S. S. Bagley (Eds.), *Higher education, policy, and the global competition phenomena* (pp. 29–41). New York, NY: Palgrave Macmillan.

Marginson, S. (2011). Higher education in East Asia and Singapore: Rise of the Confucian model. *Higher Education, 61*(5), 587–611.

Marginson, S. (2015a). Systemic challenges to educational quality and global competitiveness. In R. Bhandari & A. Lefébure (Eds.), *Asia: The next higher education superpower?* (pp. 57–74). New York, NY: Institute of International Education.

Marginson, S. (2015b). The rise of post-Confucion knowledge Economies. *International Higher Education, 69*, 7–8.

Ministry of Education of the People's Republic of China. (2010). 留学中国计划 [Study China plan]. Retrieved from http://www.moe.gov.cn/publicfiles/business/ htmlfiles/moe_850/201009/xxgk_108815.htmlhttp://www.moe.gov.cn/publicfiles/ business/htmlfiles/moe_850/201009/xxgk_108815.html

Ministry of Education of the People's Republic of China. (2013). 2013 年度我国留学 人员情况 [Statistics on study abroad in 2013]. Retrieved from http://www.moe.gov.cn/ publicfiles/business/htmlfiles/moe/s5987/201402/164235.html

Mohrman, K. (2008). The emerging global model with Chinese characteristics. *Higher Education Policy, 21*(1), 29–48.

Mok, K. H. (2007). Questing for internationalization of universities in Asia: Critical reflections. *Journal of Studies in International Education, 11*(3–4), 433–454.

Mok, K. H. (2012). Bringing the state back in: Restoring the role of the state in Chinese higher education. *European Journal of Education, 47*(2), 228–241.

Naidoo, V. (2009). Transnational higher education: A stock take of current activity. *Journal of Studies in International education, 13*(3), 310–330.

Neubauer, D., & Jiangxin, Z. (2015). The internationalization of Chinese higher education (CIQG Publication Series). Retrieved from http://www.cheainternational.org/ pdf/internationalization%20of%20chinese%20he-ver2.pdf

Obst, D., Kuder, M., & Banks, C. (2011). *Joint and double degree programs in the global context.* New York, NY: Institute of International Education.

Olssen, M., & Peters, M. A. (2005). Neoliberalism, higher education, and the knowledge economy: From the free market to knowledge capitalism. *Journal of Education Policy, 20*(3), 313–345.

Pan, J.-Y. (2011). A resilience-based and meaning-oriented model of acculturation: A sample of mainland Chinese postgraduate students in Hong Kong. *International Journal of Intercultural Relations, 35*(5), 592–603.

Pan, S.-Y. (2010). Changes and challenges in the flow of international human capital China's experience. *Journal of Studies in International Education, 14*(3), 259–288.

Punteney, K. N. (2012). International careers: The gap between student interest and knowledge. *Journal of Studies in International Education, 16*(4), 390–407. doi:10.1177/1028315311430354

Pysarchik, D. T., & Hudzik, J. K. (2015). Michigan State University: Origins and evolution of an institution toward a global frame. In J. K. Hudzik (Ed.), *Comprehensive internationalization: Institutional pathways to success* (pp. 166–174). New York, NY: Routledge.

Rhoades, G., & Slaughter, S. (2004). Academic capitalism in the new economy: Challenges and choices. *American Academic, 1*(1), 37–60.

Schwarzman Scholars. (n.d.). *Schwarzman Scholars.* Retrieved from http://schwarzmanscholars.org/

Scott, P. (2016). International higher education and the "neo-liberal turn." *International Higher Education, 84*, 16–17.

Spencer-Oatey, H. (2013). Maximizing the benefits of international education collaborations managing interaction processes. *Journal of Studies in International Education, 17*(3), 244–261.

Stanley, A. (2016, January 10). Schwarzman Scholars announces inaugural class to study in China. *The New York Times.* Retrieved from http://www.nytimes.com/2016/01/11/business/dealbook/schwarzman-scholars-announces-inaugural-class-to-study-in-china.html?_r=0http://www.nytimes.com/2016/01/11/business/dealbook/schwarzman-scholars-announces-inaugural-class-to-study-in-china.html?_r=0

Tsang, E. Y. H. (2013). The quest for higher education by the Chinese middle class: Retrenching social mobility?. *Higher Education, 66*(6), 653–668.

U.S. China Strong. (n.d.). *U.S. China strong.* Retrieved from http://uschinastrong.org/ http://uschinastrong.org/

U.S. Immigration and Customs Enforcement. (2016). *SEVIS by the numbers: March 2016.* Retrieved from https://www.ice.gov/sites/default/files/documents/Report/2016/sevis-bythenumbers–0416.pdf

Wang, Q. H., Wang, Q., & Liu, N. C. (2011). Building world-class universities in China: Shanghai Jiao Tong university. In P. G. Altbach & J. Salmi (Eds.), *The road to academic excellence: The making of world-class research universities* (pp. 33–62). Washington, DC: The World Bank.

West, C. (2015). Degrees without borders. *International Educator, 24*(4), 20–32.

Williams, R. D., & Lee, A. (2015). *Internationalizing higher education: Critical collaborations across the curriculum.* Rotterdam, The Netherlands: Sense Publishers.

Write, S. (2010). Different emirates, different models: Creating global institutions in the gulf states. In D. Obst & D. Kirk (Eds.), *Innovation through education: Building the knowledge economy in the Middle East* (pp. 7–25). New York, NY: Institute of International Education.

Wu, B., & Zheng, Y. (2008). *Expansion of higher education in China: Challenges and implications* (Briefing Series – Issue No. 36). Nottingham: China Policy Institute.

Xinyu, Y. (2008). National policy goals: PRC government activities supporting U.S.-China exchange. In S. Laughlin (Ed.), *U.S.-China educational exchange: Perspectives on a growing partnership* (pp. 35–48). New York, NY: Institute of International Education.

Yang, R. (2008). Transnational higher education in China: Contexts, characteristics and concerns. *Australian Journal of Education, 52*(3), 272–286.

Yang, R. (2012). Internationalization, regionalization, and soft power: China's relations with ASEAN member countries in higher education. *Frontiers of Education in China, 7*(4), 486–507.

Yang, R. (2014). Going global: Contemporary international networking in Chinese mainland universities. *Chinese Education & Society, 47*(1), 27–43.

Yang, R. (2016). Toxic academic culture in East Asia. *International Higher Education, 84*, 15–16.

Yuan, B. (2011). Internationalization at home: The path to internationalization in Chinese research universities. *Chinese Education & Society, 44*(5), 84–96.

Zhang, H., Patton, D., & Kenney, M. (2013). Building global-class universities: Assessing the impact of the 985 project. *Research Policy, 42*(3), 765–775.

Ziguras, C., & McBurnie, G. (2015). *Governing cross-border higher education.* New York, NY: Routledge.

About the Authors

Katherine Punteney is an Associate Professor and Chair of the MA in International Education Management program at the Middlebury Institute of International Studies at Monterey where she is delighted and challenged to help develop the next generation of international education leaders. She holds an EdD in Education Leadership from California State University, Sacramento. Punteney teaches Principles and Practices of International Education, Internationalization, Student Services, Acculturation, Biculturalism and Multiculturalism, and International Student and Scholar Services. Her research focuses on internationalization, the teaching of intercultural competency, and the role of graduate education in developing international educators. In addition to co-authoring a chapter for this book, her recent projects include conducting research on practitioner identities in international education, writing a chapter on social psychology and international education, and developing a new course about the internationalization of primary and secondary schools.

Yilin Wei holds an MA degree in Comparative and International Development Education at the University of Minnesota-Twin Cities. She holds a Bachelor's degree in dramatic literature and script writing from Zhengjiang University of Media and Communications, China. She was an English language instructor and certified TFCL (teach Chinese to foreigners) teacher before she came to U.S.A. Ms. Wei is now an educational advisor and curriculum designer with GYMI (Global Youth Mentorship Initiative) and ALo7.com. She completed her Master's paper on the topic of internationalization in China, specifically related to the "World Class Universities" initiative. She focused on the appropriateness of China's perceptions and strategies, in reacting to the country's social and political realities.

CHAPTER 4

Leveraging Confucius Institutes for International Education and Exchange

Anthony C. Ogden and Huajing Xiu Maske

Abstract

This chapter discusses the unique role of the Confucius Institute program in advancing international cooperation in higher education between the U.S. and China. Initiated by China's Ministry of Education in 2004, the primary aim of the Confucius Institute program has been to promote Chinese language and culture, support local Chinese teaching internationally, and facilitate cultural exchange. There are currently 500 Confucius Institutes operating throughout the world (in 123 countries) and 109 of them are located in the United States (Xu, 2016). This chapter provides an overview of the additional roles Confucius Institutes can play in U.S. higher education, particularly with regard to: (1) establishing new partnerships and linkages between U.S. and Chinese colleges and universities, (2) fostering educational mobility of students and scholars, and, (3) enhancing U.S. faculty engagement in international education and exchange. A case study will be presented as a model for how campus-based Confucius Institutes can be strategically leveraged to simultaneously advance all three roles. Other examples of institutional strategies will be highlighted as best practices for maximizing the role of Confucius Institutes in advancing international education and exchange.

1 Introduction

The influential rise of China in recent years, both politically and economically, has created momentum on U.S. university and college campuses toward establishing new institutional partnerships and linkages with Chinese higher education institutions. Such initiatives have primarily targeted efforts that increase educational mobility and exchange of students and scholars; but have also prioritized joint research activities; exchanges of academic materials and publications; exchange of faculty members for research, lectures, and discussions, and related forms of cooperation. Although senior institutional administrators seem to be driving this momentum, U.S. federal, state and local governments are understandably similarly invested in welcoming international students and scholars. According to NAFSA: Association of International Educators, international students contributed more than $30.5 billion to the U.S. economy and supported more than 373,000 jobs during the 2014–2015 academic year (NAFSA, 2016). Of the 974,926 international students studying at U.S. colleges and universities in 2014–2015, over 31% were from China (IIE, Open Doors, 2015), representing by far the largest proportion of students from any one sending country. According to the Institute of International Education (IIE), international students make a significant positive economic impact on the U.S., while also contributing to America's scientific and technical research and bringing international perspectives into U.S. classrooms (IIE, 2016).

The number of U.S. undergraduate students choosing to study in China has also increased in recent years. In fact, China is now the fifth largest host country for U.S. students, surpassing popular traditional destinations such as Germany, Ireland, Australia and Japan. Due in part to federal efforts such as the *100,000 Strong* initiative, which was designed to dramatically increase the number and diversify the composition of American students studying in China, approximately 14,000 students studied in China in 2013–2014 (IIE, Open Doors, 2015). Although the pace of enrollment growth appears to be slowing, China remains very popular as a study abroad destination.

Evidence of a pivot toward China in U.S. higher education can be seen in the proliferation of China offices, China area studies centers, and Confucius Institutes being established on U.S. college and university campuses. While these offices, centers, and institutes may have been established primarily to advance Chinese language study and China-oriented cultural studies, they are secondarily being leveraged to advance international student recruitment efforts within China and the establishment of new partnerships and linkages with Chinese higher education institutions. These units also have an influential role in advancing and supporting U.S education abroad programming to China.

This chapter specifically discusses the unique role of the Confucius Institute program in advancing international cooperation in higher education between the U.S. and China. Initiated by China's Ministry of Education in 2004, the primary aim of the Confucius Institute program has been to promote Chinese language and culture, support local Chinese teaching internationally, and facilitate cultural exchange. The chapter provides an overview of the multifaceted roles Confucius Institutes play in U.S. higher education, particularly with regard to (1) establishing new partnerships and linkages between U.S. and Chinese colleges and universities; (2) fostering educational mobility of students and scholars; and (3) enhancing U.S. faculty engagement in international education and exchange. A case study is presented in the paragraphs below as a model for how campus-based Confucius Institutes can be strategically leveraged to simultaneously advance all three roles. Other notable strategies for advancing international education and exchange from distinguished Confucius Institutes across the U.S. will also be highlighted.

2   Introducing the Confucius Institute Program

Under the Chinese Ministry of Education, the Office of Chinese Language Council International in China (commonly referred to as "Hanban") oversees the Confucius Institute program with the aim "to introduce Chinese language to the world and elevate the impact of Chinese language in the world" (People's Daily Online, 2006a, 2006b, 2009). Accordingly, the purpose of the Confucius Institute is to strengthen educational cooperation between China and other countries, support and promote the development of Chinese language education, and increase mutual understanding between people in China and in the world. The Confucius Institute program was initially modeled on the successful operations of the British Council, Germany's Goethe-Institut, Spain's Instituto Cervantes and France's Alliance Français. Unlike the British Council or the Goethe-Institut, Confucius Institutes are mostly established on university and college campuses.[1] In 2004, the first Confucius Institute was established in the U.S. at the University of Maryland at College Park (People's Daily Online, 2006). There are now 500 Confucius Institutes operating in 123 countries throughout the world and 109 of them are located in the U.S., in every state and the District of Columbia (Xu, 2016).

The vast majority of Confucius Institutes focus on providing Chinese language teaching in K-12 schools, Chinese language instruction for the community, and Chinese cultural events such as the celebration of traditional Chinese New Year and the Moon Festival (People's Daily Online, 2009). In the U.S. alone, there are approximately 270,000 students who are learning Chinese through the Confucius Institutes. Every year, there are over 9,000 cultural activities in the U.S. with 4 million participants (Xu, 2016). By 2016, 136,000 high school students had participated in the Chinese Bridge Summer Camp for American High School Students, which is a joint exchange program created by Chinese Vice Premier Liu Yandong and former U.S. Secretary of State, Hillary Clinton. The U.S. provides the second largest group of international students to China, largely due to the support and work of the Confucius Institutes across the country (U.S. Department of State, 2014).

Although the Confucius Institute program is largely seen as a successful initiative with regard to enhancing China's public diplomacy efforts and people to-people exchange (Xu, 2016), the institutes have been the subject of controversy, particularly in areas related to financial obligations, academic freedom, legal issues, and ideological concerns (Redden, 2014a, 2014b). "They are attractive for universities seeking engagement with China, but also seen as a threat to academic freedom" (Wang & Adamson, 2014, p. 225). In 2012, McMaster University in Canada was forced to close its Confucius Institute due to a complaint filed by a Hanban teacher accusing McMaster for discrimination against her religious freedom (Bradshaw & Freeze, 2013). In the U.S., concerns have been expressed by the American Association of University Professors (AAUP) regarding the funding model of Confucius Institutes on university campuses. In a statement released in June 2014, the AAUP warned that "allowing any third-party control of academic matters is inconsistent with principles of academic freedom, shared governance, and the institutional autonomy of colleges and universities," and recommended that universities cease their involvement with Confucius Institutes (AAUP, 2014). In 2014, the University of Chicago did not renew its contract with Hanban to continue its Confucius Institute and since then, a number of other U.S. and international institutions have done the same (University of Chicago, 2014).

In response to this criticism, many U.S. Confucius Institutes have released messages clarifying their purpose and some have prepared formal statements agreeing that there should be no third-party control of academic matters. The University of Kentucky's Confucius Institute states that "UK proudly supports multiple viewpoints in its commitment to academic freedom. Through the University's Confucius Institute, the university also demonstrates its commitment to internationalization through intercultural understanding, exchange and development" (Confucius Institute, 2016, para 5). In spite of the controversies, the Confucius Institute program continues to thrive in its work promoting Chinese language and culture, supporting local Chinese teaching internationally, and facilitating cultural exchange.

3   Leveraging Confucius Institutes to Advance International
       Education and Exchange

Despite the controversy surrounding Confucius Institutes, the rapid expansion of the program around the world suggest that the program is flourishing. Although the official purpose of the Confucius Institute program is to promote and teach Chinese culture and language around the world, the broad expertise these institutes have can be leveraged to support other educational goals. Within U.S. higher education specifically, Confucius Institutes have the potential to serve as gateways to China or as conduits for an institution's China initiatives. They can provide leadership and support by facilitating a range of China-related initiatives across the campus and in the local community and be strategically leveraged to provide support with establishing partnerships with Chinese institutions, encouraging student mobility, and supporting faculty engagement.

3.1   *Partnerships and Linkages*

As explained below, Confucius Institutes have the potential to serve as a key resource for advancing an institution's international initiatives by supporting the development of agreements and partnerships with Chinese institutions; promoting the development of cross-border education delivery schemes, establishing joint, dual, and consecutive degree programs; and facilitating access to Chinese funding opportunities.

- *Strategic Partnerships.* Confucius Institutes may be instrumental in the development, negotiation, establishment and maintenance of institutional agreements (i.e., memoranda of understanding, bilateral exchange agreements) with key strategic partners in China. Memoranda of understanding generally serve as platforms for collaborative engagement in joint research activities; exchange of academic materials and publications; and collaboration among faculty members for research, lectures, and discussions (Sutton & Obst, 2011). Exchange agreements are more specific and outline bilateral reciprocal exchanges of students and/or faculty members. Confucius Institutes may facilitate partnerships, but are often not a part of university-to-university exchange agreements.
- *Cross Border Delivery Programs.* Confucius Institutes may be very valuable to institutions pursuing cross border delivery strategies in China (Burgesss & Berquist, 2012). Such programs take many forms, including twinning arrangements, branch campuses, online learning (i.e., distance learning, e-learning, etc.), and franchising. Involvement may be limited to initial introductions or persist throughout the more complex stages of negotiation and implementation. It is important to recognize that as a de facto entity of the Chinese Ministry of Education, there may be limitations in the extent to which a Confucius Institute may be allowed to facilitate the establishment of such programming.
- *Joint, Dual and Consecutive Degree Programs.* U.S. institutions have also become increasingly interested in pursuing joint, dual and consecutive degree programs with Chinese institutions (Knight & Lee, 2012). Chinese students are often attracted to the possibility of earning two degrees from two universities located in different countries. At the institutional level, collaborative degree programs have the potential to lead to deeper

and more sustainable relationships that bring other important academic benefits in terms of the curriculum, faculty exchange, and joint research and scholarship (Knight & Lee, 2012). Confucius Institutes may provide support in surmounting the many complex cultural and logistic issues and challenges for establishing these types of initiatives.

– *Grant Identification and Support.* Agencies of the Chinese government support science and technology research, including research conducted by U.S. citizens in collaboration with Chinese researchers. Confucius Institutes may be called upon to identify potential research partnerships and related grant opportunities available from Chinese sources and support the proposal development process.

3.2   *Educational Mobility of Students and Scholars*

Confucius Institutes may play an influential role in driving the flow students and scholars between the U.S. and China. According to IIE, over 300,000 Chinese students chose to study at U.S. colleges and universities in 2014–2015, which was an 11% increase over the previous academic year. In addition to these mostly degree seeking students, another 40,000 scholars and nearly 20,000 English as a Second Language (ESL) students from China studied in the U.S. during that same academic year (IIE, Open Doors, 2015). The most influential factors that draw Chinese students to the U.S. relate to the consistently high world rankings and status of U.S. higher education institutions, the diversity and capacity of the U.S. higher education system, and the perceived quality and allure of life in the U.S. (De Wit & Rumbley, 2008).

Whereas international students are primarily drawn to the U.S. to earn degrees, U.S. students have been mostly motivated to study internationally by the idea of experiencing other cultures and developing marketable skills and knowledge (De Wit & Rumbley, 2008). Over 60% of U.S. students who study abroad participate in short-term programs of less than 8 weeks in duration (IIE, Open Doors, 2015). Nearly 14,000 U.S. college and university students studied in China in 2013–2014 and many of these students were likely drawn to China to learn the language in context and to experience Chinese culture and society first-hand (IIE, Open Doors, 2015). After South Korea, the United States provides the second largest group of international students to China (IIE, Project Atlas, 2015).

Confucius Institutes are well positioned on U.S. campuses to offer an array of student advising and support services that facilitate both inbound and outbound student and scholar mobility. Such activity has most commonly included providing support with student recruitment and program development, providing scholarship support and advising, offering assistance with Chinese language proficiency testing and Chinese language instruction, conducting pre-departure orientations, and assisting with visa and immigration processes.

- *Student Recruitment.* Confucius Institutes may provide valuable insight into informing an institution's student recruitment strategies for China, which can include facilitating senior administrator visits to China, making official introductions, and coordinating with local recruitment agents and networks.
- *Program Development.* Confucius Institutes may similarly contribute to developing attractive academic programs on campus which appeal to potential students from China. In much the same way, local university faculty members can seek guidance and partnership from Confucius Institutes when developing programs in China for U.S. students. Such support is most commonly seen in the development of education abroad programs focusing on language learning and in programming based at the affiliated Chinese partner institution.
- *Scholarship Support and Advising.* The Chinese Ministry of Education, municipal governments, and potential host institutions provide an array of generous scholarships to international students. Understanding eligibility criteria and navigating complex application instructions can be daunting. Many Confucius Institutes provide advising and support to local students and some even offer their own scholarships for study and travel to China.
- *HSK Testing.* In order to be eligible for the Confucius Institute Scholarship or other Ministry of Education affiliated programming, students must take the Hanyu Shuiping Kaoshi (HSK) examination,[2] the Chinese Language Standard Test. The HSK is a standardized Chinese language proficiency test for assessing non-native Chinese speakers' ability to use the Chinese language in their daily, academic and professional lives. HSK consists of six levels. Many Confucius Institutes conveniently serve as testing centers for the HSK (and the HSKK speaking test) and even offer free tutorials for those preparing to take the exam.
- *Chinese Language Instruction.* Many Confucius Institutes offer Chinese language instruction at multiple proficiency levels. These classes are often free to students attending the affiliated college or university. Local faculty and staff can take these courses at a greatly reduced price, as well. These courses can supplement language instruction offered by the affiliated institution and provide additional opportunities for faculty, staff and students to jumpstart their Chinese language studies.
- *On-Going Orientations.* Confucius Institutes may offer supplemental culture-specific pre-departure orientation programming for students that complements the more cultural-general, on-going orientation programming provided to all outbound students.
- *Visa and Immigration Support.* Many Confucius Institutes can provide detailed instructions and guidance with securing a visa for travel or study

in China. In some cases, they may assist with securing an official invitation letter from the Chinese host institution. This may significantly reduce the stress and anxiety for first time overseas travelers as well as the faculty who direct the programs.

3.3   *Faculty Engagement*

It has been well-documented that in order for comprehensive campus and curriculum internationalization to be successful and sustainable, an institution's faculty must be engaged as active and engaged stakeholders (Childress, 2010; Green, 2012; Hudzik, 2014; Olson, Green, & Hill, 2006). Confucius Institutes may be influential in working to further engage faculty in various aspects of comprehensive internationalization. More common approaches have included assisting faculty members with securing fellowships and grants from Chinese sources, facilitating short-term teaching abroad opportunities in China, initiating conferences and speaker series, making formal introductions with Chinese disciplinary counterparts, identifying research grants and related support, and offering ongoing faculty training and support with curriculum development.

- *Faculty Fellowships and Grants.* Confucius Institutes often provide local faculty members with financial support toward international and domestic travel for China-related conferences, research, course field trips, and curriculum development.
- *Short-Term Teaching Programming.* In order to strengthen collaborative teaching and research between the affiliated institution and Chinese institutions, Confucius Institutes may facilitate opportunities for local faculty to teach short courses over the summer in China.
- *Conferences and Speaker Series.* Confucius Institutes often sponsor academic activities such as conferences, distinguished speaker series, exhibitions and so on that may appeal to local faculty members.
- *Introductions.* Confucius Institutes may connect local faculty members with scholars at Chinese institutions in order to facilitate collaborative research. The Chinese institution sponsoring the local Confucius Institute provides a natural networking opportunity.
- *Faculty Training and Curriculum Development.* With the largest proportion of the international students in U.S. higher education being from China (IIE, Open Doors, 2015), there have increasing concerns among faculty members about cultural difference on such issues as academic integrity (Hammerschmidt, 2013). Confucius Institutes may assist with developing workshops for faculty members on how to better respond to the academic needs of Chinese students as well as orienting advisors and counselors

on cultural issues as they advise and counsel Chinese students. Moreover, Confucius Institutes may provide educational resources and teaching materials that can support faculty in including China-specific academic content in their courses and research.

3.3.1   A Case Model for Faculty Engagement

The following section presents a case model example for how a campus-based Confucius Institute can be strategically leveraged to expand beyond its official role of promoting and teaching Chinese culture and language to include the work of advancing comprehensive campus and curriculum internationalization. This particular case model highlights an innovative program partnership that enabled the University of Kentucky to further explore the establishment of strategic partnerships and linkages with Chinese institutions, to build a stronger foundation on which to increase the educational mobility of students and scholars to and from China, and to engage its faculty members in an interactive, interdisciplinary and collegial exploration of China and Chinese higher education.

3.3.2   The Institution

Nestled in the heart of Kentucky's scenic Bluegrass region, the University of Kentucky (UK) is a public, research-extensive, land grant university that was founded in 1865. UK dedicates itself to improving people's lives through excellence in teaching, research, health care, cultural enrichment, and economic development. As the flagship institution for the Commonwealth of Kentucky, the University plays a critical leadership role by contributing to the economic development and quality of life within Kentucky's borders and beyond. UK's campus now covers more than 716 acres in Lexington and is home to more than 29,000 students and 2,227 full-time faculty members.

International activity and a global reach have always been a part of the research and educational mission of the University. It was not until 2009, however, that UK approved a strategic plan for purposeful internationalization that is both fiscally responsible and sensitive to the culture of the institution's individual colleges. Today, UK annually enrolls nearly 2,000 international students and hosts over 500 J-1 research scholars or professors. Students from China represent by far the largest proportion of international students (approximately 37% of this international student population at UK), which is three times higher than the next largest sending country, India (University of Kentucky International Center, 2016). With nearly 1,300 UK students studying abroad in 2015–2016, education abroad programming has the strong support of UK's senior administration and college deans and holds a central place in the current campus-wide strategic plan. Enrollment in China-based education abroad programs has steadily increased in recent years and China is now among the top ten leading destinations for UK students.

Founded in 2010, the Confucius Institute at the University of Kentucky is a resource for Chinese language, culture, art, and business. A gateway to China for the University and the Commonwealth, the Institute serves as a conduit for many of UK's China initiatives. It facilitates a range of cultural events and activities on campus and in the community and spearheads successful partnerships between UK and Chinese institutions. The Institute also works to strengthen China studies at the University while providing leadership and support for Chinese language study. The UK Confucius Institute partners particularly closely with UK's central education abroad office to further encourage study in China. The Institute has sponsored generous scholarships for study in China, assisted numerous faculty members with developing short-term, faculty-directed programs, provided Chinese language instruction for students departing to and returning from China, offered the HSK test, and assisted with visa and immigration processes. In 2012, and again in 2014, the UK Confucius Institute was honored by Hanban as a Confucius Institute of the Year.

The University of Kentucky Confucius Institute

Founded in 2010 as the 68th Confucius Institute in the U.S., the Institute at the University of Kentucky (UK) is a center for Chinese language, culture, art and business. A gateway to China for the University and the Commonwealth, the Institute serves as a conduit for many of UK's China initiatives. The Institute works to strengthen China studies at the university, while at the same time providing leadership and support for Chinese language programs in Kentucky's K-12 classrooms, and forging important community relationships through Chinese cultural outreach to people of the Commonwealth of Kentucky.

Since its establishment, the Institute has supported the University of Kentucky's strategic plan by establishing and maintaining university-wide partnerships with Chinese universities; enhancing student academic success by developing co-curricular programming for colleges across the University; expanding and enriching student wellness and belonging by providing cultural programing on campus and in the community; and by working with the institution's education abroad office to offer student scholarships and China-specific orientation programming for students studying in China. The Confucius Institute extends the University's land grant mission by reaching out to the communities across the Commonwealth to provide Chinese language instruction and Chinese cultural programing.

In just four years, the UK Confucius Institute has played a crucial role in establishing partnerships with Chinese universities and research institutes, creating opportunities for UK faculty and students to engage more broadly with China, and at the same time contributing to campus diversity. The work of the Institute has been recognized by the UK University Senate for its contribution to the University. In visible opposition to the AAUP recommendation to sever relationships with Confucius Institutes, the University Senate issued a formal statement supporting the Confucius Institute (Senate Review Report, 2015).

Due in large part to the UK Confucius Institute's work, the University of Kentucky has since reinforced its commitment to developing China initiatives as expressed in its 2015–2020 Strategic Plan, establishing an on-campus China Office, and expanding financial support for the operation of the UK Confucius Institute.

In 2012, and again in 2014, the UK Confucius Institute was honored by Hanban as a Confucius Institute of the Year. In 2015, the UK Confucius Institute was selected as a Model Confucius Institute, thus garnering an additional $1.7 million from Hanban to expand operations on the UK campus.

UK Confucius Institute, 2016, http://www.uky.edu/international/confucius_institute

3.3.3   The Program

In 2014, UK Education Abroad approached the UK Confucius Institute with a request to develop and co sponsor a summer 2015 group site visit to China for UK faculty members. Each year, UK Education Abroad facilitates a number of international engagement opportunities for faculty and staff. The goals of these activities have been to raise awareness among the faculty of the potential of education abroad programming, to provide faculty with opportunities to explore the international dimensions of their disciplines, and to support the faculty with identifying strategies for incorporating international elements into their course content. The initial goals of this summer 2015 site visit were to offer UK faculty members the opportunity to learn about international higher education issues in China first-hand and to further enhance education abroad programming in China for UK students.

College deans interested in enhancing education abroad programming opportunities in China were invited to nominate one faculty representative (two for larger colleges) to participate in the site visit. Selected representatives needed to be in a position that could potentially influence education abroad programming within the home college. Preferred representatives were those who were: (1) prepared to advocate for curriculum internationalization, especially as it related to blending a global component into a course or refocusing a course by incorporating issues about China; (2) interested in advancing research on issues related to China; and/or (3) interested in championing the international education goals of the home college (e.g., education abroad, institutional partnerships, etc.).

With the approval and backing of Hanban, the UK Confucius Institute agreed to cover expenses in China. Participants were asked to cover international travel expenses, costs associated with visa documentation, and incidental expenses. Participants were also responsible for any meals not included in the program itinerary. UK Education Abroad provided a limited number of $500 travel grants to support participating representatives. In total, 20 participants were selected, representing 12 UK colleges and the UK Library.[3] Also included were faculty representatives with responsibilities for undergraduate research and service-learning. A member of WRFL, UK's campus radio station, was also invited and tasked with creating and broadcasting several podcasts with faculty members during the site visit.

Prior to departure, representatives attended a series of pre-departure orientation and planning meetings jointly facilitated by Education Abroad and the Confucius Institute. Additionally, representatives were expected to attend three workshops, which included: (1) an introduction to UK Education Abroad, with an emphasis on curriculum integration (Woodruff & Henry, 2012); (2) an introduction to Chinese culture, language and society; and (3) an introduction to higher education in China. Participants also received a number of publications on topics related to China, Chinese higher education, and the development of education abroad programming in China. A final meeting and group dinner was provided at which participants were to share and discuss their answers to the following five questions. A summary of responses was distributed prior to departure.

1 What are your goals for this site visit to China?
2 What will you be specifically looking at while in China (i.e., assessing academic offerings, exploring new partnerships, etc.)?
3 To what extent is education abroad programming, whether in China or elsewhere, integrated into the degree structure of your college?

4 What are the barriers to further integrating education abroad into the degree structures of your college? What are the opportunities to pursue?

5 How can UK Education Abroad better support your college in realizing its international education goals?

Once in China for the 12-day site visit, representatives attended various lectures, visited a diverse range of established and emerging education abroad programs open to students from the U.S., and participated in cultural activities in Beijing, Tianjin and Shanghai. Selected to offer a range of different institution types and contexts, participants visited Shanghai University, Fudan University, East China Normal University, Beijing Normal University, University of International Business & Economics, Beijing Foreign Studies University, and Tianjin University. Some of the Chinese cultural activities included visits to the Shanghai Museum, the Forbidden City, the Temple of Heaven, and the Great Wall, and a cruise on the Huangpu River. The delegation was also invited to the headquarters of the Confucius Institute in Beijing.

FIGURE 4.1   *UK delegation arrives at Hanban*

Upon their return, representatives attended a series of debriefing meetings to discuss the site visit and develop college-specific action plans. A final capstone meeting and reception was organized, which college deans and other senior leaders at UK attended. Participants received a custom t-shirt that included a quote from Confucius and a water bottle from the Confucius

Institute. Action plans were relatively detailed and included a wide range of short- and long-term objectives, such as the following:

— Enhance curriculum integration efforts targeting accounting and finance majors.
— Develop an interdisciplinary, service-learning program in China.
— Create a new brochure on education abroad for Fine Arts students.
— Arrange a return visit with college-level leadership to continue specific discussions started during the site visit.
— Strategically recruit faculty members with research interests in China.
— Develop a pre-departure training for students in global health programs, and a self-paced course for education abroad participants.
— Build an internship program for hospitality majors in Shanghai.
— Host a brown bag lunch for faculty members in my college to learn more about international opportunities.
— Working with dean and chairs to assemble a college-wide plan for engagement in China.
— Work with the college to determine what UK Core courses can be taken in China.

3.3.4   The Outcome

Participants completed a program evaluation after returning from the site visit. Nearly all participants completed the evaluation and unanimously agreed that the purpose and goals for the site visit were well-understood, the provided readings were useful, and the pre-departure materials were helpful in preparing for the visit. Participants found the pre-departure meetings valuable and were highly satisfied with all aspects of the visit itself, including the schedule, lodging, food, transportation, and cultural activities. When asked about their satisfaction in regard to the campus visits, participants reported that the range of institutions visited was appropriate, as was the level of engagement with faculty and administration at each location. Although considerable time was allotted to introduce each institution prior to arrival and then to subsequently debrief each visit, participants reported that still more structured group reflection was needed.

Participants were also asked to list three main takeaways from the site visit (see Table 4.1). Although comments varied, the majority could be categorized into four primary topic areas. First, comments suggested that education abroad programming is more complex and diverse than the participants had expected. Regarding China as a location for education abroad, participant comments suggested that while some remain skeptical about the feasibility of education abroad programming in China, others have begun to think more strategically about sending their students to study in China. Third, participants

TABLE 4.1   *Course and instructor evaluation*

Education abroad

"The breadth of opportunities available to our students."

"I have a better sense for which programs would be more appealing and realistic for my students."

"There are multiple types of education abroad models (and most of our students will require those that provide more support)."

"Education abroad options available to our students are more complicated than I thought."

"There is no 'one size fits all' program for all our students."

Education abroad programming in China

"To entice students, we will need to find a strong rationale for why learning about healthcare in China (compared to any other place) is important or helpful."

"China is different, but not out of the realm of possibilities for many of our students, as long as we strategically identify opportunities that respond to their needs."

"Quality of student services with regards to the different program models and institutions vary widely."

"Aside from the language barrier and some cultural and academic differences, studying in China doesn't appear to be much different than studying in other countries."

"I have a better idea about some directions in which my college can go for potential programming and exploration ideas as far as China is concerned."

"Utilizing providers to assist with faculty-led programs may be the right direction for our College."

"Some students would experience significant challenges."

Chinese higher education

"The dynamism and focus of Chinese universities."

"Chinese universities are rapidly coming on line for receiving international students."

"Chinese higher education institutions are making great strides to accommodate western students and are very flexible in their program design and options."

Interdisciplinary networking and coordinated programming

"Really strong relationships with a whole new set of colleagues from UK."

"Improved network of motivated colleagues at UK."

"We need to do more programming across colleges."

"Healthcare colleges need to join forces in order to create a student cohort large enough to go to China."

"We need to do better at coordinating our efforts as a university."

---

seemed very impressed with the momentum within Chinese higher education institutions to develop and deliver high-quality programming for international students. Finally, and perhaps most unexpectedly, the comments underscored that many of the participants did not know each other prior to the site visit and were excited to be developing a network beyond their home college. Thus, a number of participants called for more interdisciplinary programming and networking across home academic units. There were very few comments about Chinese language, culture and society. Table 4.1 provides an overview of participant comments.

FIGURE 4.2   *Working session*

All respondents stated that they felt better informed and ready to bring about effective change in their home colleges based on what they learned during the site visit. Comments suggested that they have a deepened understanding of education abroad, are more empowered to work across traditional college boundaries, and are better able to advise students and other faculty members on educational programming in China.

- A deepened understanding of education abroad, including third party opportunities, direct enrollment and other types.
- I am not sure it will generate results, but I do know a lot more than I did before about China as an option for students.
- I feel like I gained a better sense of the two main cities we visited and which might be better for our students. Just the experience was great so that I

can better advise my students and help show them that China is a location where they can study the disciplines within our college.
- Working with the other healthcare colleges, I am hoping that we can generate meaningful, practical opportunities for our students.
- I can better inform faculty and departments about the options for our students in China as well as better advise students about studying in China.
- Raising awareness of the EA (education abroad) activities going on across campus will definitely help our unit (the Libraries) support departments more effectively.

3.3.5   Next Steps

By all accounts, the summer 2015 group site visit went smoothly and was well received by all involved. Participants expressed that they learned a lot about Chinese higher education and are more empowered to further enhance education abroad programming both in general and in China. Although developing strategic partnerships and linkages was not an explicit goal of the site visit, the individual campus visits provided ample opportunities for the visiting faculty members to initiate discussions with their academic peers in China. As such, numerous follow-up meetings and visits have since progressed with this particular selection of institutions and negotiations for specific memoranda of understanding have begun. Other initiatives have included, for example, revising curriculum integration documents to include China-specific education abroad programs, developing an interdisciplinary service-learning program in China, initiating a recruitment plan to attract more faculty from China, developing a China-specific, pre-departure training for students in global health programs, and building an internship program in China's hospitality and tourism sector. Because this collaborative program was such a success, Hanban has since invited the UK Confucius Institute to make this an annual activity.

Moreover, the UK Confucius Institute and UK Education Abroad have since embarked together on several new initiatives, including the creation of a new faculty grant program to annually fund the development and implementation of a summer, UK faculty-directed education abroad program in China. The proposed program must feature some form of high-impact educational programming (Kuh, 2008), such as undergraduate research or service-learning and leverage UK's existing strengths and partnerships in China (i.e., Fudan University, East China Normal University, etc). UK Education Abroad will provide a program development grant (if needed) to support the UK faculty member or instructor to travel to China for the purpose of establishing the proposed program. The UK Confucius Institute will provide a sizeable amount toward the total cost of the program in order to lower the program fee assessed to participants. Members of the summer 2015 group site visit have asked to serve as the faculty selection committee.

4   Promising Practices from Confucius Institutes in the U.S.

Although Confucius Institutes may have been established primarily to advance Chinese language study and China-oriented cultural studies, they are now being leveraged in multifaceted ways to advance international cooperation in higher education between the U.S. and China. As the aforementioned case study exemplifies, individual Confucius Institutes are also actively investing energy and resources in innovative programming that increases the educational mobility of students and scholars to and from China, building international networks that enable the establishment of strategic partnerships and linkages with Chinese institutions, and engaging host institution faculty in interdisciplinary study of China. The case study presents a model collaboration built on common goals, mutual respect and strategic collaboration between a host institution and the local Confucius Institute. In this specific case, the Confucius Institute was able to partner with the education abroad office in an innovative way to combine resources to respond to an explicit local need while extending the overall mission of the Confucius Institute.

Such innovative programs are not rare. Confucius Institutes across the country are increasingly seeking to better understand the needs and directions of their host institutions with the goal of developing mutually beneficial and influential programming. For example, Confucius Institutes are active partners in institutions across the U.S. in developing faculty-directed, education abroad programs to China, creating bilateral student exchanges, and fostering research networks. They provide campus leadership and coordination of large-scale cultural activities and events on China, such as film festivals, concerts, and exhibitions. Moreover, Confucius Institutes are creatively partnering with local institutions to advance Chinese language studies and Chinese area studies through initiatives such as academic symposia, faculty exchange, training and development, and curriculum development. To recognize these many efforts, Hanban annually honors a select few institutes worldwide as "Confucius Institute of the Year." Table 4.2 list some of the Confucius Institutes in the U.S. that have been honored since 2013 and highlights some of their many achievements. The work of these institutes underscore the diverse ways of leveraging the Confucius Institute program to advance international education and exchange.

TABLE 4.2   *Selected Confucius institutes of the year, 2013–2015*

Host institution	Partner institution	Notable achievements
George Mason University (Est. 2009)	Beijing Language and Culture University	— Coordinated with the College of Education and Graduate School for a joint training program of master's degree in teaching Chinese. — Through the Social Studies "traveling trunk" and Baoku digital library, supported more than 30,000 elementary and middle school students learn more about China. — Represented China in hosting the Washington Euro-Asian short films festival and trilingual Chinese-English-German poetry-reading event. — Hosted the "China in My Eyes" photography exhibition multiple times, with over 20,000 people attending.
Portland State University (Est. 2007)	Soochow University	— Opened 25 Confucius Classrooms, and as such the number of people learning Chinese tripled, rapidly increasing from 2,000 to more than 6,000. — Held more than 20 international and regional conferences and seminars. The number of participants in these activities has exceeded 100,000. — Organized the compilation, translation and publication of more than a dozen Chinese language teaching research books and local Chinese teaching materials.
Rutgers, the State Univ. of New Jersey (Est. 2007)	Jilin University	— One of the few Confucius Institutes to offer credit-bearing courses in Chinese Studies. — Offers two large-scale international conferences and jointly sponsored three academic conferences.

TABLE 4.2   *Selected Confucius institutes of the year, 2013–2015 (cont.)*

Host institution	Partner institution	Notable achievements
University of Hawai'i at Manoa (Est. 2006)	Beijing Foreign Studies University	– With the Confucius Institute's support, Hawai'i's parliament announced September 28th as "Confucius Day." – Established an innovative online Chinese course for high school students in cooperation with the Myron B. Thompson Academy, funded by the U.S. Department of Education. – Successfully organized the 2015 Joint Conference of North American and Oceanian Confucius Institutes with more than 300 delegates attending the conference.
University of Michigan (Est. 2009)	Renmin University of China	– Advanced study of Chinese musical instruments and Chinese art. – Carried out a series of high-level, professional, multiple and bilateral activities to promote the cultural and artistic exchange between China and the U.S.
University of Pittsburgh (Est. 2007)	Wuhan University	– Established joint advisory group with other six sisterly Confucius Institutes in America. – Held a two-day traditional Chinese Medical seminar which attracted eight experts in Chinese medicine from China. – Established a Chinese proficiency test center and offered comprehensive language examination services concerning HSK, YCT and BCT to Chinese language learners in the six states of central U.S.A.
Pace University (Est. 2010)	Nanjing Normal University	– Offered special training for programs to China, both of which were free to students and faculty of Pace University; offered consulting services concerning China. – Offered the first Internet-based Chinese test center in Greater New York.

Host institution	Partner institution	Notable achievements
University of Kentucky (Est. 2010)	Shanghai University	— A total of around 50,000 people attend a variety of activities held by Institute. — 29 teaching sites have been established by UKCI, with a total of over 14,400 students. — Offered a number of activities, scholarships and orientation to support U.S. students studying in China. — Sent 71 university faculty to teach in China. — One of the only two Testing Centers for Chinese as Second Language Teaching Certificate in Northern America.
University of Minnesota (Est. 2008)	Capital Normal University	— Conducted rigorous academic research including the research project: *Language Development and Academic Achievement of Students in Immersion Programs*. — Received grant from the Star Talk program belonging to the federal government for six consecutive years. — Organized the HSK, HSKK and YCT tests for over 600 students in 2014. Was awarded the title of Best Overseas Test Center.
University of Texas at Dallas (Est. 2007)	Southeast University	— Holds Chinese Public Speaking Competition in Northern Texas as well as Chinese Bridge Chinese proficiency Competition for college and secondary school students.
Webster University (Est. 2008)	Beijing Language and Culture University	— Established 30 teaching sites. The number of students increased by 10% to over 2,400. — Held over 100 cultural exchange activities, achieving a year-on-year increase of 50%. Around 85,000 visitors and participants attended those activities.
Alfred University (Est. 2009)	China University of Geosciences	— Finished the compilation of Chinese language textbook, *Explore Chinese*, which is in use in each school district. — Implemented unique teaching model of refunding tuition fee with cultural activities. In 2014, Geneva school district paid its first tuition fee of 16,000 dollars.

TABLE 4.2   *Selected Confucius institutes of the year, 2013–2015 (cont.)*

Host institution	Partner institution	Notable achievements
Miami Dade College (Est. 2010)	Jiangsu Normal University	– Assisted the School of Theater and Design Technology in developing a credit bearing, education abroad program in China. – Designed a music video called *Chinese Tea* to promote Chinese culture. – Holds an annual international symposium on Chinese Film.
University of Arizona (Est. 2007)	Shanxi Normal University	– Confucius classrooms have adopted the Partial-Immersion Chinese Program, which has been well received by students and their parents. – Organizes an annual Chinese Health Day attracting over 1,000 people each year. – Coordinate an annual, week-long Chinese Culture Festival, attracting over 3,000 attendees.

SOURCE: CONFUCIUS INSTITUTE ANNUAL REPORT (REP. NO. 2013, 2014, 2015), BEIJING

5   Conclusion

As the Confucius Institute program continues to mature, it is in the interest of institutes to align themselves and their activities with the mission and strategic directions of their host institutions. Although the primary aim of the Confucius Institute program may be to promote Chinese language and culture, this chapter has attempted to clarify how Confucius Institutes can also serve as strategic campus partners in advancing international cooperation in higher education between the U.S. and China. Specifically, this chapter has attempted to provide an expanded view of the multifaceted roles Confucius Institutes can play in U.S. higher education, particularly with regard to establishing new partnerships and linkages, fostering international educational mobility, and enhancing U.S. faculty engagement in international education. A case study was presented as a model for how campus-based Confucius Institutes can be strategically leveraged to advance all three roles. Additional institutional best practices from distinguished Confucius Institutes of the Year were highlighted with the goal of providing other strategies for maximizing the Confucius Institute program toward advancing international education and exchange.

Notes

1 To establish a new Confucius Institute, the potential host institution submits a proposal to Hanban. Upon approval, a Chinese partner institution is identified and sends a "Chinese Co-Director" to the host institution to initiate the collaboration. The host institution is required to provide office space and a local director, preferably someone specialized in China studies. A financial match is also required. The budget to operate the new Institute is approved on annual basis by Hanban. In addition to the annual funding, Hanban also provides books on Chinese culture and language and full-time Chinese language instructors.
2 For more information, see http://english.hanban.org/node_8002.htm
3 Colleges included Communication and Information, Engineering, Medicine, Agriculture, Food and Environment (CAFE), Fine Arts, Arts and Sciences, Design, Health Science, Honors, Business and Economics, Education, Public Health, Patterson School of Diplomacy and International Commerce.

References

American Association of University Professors (AAUP). (2015, June 25). *AAUP urges universities to cut ties with Confucius institutes for ignoring academic freedom.* Retrieved July 25, 2016, from http://www.universityherald.com/articles/10105/20140625/aaup-universities-confucius-institutes-academic-freedom-american.htm

Bradshaw, J., & Freeze, C. (2013, February 7). McMaster closing Confucius institute over hiring issues. *The Globe and Mail.* Retrieved December 18, 2016, from http://www.theglobeandmail.com/news/national/education/mcmaster-closing-confucius-institute-over-hiring-issues/article8372894/

Burgess, P., & Berquist, B. (2012). Cross-border delivery: Projects, programs and providers. In H. De Wit, D. Deardorff, J. D. Heyl, & T. Adams (Eds.), *The Sage handbook of international education* (pp. 325–342). Lanham, MD: Rowman & Littlefield.

Childress, L. (2010). *The twenty-first century university: Developing faculty engagement in internationalization.* New York, NY: Peter Lang.

Confucius Institute. (n.d.). *'12 and '14 CI of the year.* Retrieved July 26, 2016, from http://www.uky.edu/international/About_the_Confucius_Institute

De Wit, H., & Rumbley, L. (2008). The role of American higher education in international student circulation. In H. De Wit, P. Agarwal, M. E. Said, M. T. Sehoole, & M. Sirozi (Eds.), *The dynamics of international student circulation in a global context* (pp. 199–231). Rotterdam, The Netherlands: Sense Publishers.

Green, M. (2012). *Measuring and assessing internationalization.* Washington, DC: NAFSA: Association of International Educators.

Hammerschmidt, J. E. (2013). *An investigation of Chinese graduate student understanding of academic integrity in U's higher education: Dissertations* (Paper 519). Retrieved October 30, 2016, from http://ecommons.luc.edu/luc_diss/519

Hudzik, J. (2014). *Comprehensive internationalization: Institutional pathways to success.* New York, NY: Routledge.

Institute for International Education. (2015). *Open doors.* New York, NY: Institute for International Education.

Institute for International Education. (2015). *Project Atlas.* New York, NY: Institute for International Education.

Knight, J., & Lee, J. (2012). International joint, double and consecutive degree programs. In D. Deardorff, H. de Wit, J. D. Heyl, & T. Adams (Eds.), *The Sage handbook of international education* (pp. 343–357). Lanham, MD: Rowman & Littlefield.

Kuh, G. D. (2008). *High-impact educational practices: What they are, who has access to them, and why they matter.* Washington, DC: American Association for Colleges & Universities.

NAFSA. (2016). *NAFSA international student economic value tool.* Retrieved on July 25, 2016, from www.nafsa.org/Explore_International_Education/Impact/Data_And_Statistics/NAFSA_International_Student_Economic_Value_Tool/

Olson, C., Green, M., & Hill, B. (2006). *A handbook for advancing comprehensive internationalization: What institutions can do and what students should learn.* Washington, DC: American Council on Education.

People's Daily Online. (2006a, April 29). *Backgrounder: Confucius institutes.* Retrieved July 26, 2016, from http://en.people.cn/200604/29/eng20060429_262201.html

People's Daily Online. (2006b, October 2). *Confucius institute: Promoting language, culture and friendliness.* Retrieved July 26, 2016, from http://en.people.cn/200610/02/eng20061002_308230.html

People's Daily Online. (2009, March 13). *Number of Confucius institutes worldwide to reach 500 next year.* Retrieved July 26, 2016, from http://en.people.cn/90001/90776/90883/6613754.html

Redden, E. (2014a, July 24). *Confucius controversies.* Retrieved July 25, 2016, from https://www.insidehighered.com/news/2014/07/24/debate-renews-over-confucius-institutes

Redden, E. (2014b, October 1). *Another Confucius institute to close: Inside higher education.* Retrieved July 25, 2016, from http://www.insidehighered.com/quicktakes/2014/10/01/another-confucius-institute-close

Sutton, S., & Obst, D. (2011). *Developing strategic international partnerships: Models for initiating and sustaining innovative institutional linkages*. New York, NY: The Institute of International Education.

University of Chicago. (2014, September 15). Statement on the Confucius institute at the University of Chicago. *UChicago News*.

University of Kentucky International Center. (2016). *UKIC by the numbers*. Retrieved October 30, 2016, from http://www.uky.edu/international/BYTHENUMBERS

U.S. Department of State. (2014, June 24). *U.S.-China Consultation on People-to-People Exchange (CPE)* [Press release]. Retrieved July 25, 2016, from http://www.state.gov/r/pa/prs/ps/2015/index.htm

Wang, D., & Adamson, B. (2014). War and peace: Perceptions of Confucius institutes in China and USA. *The Asia-Pacific Education Researcher, 24*(1), 225–234.

Woodruff, G., & Henry, H. (2012). *Curriculum integration of education abroad*. Retrieved March 27, 2013, from http://www.nafsa.org/epubs

Xu, L. (2016, April 22). *Opening remarks*. Presentation at National Chinese Language Conference, Chicago.

About the Authors

Anthony C. Ogden is executive director of Education Abroad and Exchanges at Michigan State University. Dr. Ogden earned his bachelor's degree from Berea College, master's degree in International and Intercultural Management at the SIT Graduate Institute, and his Ph.D. at The Pennsylvania State University in Educational Theory and Policy with a dual title in Comparative and International Education. Ogden is a career international educator and author of numerous publications related to U.S. education abroad and comprehensive internationalization, including the new co-edited book, *International Higher Education's Scholar-Practitioners: Bridging Research and Practice*, published by Symposium Books, Oxford, UK.

Huajing Xiu Maske is the Director of the Confucius Institute at the University of Kentucky as well as the Executive Director of the university's China Office. She also holds the rank of Associate Professor in the College of Education and has been a Visiting Professor at China's Jilin University and at the University of International Business and Economics in Beijing. Dr. Maske is also a committee member of the Expert Panel of International Chinese Language Teaching Materials. Dr. Maske received her PhD in Chinese Art History from Oxford University, England, her MA in International Cultural Exchange from Peking University, and her BA in English Literature from the University of International Relations, Beijing, China. She has lectured extensively in the U.S.,

Europe and Asia. She has published numerous articles and essays. Dr. Maske and the institute she directs have received national and international awards including Amici Linguarum (Friend of Languages) Award, Individual Performance Excellent Award and Confucius Institute of the Year Award.

CHAPTER 5

Developing a Multi-Institutional, Internationally-Focused Higher Education Research Partnership

Deane Neubauer and Joanne Taira

Abstract

This chapter presents a case study of a process initiated at the East-West Center in Honolulu, Hawai'i, to explore the rapidly expanding range of issues associated with the massification of education, and especially higher education in the Asia Pacific region over the past three to four decades. For the group initiating this process, the fundamental issue to be addressed was whether or not the very pace of innovation and change within this area had come to "overwhelm" the policy structures and discourses prevalent within the region, and if a focused research endeavor could be developed as an ongoing structure and process for confronting these rapidly changing policy dimensions. The study describes a multi-institutional partnership among universities and other entities in the Asia Pacific, including China, that is focused on addressing these innovative and dynamic changes in higher education in the region and the multitude of policy issues and discourses which have resulted. Through the pursuit of quality research and professional training, the Asia Pacific Higher Education Research Partnership (APHERP) has created a network of institutions and scholars dedicated to research on these issues and an ongoing and continuous exploration of the novel dimensions of change and their consequences presented by these phenomena of massification. The chapter examines the East-West Center legacy that has been the inspiration for APHERP; the evolution of this effort from a sponsored program to a membership consortium; and the process, challenges, and benefits of the resulting multi-institutional partner model.

1 Introduction

Shortly after the turn of the century, a small group of researchers at the East-West Center (EWC) in Honolulu, which is located adjacent to the University of Hawai'i Mānoa campus, began a conversation that centered on a simple but

© KONINKLIJKE BRILL NV, LEIDEN, 2018 | DOI 10.1163/9789004368361_005

compelling observation. This observation was that the contemporary world, in large part defined by what were perceived as the dynamics of contemporary globalization, was changing more rapidly than education, and perhaps they should do something to address that situation.

This served as the pretext for a set of seminars convened by the EWC (two in Honolulu and one in Hong Kong) to address this simple but compelling proposition. The seminars involved scholars with expertise in research, teaching, and administrative roles throughout Asia, with a particular emphasis on Australia, New Zealand, Southeast Asia and East Asia as well as the United States. The third such seminar was convened in Honolulu in November 2004 with the goal of first developing a set of essays that defined the issues involved and later developing a methodology that would extend the reach of such seminars to a broader audience. The essays that emerged from the event took the form of a volume of original papers edited by three of the participants: Peter Hershock, John Hawkins, and Richard Mason (2007). By this point the endeavor had acquired the name, The International Forum for Education 2020 (IFE, 2020), on the premise that this set of "conversations" would be guided by the goal of identifying and providing insight into the changes likely to occur within education in the first two decades of the century. By this point, it had also become clear to the participants that their guiding strategy would be to develop policy-relevant issues, questions, and proposals. These would be of use throughout the policy processes associated with education as participants strove to identify issues, adapt to challenges, and seek solutions. Shortly after the 2004 meeting the EWC planning group agreed that their subsequent efforts would be focused on such issues within higher education.

As a portion of the 2004 meeting, two decisions were made that would give form to IFE 2020 for the remainder of its duration until its unanticipated conclusion in 2012. One decision was to hold a seminar, which came to be called a senior seminar, signifying the effort to engage mainly senior scholars in the enterprise. The seminar would be held every year if possible. Beginning in 2005 IFE would conduct an annual event termed a "leadership seminar" intended to assist mid-level academics in developing policy-relevant perspectives on higher education. The first such seminar was held for one month with five attendees invited from five countries: the Philippines, China, Thailand, India, and the U.S. (specifically Hawai'i in this instance). The "curriculum" for the leadership institute was drawn from the content of previous IFE senior seminars.

This model would persist until the conclusion of IFE 2020 in 2012, leading to an annual senior seminar that would produce either an edited book, or a special journal issue, or both. In addition, a Leadership Institute was held with two important structural changes that differentiated it from the senior seminars. First, in 2006, senior staff decided to have fewer representatives from more countries (typically two each from nine or ten countries). Then, in 2010, the decision was made to move the institute physically from convening in Hawai'i to the Asia region. As a result, leadership institutes were held in Bangkok, Thailand in 2010; at East China Normal University in Shanghai, China in 2011; and at Northeast Normal University in Changchun, China in 2012.

A major event was set in motion in the summer of 2010, in anticipation of the November 2011 Asia-Pacific Economic Cooperation (APEC) heads of state meeting in Hawai'i. The presidents of the University of Hawai'i, M.R.C. Greenwood, and the East-West Center, Charles Morrison, requested staff at both institutions to cooperate in developing a "pre-APEC" event that would blend the strengths of the University of Hawai'i and the East West Center and would serve to focus some of the services provided by the institutions within the APEC region. Staff of both organizations worked with the U.S. Department of Education to propose an APEC Education Network project on higher education quality. The project was approved for funding by APEC, and brought forth a three-day meeting August 4–6, 2011, in Honolulu, on the subject, "Quality in Higher Education: Identifying, Developing and Sustaining Best Practices in the APEC Region." The form of this meeting and many of the participants selected to present papers were linked to the previous activities of IFE 2020, which by this time had developed relationships with many key participants in the Asia-Pacific higher education policy-relevant communities. Central to the development of this session, which we discuss in further detail below, was the structure of the meeting itself, modeled after an IFE 2020 senior seminar to ensure not merely the presentation of relevant materials, but also critical and engaged discussion among meeting participants.

Largely due to U.S. government budgetary politics resulting in wide-spread budgetary cuts in Fiscal Year 2012, IFE 2020 was notified that after the completion of its scheduled events in 2012 (which included a senior seminar at Seoul National University in May, and a leadership institute at Northeast Normal University in Changchun, China, in September), the program would receive no further funding from the East-West Center. At this time, Drs. John Hawkins and Deane Neubauer, acting Center consultants and de facto co-facilitators of the program, were confronted with the choice of either terminating the program after publishing the Seoul meeting papers with Palgrave Macmillan, or developing a new model. Up to that point, IFE 2020 had generated a significant amount of intellectual capital, a somewhat novel and viable meeting model, and a leadership institute of significant reported value to its annual participants which was financially self-sufficient.

These circumstances led to the creation of the Asia Pacific Higher Education Research Partnership (APHERP). At the point of its transition from IFE 2020 to APHERP the project had involved scholars and leadership participants from Australia, Canada, China,[1] Germany, Hong Kong, India, Indonesia. Japan,

New Zealand, Pakistan, Philippines, Korea, Malaysia, Mongolia, Singapore, Taiwan, Thailand, the United States, and Vietnam.

2   APHERP

APHERP was established in January 2013 as a membership-based organization. The planning for such an organization actually went back to the APEC meeting of August 2011. As part of the APEC project plan, the organizers conducted daily "sustainability" sessions that explored other kinds of activities that might flow from the discussions of higher education quality held during the APEC initiative. These discussions were conducted on all three days of the meeting on a voluntary basis, initially within a small designated "planning committee" and later in a group of twenty people. Out of these discussions came a desire to see some form of "quality-focused" entity developed from within the East-West Center, and a list of "pressing" topics focused on quality-related issues that could be pursued by such an entity.

Between the end of fiscal year 2012 and the beginning of 2013, assisted by a planning grant provided by the University of Hawai'i system office with additional support from the East-West Center, more than twenty people who had been involved in some way with IFE 2020 held conversations to sketch out a subsequent organization. This became APHERP, bearing the full title of the Asia Pacific Higher Education Research Partnership: Innovation, Policy, Governance and Quality, the latter an emphasis suggested by several to make clear the overall intentionality of the organization in its research endeavors.

APHERP was established with four levels of membership:

1 Core members were to provide an annual fee of $30,000 and by doing so create a relatively stable financial floor for the organization. Initially, three organizations agreed to support at this level: RMIT University in Melbourne, the East-West Center and the UH System operating as a pair, and the Hong Kong Institute of Education.
2 Foundation Members agreed to support the organization with an annual fee of $9500.
3 Associate memberships were established for institutions in countries with probable lesser resources (e.g., countries identified as "travel-eligible" by APEC) at an annual contribution of $4000.
4 After some further discussion with two U.S.-located higher education accreditation bodies, The Western Association of Schools and Colleges Senior Commission (at that time WASC, now WSCUC) and The Council on Higher Education Accreditation (CHEA) requested a modest membership

level that would provide them with "a seat at the table" to view subsequent developments.

Membership rights and activities deemed appropriate for each level were developed, and the organization formed a governance structure in which each institution would attend a biennial all-membership meeting and a seven person steering committee would meet on a timely basis to engage in major decisions. (These and other aspects of the organization can be accessed at the website, https://apherp.org/.)

A major guiding principle of the organization was to focus explicitly on value added to members at all levels. Toward this end, with the emergence of APHERP, the number of annual senior seminars was raised from one to two in order to expand the range of inquiry and opportunity for publication and dissemination of research. In March of 2014, an additional seminar was added for the purpose of engaging younger scholars, The Emerging Scholar Seminar. The annual Leadership Institute is conducted at some point during the summer months. Experience over the more than ten years of its duration in both forms has indicated that the most significant value for participants is the opportunity to work intensely but productively with representatives from member organizations, typically from seven to ten Asia Pacific countries.

The primary mechanism for assuring the value and topicality of the organization is the creation of new topics for research as an integral part of each seminar, engaging the participants of a current seminar to explore subjects of relevance and importance for future seminars. Thus, the organization is always in the process of publishing work from the past two senior seminars, while providing a research agenda decided by the membership for the forthcoming two. This is a process that has been replicated with the emerging scholar seminar. Experience has demonstrated that relatively junior scholars can work effectively within the senior scholar framework and contribute significantly.

Early on in this process it became clear that the effectiveness of the senior seminar model was of adequate relevance for some subjects, but not all. For example, the last IFE senior seminar in 2012 at Seoul National University explored, "The Social, Economic and Cultural Development of Higher Education in the Asia Pacific Region: Four Contestable Hypotheses." A subset of participating researchers proposed the creation of a "research partnership" to further pursue the overall subject of the meeting with additional means and levels of support. As one participant commented, "the senior seminar provides a great view of things from 30,000 feet, but we also need to get a closer look as well." To date, four research partnerships have been established that operate autonomously from the APHERP structure, but report their findings back to the larger APHERP group. They seek autonomous publication of their work. The organizational framework also makes provision for APHERP to operate as a grant-holding entity if desired, but to date this has not yet occurred.

3   Extending and Validating Research and Training Agendas

APHERP's multi-institutional organizational structure, methods of identifying topics for senior seminar research and discourse, and membership decision processes provide a partnership model for engaging multiple institutions, agencies, and systems across borders in discourse around shared issues. The interactive process at seminars integrates research presentations with discussion and reflection, and contributes to mutual learning and interactive reframing of concepts and approaches. This is critical to APHERP's intentional focus on the rapidly-evolving policy issues in higher education within the contemporary environment of globalization in the Asia Pacific region. The process also lends itself to differing perspectives on the history, culture, and governance of higher education in the region.

Before each senior seminar, the co-directors of APHERP announce a call for papers and issue a draft concept note centered on a central issue to members. For example, the organizing research question for the November 2015 APHERP senior seminar hosted by the Hong Kong Institute for Education and Lingnan University was as follows:

How Sustainable is the Current Massification of Asian Pacific Higher Education? We are focused on issues such as: Is the region approaching a time of reassessment of this approach of unquestioned expansion and massification, particularly as the region appears to be following a particular HE paradigm? How to conceptualize sustainability? For example, do the issues go beyond financial ones, but might they also involve questions such as those focused on state capacity/capability in managing change in higher education, as well as implications for sustainable development in cultural, social, economic and political sense, especially when modern universities are under great pressure for productivity sometimes at the expense of culture and value preservation? (APHERP, 2015)

In the case of the May 2016 senior seminar at Zhejiang University in Hangzhou, China, the organizing questions were framed around the seemingly predominant world class university (WCU) rankings model and proposed an examination of a more extensive, new flagship university model:

> The emergence of global rankings, and its co-dependent WCU ideal, has captured the attention of higher educational officials, while at the same time, is being critically appraised by many academics and stakeholders in the field of higher education. ... The New Flagship University model briefly outlined in the following introductory section ... attempts to provide a more holistic and ecological vision of what constitutes the best and most influential national universities. This includes a broad conception of the purpose and goals of these institutions that include the type of variables, like socioeconomic mobility and regional economic development, largely ignored or missing from the pronouncements, policy and funding initiatives related to the WCU desires of ministries and many universities. (APHERP, 2016)

Seminar participants in May 2016 were asked to address questions about their national universities, their missions, and the effect of these on the societies they served, as well as how the WCU rankings were affecting the traditional flagship universities and national systems of higher education. Participants were also asked to consider the notion of flagship universities within the context and history of Asian higher education and to explore core missions, roles in national systems of higher education, and management and accountability practices.

In each case, the concept to be explored in the senior seminars evolved from discussions in previous senior seminars and was deemed valuable by member organizations for future research in senior seminars. Seminar topic decisions were made during periodic steering committee meetings and the all-member meetings held in Honolulu biennially. In addition, publication of papers from senior seminars in an edited volume or journal edition, along with online communications among participants of senior seminars, emerging scholar seminars, and research cluster groups, disseminated research results and supported continuing identification and framing of questions for future effort.

The APHERP model has these key elements that appear to support a sustainable, multi-institutional international collaboration:

– Partnership is not an end in itself, but a means to provide strategic opportunities for members of academic institutions, government ministries, quality agencies, researchers, and leaders to examine the dynamics of globalization in the region and its effects on higher education. An important premise of this commitment to explore the implications of globalization is that the phenomenon itself is highly dynamic and higher education institutions in the region are in a vibrant state of change and development. This view has underscored the processes by which the subject matters for research are identified, framed, articulated and pursued.

– APHERP has built on the foundation of collaborative relationships established over many years by the East West Center's IFE 2020 project, and anticipates emerging issues through an interactive member process to ascertain and anticipate institutional agendas and interests. Each year of the partnership reveals more complex dimensions of these institutional agendas and interests, which in turn inform the research agenda. One significant benefit of the current structure is heightened exposure for junior faculty, senior graduate students, and early-experience administrators whose perspectives of their own institutions and many of the emerging issues in the region is novel. This has also contributed to the overall research agenda.

– A strong APHERP core team of co-directors, who are recognized scholars with regional and higher education experience and knowledge, contributes essential stability to the organization. In addition to capturing and honing the conceptual framework for proposed research agendas, the co-directors perform functions that are critical to the sustainability of APHERP as an international partnership of institutional members. Throughout the year, co-directors provide updates on member organizations, institutional changes in leadership and priorities, and potential members. And, as indicated above, the research partnership that follows on the experiences of IFE 2020 currently constitutes a network of 250 plus scholars, administrators, and public service employees. There is considerable exchange within this informal network, which serves to provide continued input on what members regard as important and emerging higher education issues worthy of further pursuit.

– One aspect of APHERP's structure and activities are developmental opportunities for both established and emerging scholars embedded in the iterative approach of submitting a draft paper, followed by seminar presentation and discussion, and subsequent review by senior scholars in preparation for publication in an edited volume or journal with an international publisher. After almost a decade and a half of experience, the directors and staff have been exposed to growing evidence that this particular model of addressing higher education policy issues has "migrated" into the work habits and practices of many of the scholars at all levels of experience who have participated in this practice. Feedback suggests that these practices put in place an "incremental pedagogy" for approaching such issues that extends beyond the practice of the seminars themselves.

– APHERP seminars are located at universities within the Asia Pacific region, giving graduate students from member institutions an opportunity to attend the seminar as observers. The co-directors invite students to join supplementary sessions that provide background and further analysis after each day of the seminar. Feedback from these students indicates that they find this "additional benefit" of their participation as "observers" to the seminar to be most rewarding, in many cases leading to developing novel ideas for their subsequent graduate work, and in some cases dissertation topics.

− The effort to be current with important higher education policy issues within the region has created a flexible structure for determining the themes of both senior and emergent scholar seminars. In effect, input is gained initially from the biennial membership meeting and the two-year strategic plan that is developed as a result of it, and then modified by input and discussion from periodic steering committee meetings and at each senior seminar. In practice, some subjects are advanced and some subjects are delayed as events render their relevance somewhat problematic. Such was the sequence of events that produced the cluster of senior seminars taking place between 2014 and 2016 on the "Progress of Massification of Asia Pacific Higher Education" at the Hong Kong Institute of Education and the "Sustainability of Massification of Asian Pacific Higher Education." The processes of massification and sustainability were topics linked to a seminar in 2015 at Zhejiang University on quality issues and the 2016 Zhejiang University seminar on the emerging and changing roles of Flagship Universities.

3.1   Challenges

APHERP's multi-institutional membership model links diverse partners that range in institutional mission, size, and complexity within nations that differ significantly in demographics, resources, and educational governance structures. The diversity of the membership encourages broader conversations about the many dimensions of higher education, both explicit and subtle, that can emerge through the kinds of activities conducted by the research partnership. This outcome is perhaps best exemplified by the annual Leadership Institute, an eleven-day event that takes place at the National Cheng Chung University in Chia-yi, Taiwan. Initially conceived as a longer event, this shorter, eleven-day format was developed with the realization that asking mid-level career higher education personnel to absent themselves from their work-life responsibilities for longer periods becomes impractical. Each APHERP member organization is requested to nominate a member of its choosing for the institute, which is re-constructed annually based on the cumulative inputs to the knowledge and policy focus of the partnership through the various seminars. Each institute is evaluated at its conclusion and participants are asked to nominate other subjects to be explored as well as to comment on the relative value of participation. Without fail, participants most often single out the ability to spend an extended period of time working with and learning from their colleagues from other cultures, societies, and higher education environments as of the highest value.

The explicit challenges raised within this collective framework focus on issues of relevance and the relative importance of issues addressed given the extraordinary differences of higher education structures and experiences across the diversity of the partnership's membership. Again, this is exemplified in both the seminars and the institute. In the seminars, the particular structure that allows each research presentation or paper to be discussed immediately following its presentation permits participants to raise specific questions about how discrete practices and institutional forms in one culture or society may be aligned with those of others. Leaders of the seminars find that interpersonal discussions thus initiated tend to continue on through the rest of the seminar and beyond as participants continue to interact on the issues. Often issues raised in discussions find their ways into subsequent publications. The existence of this phenomenon underscores one of the original intentions of the model, namely, to use a set of discrete policy-focused discussions to create a network of scholars who can find it useful to reach out to each other across a variety of issues and subjects, and to value each other's expertise. Some of the participants over the years have said that the partnership operates in the form of an "extended learning" community, a notion that is reinforced by its institutional membership. Seminar and institute participants appear to view this overall membership structure as a de facto, if informal, institutional relationship that offers them opportunities for extended contact.

Two challenges continue to reassert themselves. One is predicated on the vagaries of institutional membership itself. Typically, an institution will be brought into the partnership through the efforts of an individual with an expressed interest in the activities of the partnership, but given the many different ways in which institutions come to express interest in and join external organizations, the actual institutional commitment may be lodged in a different part of the organization. In the case of APHERP, this has led to considerable organization disruption when the occupants of various administrative roles shift, creating situations in which one set of institutional participants has failed to recruit and socialize its successor(s). The result has been the creation of "administrative noise" that acts as a deterrent to effective organizational performance, and in several instances institutions have dropped out of the partnership. The second challenge arises from what can be viewed as a "busy marketplace" for higher education cooperative and collaborative activity, a situation in which the relative value of one enterprise becomes difficult to weigh against that of another. One response to this situation within the Asia Pacific higher education environment has been for institutions to become bureaucratically conservative in restricting staff members, schools, and faculties from joining external networks or consortia, especially when such membership involves the payment of what are regarded as substantial sums. From the perspective of the research partnership, this climate of "membership conservatism" has been compounded in various instances by the skeptical attitude of higher levels of administration that tend to be more immediately influenced by the relative size of membership dues than the presumptive and often hard to quantify benefits to be gained by participation of individual faculty members or academic departments.

On the positive side of the equation, the unique nature of the University of Hawai'i (UH) has contributed both conceptual and practical benefits to the research partnership. The University holds membership both through its system office and its major research campus at Mānoa. The University of Hawai'i (UH) is distinctive among U.S. state public higher education systems and certainly among Asian counterparts in that it consists of seven community college campuses, two primarily baccalaureate colleges campuses, and a major research university. These ten campuses, with three institutional types, are organized into a single statewide public higher education system. They are administered by one president and a single board of regents, with each campus reporting to a separate chancellor. Dozens of research, service, education, and extension centers are spread over the archipelago on six of the eight Hawaiian Islands. The organizational diversity experienced in such a system rises to a level of complexity usually not present in Asian national systems, which tend to be organized either regionally or by the level of institutions and countries that differ significantly in size, demographics, resources, organizational structure, and development. The result is that observation of the multiple units and educational pathways operating within the University of Hawai'i give it a sense of perspective that contributes usefully and significantly to becoming aware of and formulating valuable policy issues within the Asia Pacific context of the research partnership.

4   Summary

The experiences of developing a multi-institutional partnership focused on examining the dynamic changes in higher education in the Asia Pacific region have provided several enduring benefits. APHERP's structure and processes contributed through its institutional memberships; consultative framing of topics for examination; iterative review of papers for presentation and publication; and activities that include a range of participants, both senior and emerging scholars.

The first benefit is that the experience in both the IFE and APHERP formats provided the core institutions, mainly the University of Hawai'i system and the East-West Center, with a ready and focused means for continually expanding the range of scholars to "bring into the conversation" about the evolving changes in the Asia Pacific higher education policy environment. Each senior seminar among the past six have provided at least three and sometimes more new participants. Overall, the roster of participants from inception to the current day has reached nearly two hundred. These scholars at times also have had interest in working with institutions of the partnership in other activities as well as the scheduled seminars. A second benefit is that the network created by a partnership like APHERP significantly expands the framework of consultations that the core planning group is able to include when identifying and assessing possible topics of interest and importance to a variety of institutions and their members. Third, the leadership institute, targeted at mid-level (career) individuals provides a steady influx of new participants to engage with others across the region in higher education discussions, and possibly, to participate in future research seminars. And finally, the inception three years ago of the emerging scholar seminar created both a vehicle for identifying new and talented participants for research partnership and provided a means to introduce junior scholars to the world of international publication.

Note

1   The Chinese participants included representatives from Peking University (4), East China Normal University (4), Northeast Normal University (5), Tsinghua University (2), Yunnan University (1), the Ministry of Education (1), the Henan University of Science and Technology (1), and the Tianjin University of Science and Technology (1).

References

APHERP. (2015). *Senior seminar: Hong Kong 2015.* Retrieved from https://apherp.org/ss_nov2015/

APHERP. (2016). *Hangzhou May 2016: The changing nature of the flagship university.* Retrieved from https://apherp.org/ss_may2016/

Hershock, P., Hawkins, J., & Mason, M. (Eds.). (2007). *Changing education: Leadership, innovation and development in a globalizing Asia Pacific.* Hong Kong: Comparative Education Research Center and Springer.

International Association of Universities. (2012). *Affirming academic values in internationalization of higher education: A call for action.* Retrieved from http://www.iauaiu.net/sites/all/files/Affirming_Academic_Values_in_ Internationalization_of_Higher_Education.pdf

Appendix A

Brief History of Events and Publications

APHERP has conducted the following events and produced these publications. The form and substance of these results can serve as examples for activities to be conducted by a research partnership.

APHERP adjusted to members' needs and modified the model developed during the long history of IFE 2020. The bridge between the IFE 2020 program and APHERP was the collaboration experienced during the APEC 2011 project among the East-West Center, the University of Hawai'i, and seminar participants. The project supported by APEC entitled, "Quality in Higher Education: Identifying, Developing and Sustaining Best Practices in the APEC Region," resulted in a three-day conference in Honolulu, August 4–6, 2011, and the publication of conference proceedings and papers by APEC in October 2011 (APEC Publication #211-HR–04.1).

1 APHERP Senior Seminar held at the Hong Kong Institute of Education, September 24–26, 2013. Subject: "Research, Innovation and Development in Asia-Pacific Higher Education." Resulting Publication:
   a John N. Hawkins and Ka Ho Mok, Editors. Research, Development, and Innovation in Asia Pacific Higher Education, Palgrave Macmillan. 2015.

2 APHERP Senior Seminar held at East China Normal University, Shanghai, China, November 14–16, 2013. Subject: "21st Century Workskills and Competencies." Resulting Publication:
   a Deane Neubauer and Kamila Ghazali, Editors, *21st Twenty First Century Work Place Skills and Learning Competencies,* Palgrave Macmillan. 2015.

3 APHERP Senior Seminar held at the Royal Melbourne Institute of Technology, Melbourne, Australia, March 24–26, 2014. Subject: "Changing Roles and Purposes of Graduate Education in Asia Pacific Higher Education." Resulting Publication:
   a Deane Neubauer and Prompilai Buasuwan, Editors, *Changing Aspects of Graduate Education in the Asia Pacific Region,* Palgrave Macmillan. 2016.

4 Ninth Leadership Institute held at the National Chung Cheng University, Chia-yi, Chinese Taipei, July 12–20, 2014.

5 First Emerging Scholar Seminar held at IPPTN, Universiti Sains Malaysia, Penang, Malaysia, October 9–11, 2014. Resulting Publication:

    a Deane Neubauer and Christopher S. Collins, Editors, Redefining Asia Pacific Higher Education in Contexts of Globalization: Private Markets and the Public Good, Palgrave Macmillan, 2015.

6 APHERP Senior Seminar held at the Hong Kong Institute of Education, October 16–19, 2014. Subject: "The Many Faces of Asia Pacific Higher Education in the Era of Massification." Resulting Publications:

    a Ka Ho Mok and Deane Neubauer, Guest Editors, Special Edition of *Journal of Education and Work*, June 2015.

    b Alfred Wu and John N. Hawkins, Editors, Massification of Higher Education in Asia: Consequences, Policy Responses and Changing Governance, Springer, publication expected early 2017.

7 Second Emerging Scholar Institute held at Kasetsart University, Bangkok, Thailand, March 23–25, 2015.

8 APHERP Senior Seminar held at Zhejiang University, Hangzhou, China, May 18–20, 2015. Subject: "Creating Cultures of Quality within Asia Pacific Higher Education Institutions."

    a Deane Neubauer and Catherine Gomes, Editors, *Quality Issues at the University Level: Implementing Massification in Asian Higher Education*, Palgrave Macmillan, publication expected early 2017.

9 Tenth Leadership Institute held at the National Chung Cheng University, Chia-yi, Chinese Taipei, July 22–31, 2015.

10 Senior Seminar held at Hong Kong Institute of Education and Lingnan University, November 12–14, 2015. Subject: "The Sustainability of Massification of Asia Pacific Higher Education."

    a Deane Neubauer, Ka Ho Mok and Jiang Jin, Editors, *The Sustainability of Higher Education in the Asia Pacific,* Routledge, publication expected 2017.

11 Senior Seminar held at Zhejiang University, Hangzhou, China, May 23–25, 2016. Subject: "The Changing Nature of the Flagship University."

    a John Douglass and John N. Hawkins, Editors, *The Changing Nature of the Flagship University,* University of California Press, publication expected early 2017.

12 Senior Seminar to be held at the Education University of Hong Kong, October 27–29, 2016. Subject: "Gender and the Changing Face of Higher Education in the Asia Pacific."

13 Additional Resulting Publication:
  a Deane Neubauer, John N. Hawkins, Molly Nyet Ho Lee, and Christopher Collins, Editors. *Handbook of Asian Higher Education,* Palgrave Macmillian, 2016.

About the Authors

Deane Neubauer is Professor Emeritus of Political Science, University of Hawai'i, Mānoa and Co-Director of the Asia Pacific Higher Education Research Partnership since its formation in 2013, and prior to that Co-Director of the International Forum for Education at the East-West Center. His academic work has focused variously on the varieties of national policy expressions in health care, food security, and higher education within the contemporary dynamics of globalization with particular attention to nations in the Asia/Pacific region.

Joanne Y. Taira is Senior Executive for International and Strategic Initiatives at the University of Hawai'i System of ten campuses throughout Hawai'i. She convenes the systemwide international education committee; coordinates the President's Emerging Leaders Program; and is Hawai'i's liaison for a national alliance focused on increasing higher education completion. She oversaw the APEC project, *Quality in Higher Education,* and serves on the APHERP steering committee. She earned a BA from Carleton College, and a Masters in Asian Studies and PhD in Education from the University of Hawai'i at Mānoa.

CHAPTER 6

Internationalization 2.0 and Counting: Learnings from China-U.S. Collaborations in Business Education

Anne M. D'Angelo and Lili Dong

Abstract

The purpose of this chapter is to illustrate the foundational, relational, and transformational phases of internationalization 1.0 (knowledge foundation), 2.0 (relational phase) and 3.0 (transformational phase) in the context of China-U.S. collaborations by a U.S. business school. The chapter begins with a brief history and partnership structure of a case example of a bilateral collaboration and describes the partnership's gradual progression from a foundational approach to a relational, mutually beneficial, and transformative partnership. In this chapter, we identify opportunities and challenges of the partnership and explore themes and patterns that continue to emerge today. We then analyze, compare and contrast cultural strategies and lessons learned from this partnership that others might gain deeper insight into their own China-U.S. collaborations and advance progress.

1 Introduction

Internationalization (Knight, 2003), globalization (Croucher, 2004), global leadership (Global Thinkers Forum, 2014), global mindset (Javidan & Walker, 2013), cultural competence (Livermore, Ang, & Dyne, 2015), cultural intelligence (Earley & Ang, 2003), cultural agility (Caligiuri, 2012), and global savvy (Caudron, 1991) are key concepts that are often used interchangeably by corporate and business school leaders today. As organizational priorities evolve to meet demands of the global economy, professionals, students, faculty, and staff must adapt and develop their own knowledge, abilities, and skills (Anderson, 2005; World Bank, 2003). The meaning and use of these concepts and the execution of efforts by higher education leaders vary considerably across individuals, organizations, and cultures.

© KONINKLIJKE BRILL NV, LEIDEN, 2018 | DOI 10.1163/9789004368361_006

Defining internationalization in global management education and reaching common understanding on mutual goals within an organization and among colleagues around the world is challenging. A starting point for institutions is a strategic and structural framework (Bolman & Deal, 2013) for internationalization, built upon a strong, theoretical foundation. Knight defines internationalization at the national/sector/institutional levels as "the process of integrating an international, intercultural, or global dimension into the purpose, functions, or delivery of postsecondary education" (Knight, 2003, p. 2). This framework assists higher education leaders to explain and integrate the components of internationalization with colleagues and across present-day higher education systems.

A preliminary outline of foundational components often includes the following aspects:

— Who? (faculty, staff, students, partners, corporate community, alumni);
— What? (internationalizing the curriculum, designing and implementing programs including joint degrees, study abroad, international student recruitment, faculty and staff development);
— Where? (Internationalization at Home [Mestenhauser, 2003], global partnerships around the world);
— Why? (strategic mission, organizational talent development, student/ professional development, alumni satisfaction, rankings);
— How? (courses, programs, teaching, learning and research development); and
— To What Extent? (strategic priorities and contextual fit).

These are some examples of the most typical components we focus on during the initial stage of internationalization, internationalization 1.0, or what we call the foundational stage. In general, Internationalization 1.0 is mainly focused on understanding processes and identifying how they might be used to support the mission of an institution.

Internationalization 2.0 suggests a progression from such foundational components and implementation of internationalization to collaboration with deliberate attention to deepen key relationships and partnerships, understand cultural norms and nuances in the context of global partnerships, and collaborate in more meaningful ways beyond initial purposes. Most importantly, and critical to the success of advancing from a foundational to a relational and ultimately transformational methodology, is a focus on professionals – the significance of faculty, staff and community member roles, and their preparedness with the necessary knowledge and experience to create, guide and develop this progression. Given the complexity of global collaborations today, the progression from foundational to relational to transformational is not linear but manifested in diverse and disruptive ways. Expertise in knowledge and practice of international education, policy, global and cultural competence, integrated with disciplinary teaching, research and professional practice, is increasingly warranted for deepening engagement and the promise of new and emerging collaborations.

Internationalization 3.0 integrates and builds upon the foundational and relational stages and creates a greater sophistication of collaboration that is transformational – shifting from awareness to more familiarity and agility with

TABLE 6.1   *Summary of internationalization 1.0, 2.0 and 3.0*

	Definition/Criteria	Examples
Internationalization 1.0	Initial and foundational stage in international collaborations	Establish partnerships & sign agreements, e.g. student and faculty exchanges Design and establish joint degree programs Hire faculty and staff for programs Partnership may not be completely equal
Internationalization 2.0	Relational stage with increased mutual understanding and respect	Strive to deepen partnerships by learning cultural norms and nuances Expand and experiment with internationalization efforts Deepen collaborations beyond initial joint degree programs, e.g., new geographies and additional partners, joint research, etc. Relationship building, mostly equal partnership
Internationalization 3.0	Transformative partnership	Gain full trust and commitment towards joint endeavors by both partners Explore new ventures and innovation Fully equal partnership and co-culture creation

cultural norms and nuances, considering ways to learn from, adapt to, and embrace differences, and creating new ways to collaborate while assessing the effectiveness and impact of global collaborations. It encompasses doing the work together and observing the effectiveness of the work for mutual benefits. Table 6.1 summarizes the criteria for each internationalization stage, and some examples for each of these three stages.

2   China-U.S. Collaborations in Business Education: The Case of the
       Carlson School of Management at the University of Minnesota and
       Lingnan (University) College at Sun Yat-sen University

China-U.S. collaborations in business education date back to 1984, with the founding of the National Center for Industrial Science and Technology Management Development in the coastal city of Dalian, China. This initial partnership was announced during President Ronald Reagan's diplomatic trip to China that year. Supported by the Chinese Ministry of Education and the U.S. Department of Commerce, the Dalian-based program offered Master of Business Administration (MBA) courses provided by the State University of New York at Buffalo, complemented by courses on China's enterprise management practice delivered by the then Dalian Institute of Technology (State University of New York at Buffalo, 2016; Zhen, 2005).

    Since this initial China-U.S. educational collaboration, partnerships have proliferated in institutions in China and the United States. One of these institutions is the University of Minnesota (U of M). Founded in 1851 as the state's land-grant institution, the U of M is a university system with five coordinate campuses in the state of Minnesota. The University's connection with China began in 1914 when the first three Chinese students were admitted to a U.S. university. In 1979, University Board of Regents Chair Wenda Moore led the first university delegation to China, making the U of M one of the first universities to have leaders visit China after the reform and opening-up policies were in place in 1979. In the same year, the U of M Office of International Programs formed a "China Desk" to manage exchanges with the People's Republic of China, which later became the University of Minnesota's China Center. The University set up its China Office in Beijing in 2009 to help with the University's various programs and activities in China (University of Minnesota China Center, 2016).

    The University of Minnesota's business school, the Carlson School of Management, also has a variety of well-established partnerships with institutions in China. The school has several student exchange partner schools in China, managed through the Carlson Global Institute, including Antai College of Economics and Management at Shanghai Jiao Tong University, City University of Hong Kong College of Business, Hong Kong University of Science and Technology (HKUST) School of Business and Management, Lingnan (University) College at Sun Yat-sen University, and Tsinghua University School of Economics and Management. The Carlson Global Institute also manages Global Business Practicum courses, an experiential learning model in partnership with an overseas business school and a corporate sponsor. Partners in China include Lingnan and Tsinghua, as well as Cheung Kong Graduate School of Business. Most recently, in March 2016, Carlson and Antai also unveiled a joint research center to facilitate faculty and student exchanges and research activities between the two schools.

The Carlson School's longest collaboration with a higher education institution in China is the China Executive MBA program (CHEMBA), in partnership with Lingnan (University) College at Sun Yat-sen University. Lingnan (University) College was a private university established by a group of American missionaries in 1888, and was later reestablished in 1988 within Sun Yat-sen University in Guangzhou to be one of the top schools of economics and management in China. CHEMBA students participate in weekend modules co-taught by faculty from Carlson and Lingnan on the Lingnan campus in Guangzhou, China over a period of 20 months.

Each year a dozen Carlson School faculty travel to Guangzhou to teach in CHEMBA. As a result, faculty from both institutions have interacted regularly and formed professional and personal relationships. Moreover, the collaboration not only benefits faculty members and their teaching and research, but also all students and faculty they interact with at their home campuses. The CHEMBA program's team teaching model enables faculty from both schools to learn from each other as well as the students, both inside and outside of classroom learning. Student learning experience and achievement improved significantly as a result of team teaching (Zaidi & Norman, 2014). In some instances, Chinese cases related to strategy or marketing, for example, provide insights for U.S. faculty and students to understand the unique perspectives of executives in corporations in China today. Further exploration about how faculty and student development occur are forthcoming.

In their second year, CHEMBA students participate with their peers in the U.S. Carlson EMBA program (CEMBA) and Vienna EMBA program (VEMBA) in the Virtual Team Project, an experiential learning model in which cross-cultural student teams work virtually for six months to develop innovative business plans. The program is designed to help participants develop the skills needed to do business in complex and competitive economies as well as provide executives opportunities to compare and contrast their own business, economic, and cultural contexts with other business perspectives on a global scale. After graduation, students report that the lessons they learned from the Virtual Team Project have helped improve their communication across cultures, especially understanding factors such as time, cultural norms and traditions, and communication preferences. Since the founding of CHEMBA in 2001, more than 400 executives from China have graduated from the program. A survey of seven different cohorts of graduates found general satisfaction towards their EMBA program experience and return on investment, with many graduates achieving career advancement and an expanded professional network (Zaidi & Norman, 2013). Moreover, some graduates have gone on to become entrepreneurs and develop their own small businesses.

3 Internationalization of Chinese Business Schools

At Peking University's 100th anniversary celebration ceremony in 1998, then President of China Jiang Zemin called for the establishment of world-class universities to help further develop the Chinese higher education system in the 21st Century (Li, 2012). Top Chinese research universities have since started to pay more attention to internationalization, especially in promoting education and research quality. Studies done by Ma and Yue (2015) indicate that disciplines such as economics, education and management have a higher level of internationalization than other disciplines. They argue that disciplines such as economics and management are based on a Western theoretical framework, indicating why business schools tend to be among the most internationalized and with a higher level of student and faculty mobility.

Cao and Liao (2013) characterize the internationalization of Chinese business schools in four different ways: (1) internationalization of the student body by recruiting non-Chinese students including exchange students; (2) internationalization of the faculty body, hiring Chinese nationals with non-Chinese degrees and non-Chinese visiting faculty members; (3) internationalization of teaching and curriculum by adapting international case studies and providing students overseas study and internship opportunities; and (4) strengthening international programs with non-Chinese business schools and strengthening corporation relations. This is consistent with the key internationalization indicators of top Chinese universities, namely student and faculty mobility, curriculum and program internationalization, and international research and partnership (Ma & Yue, 2015).

The Chinese Universities Alumni Association (CUAA) has been releasing annual Chinese university rankings for over 30 years. It was not until 2015 that CUAA started to include university internationalization as one ranking category. The key measures and weight of each indicator are summarized in Table 6.2, together with examples of some of the detailed measurements (Cai, Zhao, & Feng, 2016; CUAA, 2015).

TABLE 6.2   *Chinese university internationalization ranking methodology*

Indicators	Key measures	Weight	Examples
International faculty	Internationalization of teaching force	20%	International and domestic awards received by faculty members
International alumni	Career prospect of graduates	20%	Members of overseas academy of science/engineering, head of Fortune 500 companies
International academic management	Opportunities for current students	18%	Sponsored visiting student opportunities at overseas institutions; Sino-foreign joint academic programs approved by the Ministry of Education, hosting Confucius Institutes
International research	Recognition by international peers	11%	Publications in peer reviewed top international and domestic journals
International teaching	Bilingual teaching and academic management system	11%	Bilingual/multilingual courses and curriculum, bilingual teaching management system, bilingual credit transfer system
International innovation base	International talent training base	10%	International joint research centers, international research collaborations
International influence	External influence	10%	Major international rankings, visits from international leaders, major international media reports, number of international conferences

NOTE: BASED ON CAI ZHAO, AND FENG (2016) AND CUAA (2015, DECEMBER 30),
RETRIEVED FROM HTTP://WWW.CUAA.NET/CUR/2016/06

Information is unclear about how the rationale for these criteria and their respective weights were determined. However, various reports about the new CUAA ranking all mentioned one example – the number of visits made to a university by foreign heads of state and government. Peking University, the most internationalized university according to the CUAA ranking, received 56 Heads of State and Government (CUAA, 2016; Science Net, 2016; Sohu, 2016).

Visits by international leaders is one example of the indicator, international influence, which counts for only 10% of the overall ranking. The fact that this one measurement is called out by multiple reports, including CUAA's own summary report, is significant because, at the minimum, it shows this indicator is popular with the general public.

4   Challenges for Internationalization of Chinese Business Schools

Business education in China has not been able to keep up with China's economic development, as well as the market demand for talent. Top Chinese business schools continue to lag behind their counterparts around the world, as shown in the lack of internationalization of research and teaching and student admission numbers. For example, Huang (2012) pointed out that the number of MBA graduates is only 5% of the total number of Master's degree graduates, similar to the percentage in the U.S. in the 1950s. The focus of internationalization has primarily been on "importing" – importing non-Chinese faculty and students and new curriculum design and teaching methods as compared to exporting Chinese pedagogy in terms of international collaborations (Huang, 2012).

The focus on "importing" has been rewarded by CUAA rankings mechanisms. The number of international partners, number of non-Chinese faculty and students, number of international programs, number of international accreditations claimed by an institution supports higher CUAA ranking for internationalization. This International 1.0 approach has been common in both the U.S. and China as a way of measuring outcomes of international investments in institutions.

Internationalization, however, is emerging in a highly contextualized way in China. Huang (2012) argues that merely copying from top non-Chinese business schools, or aligning teaching and curriculum with the needs of mainstream higher education markets, is an ineffective approach. Unlike the business education market in other countries (specifically the U.S.), it is common for people in China to become successful entrepreneurs first before they return to campus to further their academic studies. Executive MBA programs have become popularized because of the rapid economic development in China in the past decades (Lin, 2015). International officers in Chinese higher education institutions have looked to Executive MBA programs as a way to benefit from international partnerships and meet the current needs of the Chinese economy. This thoughtful approach moves beyond the counting of partnerships to the strategic initiation of programs to meet contextualized needs. The following paragraphs will describe the initiation and evolution of a partnership between two business schools in China and the U.S., specifically related to Executive MBA Education.

5   Development Phases of a China-U.S. Collaboration: A Case Study

Most bi-lateral and multi-lateral collaborations between the U.S. and China begin with a relationship between or among faculty or professional staff colleagues. Institutional reputation and alignment are at the forefront of forming such a relationship and a drive to enhance global collaborations for the institution and its faculty, staff, and students. Internationalization and its phases of development are best illustrated through examples and the strategies, challenges, and perceived benefits of the cross-national collaboration. In the following paragraphs, we will trace the U of M/Lingnan (University) College through three phases of internationalization and partnership.

5.1   *Internationalization 1.0: Transactional Phase – A Knowledge Foundation*

At the start of the Carlson School's China Executive MBA program, Chinese and U.S. faculty and professional staff worked together to construct and design key components of the collaboration beginning with the viability of Chinese professionals earning a U.S. degree while studying in China for the majority of the program. Early on, faculty and staff leaders determined the minimum enrollment numbers needed for financial sustainability and explored market interest for success. At that time, and still today, Lingnan (University) College is not issuing its degree due to regulatory quotas and limitations by the Chinese government, therefore the U.S. degree is solely issued. Consequently, faculty began with a U.S.-designed framework for the syllabus and negotiated half of the classes taught by Chinese faculty and half taught by U.S. faculty. The equal splitting of teaching had three intended effects. First, it was not feasible to fly all U.S. faculty to China to teach courses; technology-based courses also were not valued by either partner due to the lack of in-person interactions between students and faculty. Second, Chinese faculty offered unique perspectives and examples based on specific lived examples in the Chinese economy, where U.S. instructors could provide different viewpoints for comparison. Third, the exposure to a multinational faculty provided unique opportunities for student development because of the exposure to a variety of teaching and communication styles.

A primary working purpose at the early stages of this partnership was the development of content and delivery, with attention to quality and evaluation methods based on U.S.-driven business accreditation standards by AACSB International: The Association to Advance Collegiate Schools of

Business, an important recognition that both institutions now share. Once all components were identified and designed, leaders signed a Memorandum of Agreement (MOA) outlining the necessary structure, degree issuance, and financial outlook of the collaboration. Subsequently, professional staff were hired to execute the transactions of the agreement including marketing, recruiting, and student admissions, hiring U.S. and Chinese faculty, organizing travel, courses, and evaluations, and ensuring quality for successful degree completion. In short, the early years of the program focused heavily on developing organizational structure.

While constructing and reviewing the Lingnan–Carlson MOA, we learned that our approaches to the agreement and what was necessary to outline within the agreement varied. A U.S. approach is decentralized and more regularly emerges from the bottom up – details about market demand by students, curriculum, teaching schedules, financials, and adhering to quality standards outlined by accreditation standards drive the development of the MOA. A Chinese approach is centralized and generally more top down – signing a formal Memorandum of Understanding (MOU) at the onset and then negotiating the details later. Because of the litigious culture of U.S. higher education, all details are typically negotiated in advance of signing any agreement. The legal nature of agreements "locks in" institutions to the procedures outlined in the document. Conversely, the nature of Chinese higher education institutions is to sign an agreement first, both for governmental documentation and to confer an intent to work out details. These opposing approaches to signing agreements sometimes leads to challenges in the negotiation process.

In the case of the Lingnan–Carlson collaboration, since the U.S. degree was solely issued, Carlson School faculty and professional staff led the development of the MOA and decision-making approach. Additionally, this bilateral relationship was the first of its kind in the Guangdong province and a new "global" collaboration for Lingnan (University) College, therefore the experience of Carlson School leaders in internationalization, and more specifically with offshore EMBA programs, helped establish the initial, structural parameters and transactions. The expertise of Carlson faculty helped to set the parameters of the agreement, but the structure of the first round of the agreement did not allow for strong inputs from Lingnan faculty.

This foundational, or transactional, approach at the early stages of the Lingnan–Carlson collaboration confirms what researchers observe more broadly in China. There are three stages that are most typical for international collaborations for Chinese business schools. During the first stage, Chinese business schools are not able to make many decisions, but rather follow the recommendations of their international partners. In the second stage, disagreements start to surface when Chinese business schools start to negotiate terms. The third stage is when collaborations deepen and partners reach a more equal relationship, it is easier to solve issues in a consultative capacity (Ye, 2016).

One of the reasons why newly global Chinese institutions may initially be disadvantaged in relationships is that the style of "signing first – agreeing on details later" provides time to understand context, needs, and initial failures. Rather, locking in details at initial stages of agreements may be advantageous to U.S. institutions that have prior experience with agreements. If partnerships can be created within the structure of Internationalization 1.0, however, new opportunities may emerge in the second phase.

5.2   *Internationalization 2.0: Relational Phase – A Cultural Imperative*

Before a formal institutional collaboration occurs, faculty and professional staff explore potential schools for the right fit for such a partnership. Factors that drive decisions include building upon an already existing faculty or staff relationship, institutional reputation, or institutional strategies and goals. A relationship begins to form and often deepens as faculty and professional staff work together through the structural components described in the foundational phase.

In the case of the Lingnan–Carlson collaboration, as years passed and leaders from both institutions interacted more regularly with each other, relationships grew. Mutual understanding and exchange of ideas emerged with each transaction and illuminated challenges and perceived benefits of the cross-national collaboration. One major benefit is mutual collaboration as a differentiation for both institutions, especially as it relates to expansion of internationalization efforts. The two schools have since collaborated on several joint efforts, including the graduate global business practicum program, a live business project in collaboration with a corporate sponsor, and undergraduate exchanges. Through the partnership, Lingnan has also been working with one of Carlson's international partner institutions, Wirtschafts Universitat Wien (WU), Vienna University of Economics and Business, on global residency programs and WU faculty have had opportunities to teach at Lingnan. Moreover, Lingnan was able to highlight the relationship with Carlson and WU, as they sought and acquired AACSB accreditation, along with EQUIS, the European accreditation.

The relationships that grew were important for navigating unforeseen challenges. One key challenge has been the variability of institutional policies that has impacted the effectiveness of implementing the EMBA program. The partnership began in 2000, a time when Chinese higher institutions were just beginning to deliberately seek more diverse and global collaborations. China opened up rapidly and professionals sought U.S. MBA credentials aggressively.

As time progressed, more government and university policies were enacted that impacted the program and the institutional relationship. These changes are outlined in the following paragraphs.

In March 2016, the Chinese Ministry of Education announced that starting from 2017, EMBA programs offered by Chinese universities will no longer be allowed to use their own admission assessments. All applicants will be required to take the national postgraduate entrance examination (Ministry of Education of the People's Republic of China, 2016). This is a step further in the Chinese government's determination to tighten regulations on EMBA programs. Moreover, back in 2014 as part of its anti-corruption campaign, the government banned the use of public funds to pay for EMBA program tuition for both government officials and state-owned enterprise executives.

While U.S. partner school leaders were made aware of Chinese government policy changes, we were not aware of the complexities of certain policies and their short- and long-term influences on the daily work of our Chinese partners. The government's anti-corruption campaign, for example, put our Chinese partner university colleagues under stricter audits for fund transfers and program expenses, including expense approvals, reimbursements and foreign wire transfers, making each transaction a more time-consuming process. On the other hand, our Chinese colleagues have helped our collective navigation by explaining the policies better to partner universities and providing detailed timelines for financial transactions to avoid further delays.

The government policies described above slowed the ease at which Lingnan–Carlson professional staff were able to transfer funds and approve program expenses. At the same time, U of M policies were also changing, including tightening of checks and balances on such global partnerships, greater legal control by way of additional statements about liabilities by Lingnan and other partners, and increased internationalization strategies without attention to unique implications for Chinese partnerships. In this case, the Carlson School became the cultural guide in helping its partners to understand U.S. policy changes, procedures and implications.

The increased control by Chinese and U.S. policy makers at the government and university levels naturally increased frustration over the lack of control by Lingnan–Carlson faculty and professional staff involved. New tensions began to emerge in these new policy environments. Rather than talking early on about the implications of these policies on the working relationship, Lingnan–Carlson colleagues continued to focus on the issues with the assumption that the challenges were solely transactional in nature, without stepping back and realizing the impact of the policy implications on the relationship. Through this process we have learned by examination about the unconscious assumptions partners can make that often lead to unnecessary frustrations and confusion. One relational approach learned by both sides was that, in the midst of changes beyond our control, sharing together at the onset of new policy conditions deepens our relationship and helps us work towards mutually beneficial goals.

Another key learning principle was that of respecting difference. People and cultures are different, and our higher education systems are different, just as one Chinese saying 求同存异 (*qiutong cunyi*) goes – seeking common ground while respecting each other's differences. In our Internationalization 2.0 phase, we learned that it is important for both partners to recognize one another's differences and strive to reach the common goal(s) – in our case, to run a successful program that benefits faculty and student learning experiences. Differences may make collaborations more challenging as we try to understand them, but they also bring opportunities for mutual learning and bridge building.

We highlighted the significance of program agreements in the first transactional stage. As Chinese institutions become more fluent in working with overseas partners in joint degree and non-degree programs, re-negotiating agreement terms may become a norm. Program agreements are often renewed every four years. The renewal and approval process can be prolonged when there is a change in university leadership or government policies related to joint programs. Changes on certain agreement terms and language are often required either by the Chinese university leadership, or the approving government agencies – including municipal education commissions and the Ministry of Education. Sometimes it may take several rounds of approval processes, between change requests initiated by either the Chinese or U.S. institutions, reviewing and approval procedures conducted by Chinese universities and government agencies, as well as reviewing and approval processes required by U.S. institutions (university regents, president and provost offices and office of general counsels).

5.3   *Internationalization 3.0: Transformational Phase –*
An Aspirational Goal

Establishing a transformative partnership is rare and requires time, leadership, and capacity of partners to manage unforeseen factors. To achieve this phase is aspirational and requires building relations over many years, increasing and sustaining interactions with colleagues, mutual learning, adapting, and growing together, innovating and advancing new collaborations. Exceptions exist but examples are few.

Policy implications as stated in the relational phase can easily impact a relationship and prevent it from moving forward. To be in a transformational phase, full trust, commitment, and willingness to explore new ways to collaborate and take on more risks together are essential. Learning and growing together are at the core of the relationship and a newly established co-culture (Orbe, 1996) is able to emerge organically. This does not often pertain to the entire institutional partnership but could exist in certain aspects.

In the Lingnan–Carlson collaboration, faculty and professional staff strive to work together as one team. Most interactions are done virtually via technologies such as WeChat, Skype, QQ, and traditional e-mail. At the program orientation in China and the conclusion at graduation in the U.S., the team meets in person with each other and with the EMBA cohort of students and faculty, further solidifying the working relationship. The investments of travel, time, and hosting are invaluable to the sustainability of the partnership and its progress.

At the same time, Carlson professional staff have been dedicated to seeking degrees in organizational leadership, policy, and development with a focus on international education, intercultural communications, and advancement of internationalization at institutions. The pursuit of advanced knowledge to enhance work experience has resulted in staff expertise to integrate study and practice, leading to research applied to the development of the Lingnan–Carlson relationship. This shift from transaction to researching, analyzing, and making sound recommendations for improvement illustrates a new way of understanding and deepening the partnership.

A former Carlson program director, who managed the China EMBA program from 2006–2014, dedicated his dissertation study to an examination of the teaching and learning in the CHEMBA classroom. Goode (2013) provided a deeper understanding of the program learning environment from the viewpoint of faculty, students and alumni of the program. He identified gaps in faculty and student expectations and perceptions of the learning environment, challenges and corresponding responses, previous experience working with people from each other's culture, and their preparatory experiences. Each of these gaps is fundamentally culture-related and calls for better understanding of one another's cultural differences.

Goode (2013) also provided strategies for faculty and students to address these gaps, including ways to engage each other, preparation for such a learning environment, and the role of English language competency in student success. Due to the offshore nature of the program, staff turnover and regular flow of new instructors traveling to teach in China, these strategies rely on adequate program orientation, faculty training and learning from alumni experience.

Institutional leaders in both China and the U.S. value relationships, and look for different signals that a partner is invested in the process. For many of the Lingnan participants, the importance of 关系 (*guanxi*) [personal relationships and networks] was cultivated by collaborative work. Communication in this relationship was aided by Lingnan faculty who patiently waded through bureaucratic curricular discussions and through their welcome of U.S. faculty. The same is true for Carlson faculty and staff who showed genuine interest in Chinese culture and a willingness to learn. These efforts go a long way. Carlson faculty have brought their family members with them to China and found the experience profoundly changed their world view and positively influenced their families as well.

The CHEMBA team arrangement with faculty from Lingnan and Carlson co-teaching the same course has offered great opportunities for faculty to learn from each other academically, culturally and personally. In terms of the administrative structure in China, most of the previous CHEMBA directors are program graduates who know the program inside and out. CHEMBA staff all have developed close relationships with key program alumni and continue to play an important role in strengthening our alumni network.

The final piece of the relationship is students. Chinese students reported that once they adapted to U.S. teaching and learning methods, such as case studies and interactive teaching methods, their learning experience improved. As students become alumni, their voices continue to be heard in the program. CHEMBA alumni have always played an indispensable role in each transitional period and beyond. Because of the positive and transformational experience students have had on the program, CHEMBA has a strong and committed alumni network. Alumni develop close relationships with each other and remain dedicated to the program. They organize sports teams, charity activities, and annual alumni gatherings sponsored and organized collaboratively by the graduating class and the alumni club. In 2009, CHEMBA graduates started a Mingling Foundation, to care for children and adolescents in poverty. The name *Mingling* (明岭) is composed of the first characters for the acronyms of the University of Minnesota (*Ming*) and Lingnan (University) College (*Ling*). The foundation also built an elementary school with the same name *Mingling*. CHEMBA alumni are also instrumental in program promotion and recruitment for future cohorts.

One exceptional example of alumni support for the program is Eric Jing, CEO of Ant Financial Services and CHEMBA alumnus, who recently announced a \$5 million gift to the Carlson School to further strengthen the school's relationship with China, by increasing access to graduate programs at the Carlson School and promoting research and exchange activities with Chinese institutions. Jing's philanthropic gift is a unique phenomenon in mainland China and illustrates the transformational impact such a learning development experience can have on one's perspective, career, life and subsequent decisions for action. His contributions also make it possible for the Carlson School to further explore, adapt, and integrate its thinking while doing it together. As a role model for other alumni and aspiring students, Jing credits his own success to the transformative experience of the CHEMBA program (Figure 6.1).

FIGURE 6.1.   *Photo of China EMBA 15th year reunion, taken at Carlson school 2017 commencement ceremony. Eric Jing (6th to the right) was the keynote speaker. Copyright 2017 by Carlson School Communications (reprinted with permission)*

6   Conclusion

The long-standing Lingnan–Carlson collaboration illustrates the progression of its partnership from the origins of a foundational or transactional phase to a deeper understanding of a relational phase and the impact of an aspirational, transformative phase. These phases depict the mutual benefits, continued challenges, and emergence of new initiatives indicative of internationalization 1.0, 2.0 and 3.0. We, as the authors of this chapter, as well as faculty and professional staff who are instrumental in the development and implementation of the Lingnan–Carlson partnership, highly value the relationships and evolution of this partnership. At the same time, we understand changes in institutional and governmental policies and procedures could alter or even hinder the relationship.

6.1   *Internationalization 3.0 and Beyond*
Through this partnership and subsequent relationships, we have experienced significant learning and growth related to collaborations and communication with our partners. From basic communication tools including email, phone calls and Skype in the early stages of the relationship, we began to rely

more on emerging platforms in China such as WeChat to connect with our colleagues. Many schools and universities in the U.S. now have public WeChat accounts, where communication channels with prospective and current students, as well as alumni, are shifting. Moreover, programs are now commonly promoted through WeChat, surpassing traditional brochures and promotional website content for Chinese audiences. Technology continues to evolve, grow, and change approaches while successfully helping to build stronger and more personal connections with Chinese colleagues. Documenting our interactions and decision-making is crucial in building strong communications and relations with our Chinese partners. Consistent communications outlining all discussion and agreements for action help to ensure all parties are in agreement and serve as a reference when issues and disagreements emerge. It also helps to minimize any miscommunication or misunderstanding due to language, cultural nuances and differences, or unconscious assumptions. Intentionality about every communication is a learned technique and one that we and our colleagues have discussed and developed together.

Strong commitment by all parties is crucial for a joint program across different continents to be successful. Multiple stakeholders need to work together – institutional leadership, faculty, students, alumni, and professional staff. Professional staff are the backbone of the program. Their work and dedication ensure smooth program strategy and operations, from academic and administrative provisions to faculty and student teaching and learning support, thus making staff retention crucial for program development and relationship management. Over the course of 16 years of the CHEMBA program, regular staff transitions remain one of our biggest challenges. We continue to strive toward more effective ways to highlight the relevance of staff expertise and professionalism in support of our colleagues in China amidst continuous change, challenges, and opportunities.

References

Anderson, L. C. (Ed.). (2005, August). *Internationalizing undergraduate education: Integrating study abroad into the curriculum*. Minneapolis, MN: The Learning Abroad Center, University of Minnesota.

Bolman, L. G., & Deal, T. E. (2013). *Reframing organizations: Artistry, choice, and leadership* (5th ed.). San Francisco, CA: Jossey-Bass.

Cai, Y., Zhao, D., & Feng, Y. (2016). Research on annual evaluation of internationalization level of the Chinese universities and colleges. *Journal of Yunnan Agricultural University (Social Science)*, 10(2), 20–24.

Cao, L., & Liao, Z. (2013). Zhongwai shangxueyuan guojihua bijiao yanjiu [Comparative study of internationalization patterns of Chinese vs. non-Chinese business schools]. *Pioneering with Science & Technology Monthly, 2013*(5), 116–118.

Caudron, S. (1991). Training ensures success overseas. *Personnel Journal, 70*(12), 27–30.

Croucher, S. L. (2004). *Globalization and belonging: The politics of identity a changing world*. Lanham, MD: Rowman & Littlefield.

CUAA. (2015, December 30). 2016 *zhongguo daxue guojihua shuiping paihang bang* [2016 internationalization ranking of Chinese universities]. Retrieved from http://www.cuaa.net/cur/2016/06

CUAA. (2016). 2016 *zhongguo daxue pingjia yanjiu baogao chulu* [2016 Chinese university evaluation research report came out]. Retrieved from http://www.cuaa.net/cur/2016/

Earley, P., & Ang, S. (2003). *Cultural intelligence: Individual interactions across cultures*. Stanford, CA: Stanford Business Books.

Global Thinkers Forum. (2014). *Insights on successful leadership models in a fast transforming world*. London: Global Thinkers Forum, Ltd.

Goode, M. L. (2013). *'Bridging the gaps': A case study of faculty and student expectations, perceptions, challenges, and responses in the Chinese 'teach-abroad' learning environment* (Doctoral dissertation). Retrieved from ProQuest Dissertations and Theses database. (UMI No. 3596317)

Huang, B. (2012). Zhongwai shangxue jiaoyu fazhan de bijiao fenxi jiqi qishi [Comparative analysis of Chinese and foreign business education development and its lessons]. *Foreign Economic Relations & Trade, 216*, 133–135.

Javidan, M., & Walker, J. L. (2013). *Developing your global mindset: The handbook for successful global leaders*. Edina, MN: Beaver's Pond Press.

Knight, J. (2003). Updating the definition of internationalization. *International Higher Education, 33*, 2–3.

Knight, J. (2004). Internationalization remodeled: Definition, approaches, and rationales. *Journal of Studies in International Education, 8*(1), 5–31.

Li, J. (2012). World-class higher education and the emerging Chinese model of the university. *Prospects, 42*(3), 319–339.

Lin, H. (2015, March 17). *Zhongguo xuyao shijieji de shangxueyuan* [China needs world class business schools]. Retrieved from http://www.ihuawen.com/hw/article/1005.html

Livermore, D., Ang, S., & Dyne, L. V. (2015). *Leading with cultural intelligence: The real secret to success* (2nd ed.). New York, NY: AMACOM.

Ma, W., & Yue, Y. (2015). Internationalization for quality in Chinese research universities: Student perspectives. *Higher Education, 70*(2), 217–234.

Mestenhauser, J. (2003, Summer). Building bridges. *International Educator, 12*(3), 6–11.

Ministry of Education of the People's Republic of China. (2016, March 28). *Jiaoyubu guanyu jinyibu guifan gongshang guanli shuoshi xuewei yanjiusheng jiaoyu de yijian*

[The ministry of education on further standardize MBA education]. Retrieved from http://www.moe.gov.cn/srcsite/A22/moe_836/201604/t20160406_236783.html

Orbe, M. (1996). Laying the foundation for co-cultural communication theory: An inductive approach to studying "non-dominant" communication strategies and the factors that influence them. *Communication Studies, 47*(3), 157–176.

Science Net. (2016). *2016 zhongguo daxue paihangbang: Beijing daxue qinghua fudan chanlian sanjia* [2016 Chinese University ranking: Peking University, Tsinghua and Fudan reelected the top three]. Retrieved from http://news.sciencenet.cn/htmlnews/2016/1/335946.shtm

Sohu. (2016). *Daxue paihangbang: Beida 9 lianguan shouping qisuo qixing daxue* [University Ranking: Peking University ranked first for 9 consecutive years; first batch of 7 "seven star university" selected]. Retrieved from http://news.sohu.com/20160111/n434167593.shtml

State University of New York at Buffalo. (2016). *School of management: History*. Retrieved from https://mgt.buffalo.edu/about/history.html

World Bank. (2003). *Lifelong learning in the global knowledge economy: Challenges for developing countries.* Washington, DC: The World Bank. Retrieved from http://documents.worldbank.org/curated/en/528131468749957131/Lifelong-learning-in-the-global-knowledge-economy-challenges-for-developing-countries

Ye, L. (2016, March 2). *Shangxuyuan shi guojihua rencai de menggongchang ma* [Are business schools DreamWorks for internationalized talents]. Retrieved from http://weibo.com/ttarticle/p/show?id=2309403948565008355048

Zaidi, M., & Norman, T. (2013). Transferring western management knowledge to China: Perceptions of graduates from an American executive MBA program. *Frontiers of Business Research in China, 7*(1), 82–105.

Zaidi, M., & Norman, T. (2014). Transferring western management knowledge to China. *EFMD Global Focus, 8*(1), 72–75.

Zhen, Y. (2005). *Thoughts on Chinese MBA education development strategy* [Guanyu zhongguo MBA jiaoyu fazhan zhanlue de ruogan sikao]. Proceedings from China Education Society of Electronics (CESE) Higher Education Annual Conference '05, Kunming, China.

About the Authors

Anne M. D'Angelo is assistant dean of Global Initiatives at the Carlson School of Management at the University of Minnesota. She oversees the business school's internationalization strategy including institutional partnerships, education abroad programs, and offshore global executive programs. For more than a decade, she has collaborated closely with Chinese colleagues and their institutions on internationalization initiatives, program and policy development, exchanges and new innovations. Previously, Anne worked overseas in international education, training, and development in Central and Eastern Europe, Northern Africa, the Republic of Georgia, and Japan. Anne earned her M.A. and Ph.D. from the University of Minnesota in Organizational Leadership, Policy, and Development with a specialization in Comparative and International Development Education. She also serves as a teaching faculty member in the U of M's College of Education and Human Development. Among her achievements, she received a U.S. State Department Meritorious Honor Award, U.S. Fulbright-Nehru Award to India and the 2016 Distinguished Award for Global Engagement from the University of Minnesota.

Lili Dong is the director for Global Executive programs at the Carlson School of Management. She has previously worked for Georgetown University, University of Minnesota China Center, and University of California, Berkeley on international programs. Lili has worked collaboratively with students, faculty and administrators around the world, and especially in China, and has experience in program development, marketing and evaluation. Lili holds a Ph.D. in Comparative and International Development Education from the University of Minnesota's College of Education and Human Development, an M.S. in Learning and Instruction from University of Southern California, and a B.A. in English Language and Literature from Shanghai International Studies University.

CHAPTER 7

The New Normal: Student and Faculty Mobility Programs between Public Teacher Education Institutions in China and the U.S.

Mary Schlarb, Shufang Strause, and Lu-Chung Dennis Weng

Abstract

In recent years, universities and colleges in the United States are increasingly turning towards China as they consider how to prepare their students, faculty, and staff to respond to the forces of globalization. As the role of China in the world economy expands, and as the country's political and cultural reach extends, graduates experienced engaging with China, Chinese people, and their culture will have an advantage in the workplace and their communities. International educators at many higher education institutions, recognizing the importance of building student cultural competence, are creating opportunities for students, faculty, and staff to experience China through mobility partnerships and study abroad programs. In this chapter, we explore how one public institution, the State University of New York College at Cortland (SUNY Cortland), has worked with three universities – two in mainland China and one in Taiwan – to expand student, faculty, and staff mobility opportunities. We will discuss both the factors that have supported these partnerships and the challenges the partner institutions have faced in facilitating mobility. The college has leveraged its limited resources and faculty experience with China to maintain and develop these partnerships, while overcoming challenges that include balancing diverse constituent needs, limited student funding, lack of U.S. student demand for Chinese study abroad programs, concerns over student preparation, technological issues, and cultural differences.

1   Introduction

In recent years, universities and colleges in the United States are increasingly turning towards China as they consider how to prepare their students – and their faculty and staff – to respond to the forces of globalization. As the role of China in the world economy expands, and as the country's political and cultural reach extends, graduates experienced engaging with China, Chinese people, and their culture and language will have an advantage in the workplace and their communities. President Obama foreshadowed the importance of Sino-American collaboration in 2009 when he declared "the relationship between the United States and China will shape the 21st Century," speaking of a complex relationship in which global peace, security, and climate change, among other issues, are at stake (McGiffert, 2011, p. 5). International educators at many higher education institutions in the U.S., recognizing the importance of building student cultural competence for engaging with other cultures, including those of China, are creating opportunities for students, faculty, and staff to experience China through mobility partnerships and study abroad programs.

At the same time, higher education institutions in China have responded to, and functioned within, an emerging neoliberal context. Up to the early 2000s, observers of China's higher education would argue that all the Chinese universities have been faithfully carrying out the development policy of neoliberalism in China's globalization trend (Chan & Lo, 2007). Unlike the Maoist period, when the higher education institutions attempted to incorporate the Soviet Union education system, and were strictly controlled by the central government, the post-Mao higher education development went hand in hand with China's economic reforms. At this time, universities had some autonomy to make their own decisions. In order to fill the vacuum of human capital due to the Cultural Revolution, the need for well-educated college graduates increased rapidly. While in the western context, scholars argued that neoliberalism would bring a businesslike atmosphere to higher education, thus diminishing the importance of university's role in promoting democratic citizenship, it was not the primary concern for China's higher education system. With Confucian culture firmly embedded, China's central government believed that the democratic spirit would not spread in China as the higher education sector started to engage with the Western world. On the contrary, when economic reform began in the late 1980s, higher education in China was given a particular mission of nurturing elites for the country's economic development. Following Deng Xiaoping's guideline for China's development that "it doesn't matter whether a cat is white or black, as long as it catches mice," universities in China were eager to find the solution for China's development. Facing modernization and the new wave of globalization, the state government realized that higher education needed to provide cutting-edge knowledge to equip China's new generations. Due to the Cultural Revolution, there were not many qualified instructors available to teach in the universities, let alone conduct innovative research. Given the lack of advanced knowledge and modernization, and the need for high-quality human capital, promoting internationalization in China's higher education became indispensable.

Across the Taiwan Strait, higher education in Taiwan now also embraced internationalization as a path of development; however, it was approached very differently. Since Chiang Kai Sheik retreated from the mainland China in 1949, the Kuomintang (KMT) government received various amounts of foreign aid from Western democracies, including support for higher education. Despite incorporating different educational models and different sources of foreign aid, the higher education systems on both sides of the Taiwan Strait were marked by centralization as a means to ensuring that higher education followed the plan and outlines provided by the government. Both Chinese higher education systems adopted a series of "state-centric" education policies in which the universities complied with the government's orders corresponding to the country's development. For instance, while Taiwan started to transform from an agricultural economy to a knowledge-based economy in the 1960s, the government provided governmental scholarships to support elite students abroad in the hope of bridging the knowledge gap between the Western world and Taiwan. When these elite students obtained higher degrees and returned from overseas, most of them utilized their connections in the West to create opportunities for international cooperation. It was a great success as Taiwan took the opportunity to gather high-quality human capital to develop its now renowned high-tech industry.

The first stage of higher education internationalization and the KMT's state-centric education policy came to an end in the late 1980s. In response to globalization, the "neoliberalism model" of higher education was placed at the center of Taiwan's education reform by the government. The government decided to open up the higher education market in order to expand the university student population and increase the country's overall education level. For instance, while there were only seven higher education institutions in the 1950s, the number increased fifteen-fold, to 105 institutions, by 2000 (Wang, 2005). University student enrollment was only around 6,000 in the 1950s, but had increased to around 400,000 by the late 1980s, and then by 2016, the total university student population had more than tripled to 1.25 million. Since this rapid expansion, universities under the "neoliberalism model" of higher education system in Taiwan have had to compete against each other for rankings, government funding, and more importantly, student enrollment. Given Taiwan's more advanced economic development, studying abroad is currently not a big financial burden on most families, and therefore most college-age students have had some international experiences growing up. With the neoliberalism model, Taiwan's universities began to utilize their internal programs to promote their school and recruit students. Despite pursuing different purposes, the higher education systems in Taiwan and China are now embracing internationalization as the common goal.

According to the Institute of International Education (IIE), growth in student and scholar mobility between Chinese and U.S. higher education institutions has been extraordinarily rapid since 1978, when Deng Xiaoping began sending students and scholars abroad on educational programs with an eye towards economic modernization (Laughlin, 2008). Although the first Fulbright Program in the world was established with China in 1947 (Goodman, 2011), Cold War-era bilateral relations were such that exchange was driven to a standstill (Laughlin, 2008). With China's entry into the World Trade Organization in 2001 and the parallel liberalization of the education sector, the door also opened wider for students in the U.S. and elsewhere to access educational programs in China, with an over 500 percent increase of U.S. Americans studying in China between 1996 and 2006 (Laughlin, 2008). IIE suggests that U.S. student interest in studying in China has also been piqued by its growing political and economic status in the world.

In this chapter, we will highlight the case of how one public institution, the State University of New York College at Cortland (SUNY Cortland), has worked with three universities – two in mainland China and one in Taiwan – to expand student, faculty, and staff mobility opportunities. We will discuss both the factors that have supported these partnerships and the challenges the partner institutions have faced in facilitating mobility. In particular, SUNY Cortland, a four-year, comprehensive college within the public SUNY system, has leveraged its limited resources and faculty interest and experience with China to maintain and develop these partnerships and overcome challenges including balancing diverse constituent needs, limited student funding, lack of U.S. student demand for Chinese study abroad programs, concerns over student preparation, technological issues – particularly in virtual collaborative teaching- and cultural differences.

The *Open Doors* 2013–2014 report by the Institute of International Education noted that China is the fifth most popular destination for U.S. students studying abroad, and the most popular destination outside of Western Europe, with 13,763 students participating in credit-bearing programs in China out of a total of over 304,000 U.S. students studying abroad (Farrugia, 2016). Although this represents a 4.5% decrease from the previous year, China still remains a highly sought-after study abroad destination. This is still a modest number compared to the overall number of U.S. students studying abroad, and certainly compared to the large flow of Chinese students to the U.S.; however, the growth in the number of U.S. students has been astonishing, with the ratio of Chinese to U.S. students decreasing from 31 Chinese to one U.S. student, to seven to one in 2005–2006 (Laughlin, 2008). The program options available to U.S. students have expanded, too, with more students participating in short-term programs, non-credit programs, internships, and volunteering. A 2013 pilot study published by IIE revealed that an additional 11,000 U.S. students engaged in education-related activities in China, beyond the activities generally counted by the *Open Doors* study (Belyavina, 2013).

At the same time, universities and colleges in the U.S. are seeking to recruit more students from China, both out of an interest in diversifying their student bodies in order to enrich the campus community, and as a strategy for expanding enrollments. As institutions respond to shifting U.S. demographics and a declining number of high school students, (and consequently, a reduced population from which to recruit prospective students) many have developed recruitment strategies and support structures to attract international students. In 2014–2015, nearly 975,000 international students studied in the United States, a 10% growth over the previous year (Farrugia, 2016). This growth is a result of increased interest in studying abroad and the efforts of higher education institutions to recruit international students, including tapping into the growing number of Chinese students with the family means and interest to study abroad in countries such as the United States. The IIE (Farrugia, 2016) reports that in 2014–2015, China was the top country of origin for international students at U.S. institutions, with 304,040 Chinese students studying in the U.S., or 31.2 percent of the total. This total was a nearly 11 percent increase over the previous year, an upward trend for seven years running (Farrugia, 2016). IIE separates out the Taiwanese student data, which shows that Taiwan sent 20,993 students to the U.S. in 2014–2015, just over 2 percent of total international students and a slight increase over the previous year (Farrugia, 2016).

Scholars visiting the U.S. from China follow the trend in student mobility. The IIE reports that in 2014–2015, 40,140 Chinese scholars were hosted by U.S. campuses as visiting researchers and lecturers, a 10.4 percent increase over the previous year. Chinese scholars represented over 32 percent of all international scholars in the U.S. – nearly four times the number of scholars from the next largest group from India.

Host institutions should ensure that the services and structures necessary to support visiting students and scholars are present in order to help them adjust to their new environment and be academically successful. The National Association of College Admissions Counselors (NACAC) advocate for campuses being adequately prepared to host international students, with a concern that it

> is often the case that institutions begin enrolling, or increasing enrollment of, international students without the proper planning having taken place. It is critical that investments in campus infrastructure and programming

be made *before* international students arrive on campus rather than in a reactive manner or only after challenges arise. (NACAC, n.d., para. 1)

NACAC suggests a number of services and programs to consider, including faculty training and preparation to teach international students, adequate room and board arrangements, immigration and cultural support services, language training, academic and writing support, and purposeful programming to encourage international and domestic student integration.

2   Background on SUNY Cortland and its China Partners and Strategies

2.1   *SUNY Cortland*

The State University of New York College at Cortland (SUNY Cortland) is a mid-sized, four-year comprehensive college that is part of the 64-campus State University of New York (SUNY) System. Located in central New York State, the college was founded in 1868 as the Cortland Normal School focusing on teacher education. It became a Bachelor's-granting college in 1941, joining the SUNY System as a founding member in 1948. Today, the campus offers a comprehensive set of Bachelor's and Master's programs, and is comprised of three schools: Arts and Sciences, Education, and Professional Studies. These three schools house a combined total of 28 academic departments overseeing 62 undergraduate and 35 graduate majors. The college enrolls over 7,000 students, and employs 585 faculty and 815 staff.

Internationalization has become an imperative at SUNY Cortland, as it has at many higher education institutions in the U.S. and worldwide. The principal goals of internationalization relate to preparing students for an increasingly globalized world by infusing the Cortland experience with diverse perspectives, internationalizing the curriculum, and expanding education and work abroad experiences. College leaders also look to internationalization as a means to increasing the visibility of the institution, enhancing the college brand, and expanding student enrollments. The college has marked its progress towards these goals using the international education indicators most U.S. American colleges typically use, including study abroad, exchange partnerships, and international student enrollment. Over 17 percent of undergraduates study abroad, but only just over one percent of the student body is international (defined by visa status). The College's portfolio of international partnerships and programs has expanded significantly over the past six years, increasing from 32 to 48. Many of the new programs are faculty-led programs, with an increase from four in 2010 to 18 in 2016.

2.2   *Overview of China-Related Activities and Partnerships*

SUNY Cortland offers several China-related courses, programs, and partnerships that provide students, faculty and staff with opportunities to learn about China and engage with Chinese students and scholars through study, research, and teaching. SUNY Cortland also offers an interdisciplinary minor program in Asian/Middle Eastern Studies (AMES). The minor is available to students majoring in any subject who are interested in topics related to Asia, the Middle East, and Asian American issues. The program consists of an introductory course on Asia and the Middle East and 15 upper-level coursework credits in at least two departments. Participating students may take courses in the fields of anthropology, art history, economics, geography, history, philosophy, political science, health, international studies, and sociology. In addition, SUNY Cortland offers Chinese language training from the 101 (Beginning) up to 202 (Intermediate II) level. Some Chinese-speaking faculty also offer individual intensive language training as independent study credits.

The Cortland campus benefits from the active engagement of faculty of Chinese and Taiwanese descent in both China-related and internationalization initiatives. These faculty, as well as additional faculty interested in the region, voluntarily serve as resources for Chinese and Taiwanese students and visiting scholars. They host formal and informal Chinese cultural events and speaker seminars and have worked with the International Programs Office to develop the College's institutional partnerships with Chinese and Taiwanese universities. Other faculty have strong connections with China through research and teaching, or a desire to develop their interests in the region through participating in exchange, teaching, leading study abroad courses, and forming research collaborations.

Counter to the national trend in the U.S. of over five-fold expansion of student participation in study abroad programs in China (Laughlin, 2008), SUNY Cortland student engagement in study abroad to China has been low, with an average of one student studying through its semester-long Beijing program. The College has had greatest success in promoting study in China through a shorter-term, faculty-led course that has been shuttered for several years due to the faculty leader's shift in research to another region. Based on the success of this model, however, several faculty are currently developing a new short-term course that will be discussed in depth below.

These dedicated faculty have been instrumental both in maintaining and expanding SUNY Cortland's portfolio of exchange partnerships with Chinese and Taiwanese universities. The College in general has historically, and continues to select, partnerships based on faculty connections and interest. It currently operates a long-time partnership with Capital Normal University in Beijing and has developed new partnerships in Shandong Province and Taiwan, where faculty were students, in the past two years. Periodically, other Chinese institutions have approached SUNY Cortland to propose pathway and exchange partnerships. Given limited resources, however, the College's leadership has chosen to pursue a limited number of partnerships based on existing relationships through faculty, institutional curricular fit, and projected demand from students and faculty. Each partner institution and partnership is described below.

3 Partners and Student Mobility Agreements and Activities

3.1 *Capital Normal University (Beijing): Revitalizing a Long-Term Partnership*

SUNY Cortland and Capital Normal University (CNU) entered into an exchange partnership starting in 1981. CNU was founded as a public university in 1954 with programs in the humanities, sciences, engineering, education, management, foreign languages, and fine arts. For decades, CNU was a teacher-training institution. Although in recent years the school has put more emphasis on academic research and created many other majors, teacher training on both elementary and secondary levels is still a very important mission of the institution. CNU and SUNY Cortland are similar in this area, which provides a common ground for faculty and administrators at both institutions to share experiences and discuss related issues.

Today, CNU offers programs at the junior college, Bachelor's, Master's, doctoral, and post-doctoral levels. CNU enrolls approximately 30,000 students and employs nearly 2,550 teaching faculty, of whom over 90% have Master's degrees or higher. Declared by the Ministry of Education as the "Outstanding University of Undergraduate Teaching" in 2003 and founded as a normal school, CNU has a focus on undergraduate teaching and teacher education that resonate with SUNY Cortland's mission and history.

CNU has a long history of active engagement in international academic and cultural exchange. The university has operated both short- and long-term cultural exchange programs with over 200 university partners in 36 countries, and enrolls international students from around the world. Its international center houses hundreds of international students and visiting scholars, and serves as the center for international student services and programming. CNU operates six Confucius Institutes around the world, including one in collaboration with SUNY Cortland's sister institution, the University at Buffalo.

Over the 35 years of SUNY Cortland and CNU partnership, the mobility program has been characterized by flexibility, careful negotiation on financial arrangements, and an often robust flow of students and faculty between the two institutions. From the beginning of the agreement and up until its most recent renewal in 2012, CNU faculty, the majority of whom did not have graduate degrees, came to SUNY Cortland for Master's degrees in exchange for SUNY Cortland students going to CNU to learn Chinese language and culture. As an increasing number of CNU faculty obtained graduate degrees in China, the relevance of this faculty-student exchange arrangement shifted, and the two partners agreed to change the agreement to target student exchange between CNU graduate and undergraduate students, and SUNY Cortland graduate students. As we shall discuss below, because demand from SUNY students has been low, with an average of only one student studying in China every year, the partners are once again reconceiving the mobility arrangement, this time with a focus on developing a "gateway" short-term, faculty-led program that will take SUNY students to CNU and the other two partners. This will expose SUNY students to mainland China and Taiwan and promote longer-term, semester-long exchange.

In addition, a healthy flow of faculty and administrators has moved back and forth between the two institutions. While on exchange, these SUNY Cortland and CNU faculty and administrators have taught, collaborated on research, or observed courses to familiarize themselves with host institution teaching methods. Over the years, delegations from each institution have visited the other's campus, including a large delegation of 15 faculty and administrators from SUNY Cortland visiting CNU in 2007. The goal of this program was to broaden SUNY Cortland's connection to, and interaction with, Asia in general and China in particular, as well as to support the internationalization of the curriculum, academic research, and service. This program spawned collaborations between several faculty members on teaching projects.

In 2009, SUNY Cortland entered into a partnership with the Beijing Teacher Training Center for Higher Education (BTTCHE) at CNU on the Senior Visiting Scholar Research Program for Young Elite Teachers in Higher Education. Through this project, several senior doctoral-level faculty members from Chinese institutions stayed at SUNY Cortland for training periods of six months to one full year. The purpose was to build faculty capacity to engage in collaborative research and familiarize faculty with U.S. academic culture, in addition to honing their English proficiency, particularly in their scholarly writing. Activities included attending academic meetings and conferences, enhancing teaching and research abilities, and fostering innovation in research. Participants were hosted by SUNY Cortland faculty, providing intercultural exchange opportunities for both individuals and departments.

3.2   *Qufu Normal University (Qufu, Shandong): Establishing a New Partnership*

Qufu Normal University (QNU) is located in Qufu, Shandong Province, the birthplace of Confucius and the cradle of Confucianism. Its rich cultural heritage and historical importance have always drawn the attention of the world and in 1994 it became a UNESCO World Heritage Site. Inheriting Confucius' teaching philosophy and practice, QNU was founded in 1955. Since then, it has taken Confucius' words as it motto: 学而不厌，诲人不倦 (Never be content with one's study, never be impatient with one's teaching). Located in the rural suburbs of Qufu, QNU shares characteristics and mission with SUNY Cortland. It is a state/provincial college in rural China where the majority of students are from working-class families and aspire to be teachers and educators.

QNU is one of the leading universities in Shandong Province. As of spring 2015, there are 1,217 full-time faculty, 32,956 undergraduates, 3,546 graduate students (doctoral and master's), and 16,000 continuing education students. The university has 29 schools and 28 research institutes. The University offers 83 undergraduate/bachelor programs, and a great number of master's-level and doctoral-level programs. In the past 60 years, over 160,000 graduates from QNU have entered the teaching profession.

In its recent efforts around internationalization, QNU has shown strong interest in SUNY Cortland by establishing a formal exchange relationship with the SUNY campus. The new program provides a unique exchange program distinct from the existing partnership with Capital Normal University in Beijing. It offers opportunities for students and faculty to study or conduct research in a city strong in historical tradition and distinct from the cosmopolitan center of Beijing. During the last three to four decades, most of the Chinese schools with which American schools have built relationships are located in major cities. Rarely have exchange programs been established with schools in small cities like Qufu. SUNY Cortland's partnership with QNU helps fill this gap and strengthens the time-tested exchange programs of SUNY Cortland with China.

The rich historical, cultural, and academic resources offered by Qufu and QNU will provide faculty with unique opportunities for research and teaching through the partnership. In recent years, the Research Institute of Confucianism (RIC) was founded in Qufu. With over 60,000 square meters of exhibit and collection space, the RIC has become a central locale for the collections of primary and secondary sources related to Confucius and Confucianism. It houses/hosts academic research, information exchange, training, and a cultural relics exhibition. The RIC hosts residential scholars to conduct long-term and short-term projects and will gradually be developed into a center of Confucius and Confucianism study worldwide. A partnership with QNU will provide faculty access to these resources. In return, as an institution with teacher education programs and professional studies, SUNY Cortland offers faculty from QNU opportunities for collaborative research and teaching in various fields. In short, the partnership will provide faculty from both institutions opportunities to collaborate on research and teaching at both universities.

With a long tradition of internationalization, QNU has built university partnership relationships with over 50 countries and is among the 200 universities in China that are qualified for enrolling overseas students. It started accepting international students from 1992, and about 1000 foreign students have studied in QNU, from over 10 countries including Japan, Korea, Great Britain, France, and the United States.

A substantial challenge of the partnership between QNU and SUNY Cortland is the language barrier for students at SUNY Cortland, which only offers Chinese language instruction up to the intermediate level. One path for international students at QNU to develop their language skills and learn about Chinese culture is to enroll and study in the International Exchange College. Founded in 2001, the International Exchange College offers Chinese language study in speaking, listening, reading, writing, and the Chinese Language Proficiency Test (HSK-Hanyu Shuiping Kaoshi), ranging from beginner to intermediate and advanced levels. The International Exchange College also offers courses and seminars in English, including Chinese history, Introduction to Chinese culture, Chinese calligraphy, folk art, traditional music, literature/poetry, foundations and systems of education in China, Confucius and Confucianism.

Both credit-bearing and non-credit courses and seminars offered at Qufu Normal University will provide SUNY Cortland students with opportunities to learn about traditional and modern values of Chinese people and society and initiate in-depth inquiries to examine different aspects of Chinese culture and society. Given that the number of SUNY Cortland students studying abroad in China has been low, we will initiate faculty-led and short-term summer/winter courses as concentration requirements or electives. Depending on a SUNY Cortland students' specific needs in taking credit-bearing courses, a number of courses offered at QNU could satisfy a range of minor degree requirements, for instance, for Asian/Middle Eastern Studies minors, who could benefit tremendously from such an exchange experience. If approved, it is possible that a wider range of courses (semester-long) or seminars (during summer/winter breaks) be offered or customized for Cortland students through negotiation.

SUNY Cortland and QNU are compatible in terms of their mission statement, goals, and strong focus on teacher education programs. Both institutions are committed to international and global education to promote global awareness in students. As SUNY Cortland is well-known for its teacher education programs, QNU is one of the most famous teachers' college in Shandong Province. QNU teacher education programs are accredited by the Ministry of Education of China, which is an equivalent institution to the Department of

Education in the United States, but has far more authority in implementing curriculum and standards than its American counterpart.

To date, starting in Fall 2016, the new partnership has facilitated the arrival of two students and one international education staff member from QNU, who is helping to promote study in China and plan the short-term trip to China for SUNY students and their faculty leaders. The partners are also in the process of arranging further faculty exchanges and promoting semester-long study abroad for SUNY students. Additional discussions have centered on organizing cross-disciplinary workshops among faculty from both institutions and joint research.

3.3 *Tamkang University (Taiwan): Becoming a U.S. Study Abroad Destination for Taiwanese Students*

In February 2016, SUNY Cortland entered into a new partnership with Tamkang University (TKU) in New Taipei City, Taiwan. The partnership was championed on the Cortland side by a new faculty member who had attended TKU as an undergraduate. Founded in 1950 as a junior college of English literature, TKU is Taiwan's first private college, and since 1980 has been a comprehensive university comprised of 11 colleges offering degrees at the bachelor's, master's, and doctoral levels. The university enrolls over 27,000 students and employs nearly 2,100 faculty and staff at its three physical campuses in New Taipei City, Taipei City, Lanyang in Jiaoxi Township, and the online Cyber Campus.

TKU is actively engaged in international partnerships, with over 100 partner institutions in 28 countries. Students from 50 nations make up TKU's diverse student body. In 2005, when internationalization was one of the primary goals stated in its strategic plan, TKU University decided to establish the first and the only university campus in Taiwan to offer an exclusively English learning environment. This newly established Lanyang campus is not only an English campus, but also a residential college where all the faculty members are asked to connect with students in and outside of the classroom. Furthermore, while equipping graduates with sufficient foreign language skills and international awareness is the primary goal, the Lanyang campus adopted an aggressive approach to encourage its students. It created a compulsory "Junior Abroad Program" and attempted to establish sister institutions around the world for its students. While some universities in Taiwan require students to receive a certain score on a foreign language test before graduation, Lanyang campus set an even higher graduation requirement in that it requires students to spend a full year abroad to advance their language skills.

As international recruiting staff members would agree, recruiting students for a short-term study abroad program is not an easy task. Convincing students to attend a long-term program on the other side of the world is even more difficult. Among all the difficulties, perhaps the most common obstacle is financial support for students' long term overseas experience. However, this is not a problem for Lanyang students. Since the admission office at Lanyang campus notifies the parents and students about the "Junior Abroad Program" and the graduation requirement before the students actually enter the college, all the admitted students and their family have the financial support prepared in advance. Furthermore, to ensure students can afford this study abroad program, students are required to submit a financial support statement along with their application for the program abroad at the end of their sophomore year. Because this full year abroad experience is included in Lanyang Campus's core curriculum, if any student cannot complete this program abroad for any reason, they will have to transfer to another of the university's campuses, or even another university. In other words, students and their family know this program abroad is not optional and they begin preparing for the junior experience from the first day in college.

Although student funding is the most pressing concern, Lanyang Campus also has another challenge: finding foreign sister institutions. From Lanyang parents' perspective, sending their child to study at a university's foreign sister institution implies that the university will take care of the students as they do for the students at home. This *in loco parentis* expectation forces the universities to select and vet their sister institutions very cautiously. For most East Asian universities, the only exception that may expedite the process of building partnership would be a pre-existing relationship. With a pre-existing relationship intact, U.S. universities may approach Asian universities more easily because trust already exists. This relationship also allows Asian partners to gain confidence in building a closer tie with the university in the U.S.

The SUNY Cortland and Tamkang-Lanyang Campus exchange program exhibits how important a "pre-existing relationship" is. The faculty member who proposed this exchange program is a graduate of Tamkang, and he has a strong personal connection with faculty and staff at Tamkang university. This pre-existing relationship mitigates concerns at both ends quickly and the discussion proceeds rapidly to the details of the program. Since both universities have previous experience in establishing foreign partnerships, the memorandum of the SUNY Cortland and Tamkang- Lanyang exchange program was approved by both institutions within three months. The first group of Taiwanese students arrived in Cortland the following year.

3.4   *Themes and Challenges*
SUNY Cortland's experience working with its Chinese partners is characterized by several opportunities and challenges. In particular, as a public institution, SUNY Cortland has limited funding and resources for developing a large

portfolio of exchange partnerships to foster student, faculty, and staff mobility. To optimize the opportunities and address challenges, SUNY Cortland has pursued a strategy of engaging with Chinese institutions with which we share common history, interests, and goals. The college generally initiates partnerships with universities with which one or more faculty members have connections they would like to leverage on behalf of the college. In the case of China, each partnership has a faculty champion who has forged a connection because they know both institutions well, and believe there is a close institutional fit in terms of curricula, mission, and vision; faculty teaching and research interests; student profile; and student support services. Both CNU and QNU, like SUNY Cortland, were established as Normal universities with extensive teacher education programs. SUNY Cortland offers courses in several of the fields of interest to Tamkang students. The key to this approach is to work with partner institutions to identify a mutually beneficial set of activities and goals to provide students, faculty, and staff with mobility opportunities in study, research, and teaching.

3.5   Challenge: Demand by Chinese Students, Faculty, and Staff

Uneven demand for participation by U.S. and Chinese student and faculty mobility participants has been both an opportunity and a challenge. Over the past eight years, an average of four Chinese exchange students per year have studied at SUNY Cortland, while only one SUNY student per year has studied in China for a semester. Demand from Chinese students was historically hampered by cost and lack of family financial resources, and SUNY Cortland worked both internally and with Chinese partners to provide scholarships and keep costs down for students and visiting faculty. SUNY Cortland agreed to offer CNU students a $2600 scholarship per year, and beginning in 2016–2017, they will receive double that amount. In 1998, a long-time SUNY Cortland administrator, Yuki Chin, established a scholarship to honor the memory of his wife, Wah Chip, and to support student and scholar exchange between SUNY Cortland and Asian countries. Through this scholarship, dozens of students from China and SUNY Cortland have received funding for exchange through SUNY Cortland's partnerships with Chinese and other Asian institutions. Preference is given first to students coming from or going to CNU, and then mainland China universities or other institutions in Asia, for one or more semesters.

As Chinese families' financial wealth has increased, this issue has changed significantly. China has emerged as the second largest economy in the world. Chinese families are motivated to provide their students with study abroad experiences and they have the resources to do so. Although studying abroad in the U.S. can still be a heavy financial burden for many Chinese families, a

growing middle class means that an increasing number of students can afford
to study abroad. The challenge for U.S. institutions in attracting Chinese
students is the competition among U.S. and other Western institutions for the
growing number of students seeking to study abroad. SUNY Cortland is now
looking at scholarships as a means to attract Chinese students whose families
can now afford studying abroad, but who have many options for destination
universities.

Chinese institutions and government agencies at the national and regional
levels have also increasingly provided funding for faculty and staff exchange. As
described above, several Chinese scholars have visited SUNY Cortland for one
or two semesters with full funding from the Beijing Teachers' Training Center
for Higher Education, while others from a variety of non-partner institutions
in mainland China have been sponsored by their provincial or national
governments. Due to this funding, SUNY Cortland has been able to host three
exchange visitors from China per year, including from partner institutions.

The other recruitment challenge, particularly in terms of recruiting
degree-seeking students, is the importance of institutional status and name
recognition. While some of SUNY's campuses, particularly the system's
University Research Centers, are recognized by students seeking admission to
U.S. universities, four-year comprehensive colleges within the system, such as
SUNY Cortland, do not have strong name recognition. To facilitate recruitment
of Chinese students to campus, SUNY Cortland has therefore pursued
partnerships with Chinese institutions with similar academic programs and
student profiles, and with which our faculty have existing connections.

3.6   Challenge: Recruiting U.S. Students to Study in China

On the SUNY Cortland student side, recruiting U.S. students to study in China
presented a different set of difficulties than recruiting Chinese students.
Although cost is an issue for SUNY Cortland families, it is less so because the
cost of studying for a semester at a Chinese partner institution, including
tuition, airfare, housing, and meals, is less than the cost of a semester on the
Cortland campus. Substantial study abroad scholarships are also available
to Cortland students through endowed and other scholarships. The U.S.
government, through President Obama's 100,000 Strong Initiative and other
U.S. and Chinese government scholarship programs, offers substantial funding
for U.S. students seeking to study in China (Belyavina, 2013). The challenge has
been to effectively advertise the lower cost of studying abroad in China and
the availability of scholarships. And yet, despite the lower costs, recruiting
Cortland students to study in China has been challenging, with no more than
one or two studying at a partner institution per year, if any. Further research on
student motivations for and barriers to students studying in China is needed,

but anecdotally, students have cited concerns about lack of Chinese language proficiency, cultural difference, and even "fear of missing out," or FOMO, by leaving campus. As will be discussed below, SUNY Cortland has had greater success promoting short-term, faculty-led courses in China, and so faculty and administrators are turning efforts towards developing such a course as an introduction to China.

4   Strategies

4.1   *Flexible Mobility Models*
In any exchange partnership, one goal is to achieve parity of numbers of students and faculty participating over time. In the case of SUNY Cortland's longtime partnership with CNU, however, this parity has not been achieved to the extent needed to expand the exchange program as the partners have desired. Realizing that the interests of the Chinese and U.S. students are different, SUNY Cortland and each of its partner institutions have worked together to develop asynchronous exchanges that differ from traditional one-to-one exchange programs where students from each institution spend one or two semesters abroad at the host institution. For example, until CNU and SUNY Cortland renewed their exchange agreement in 2012, the institutions agreed that faculty and graduate students from CNU would come to Cortland for one or two semesters, while SUNY Cortland undergraduates would also go to CNU for one or two semesters. This met the interests and needs of CNU faculty and advanced graduate students for professional development, while providing Cortland undergraduates with an opportunity to study abroad in China. By the time the two institutions renewed the agreement, however, an increased number of CNU faculty already had doctorates, so demand to spend a semester in the U.S. was lower. The agreement is now a more conventional one, encouraging student-to-student exchange. Because of reduced demand among Cortland undergraduates and faculty for exchange and study in China, SUNY Cortland has worked not only with CNU, but also with QNU and TKU to develop a short-term, faculty-led program to introduce U.S. students to mainland China and Taiwan. This provides a structured opportunity with close faculty support to experience different environments across China and Taiwan. In this way, the institutions can achieve parity by turning the expense of a larger number of participants in a short-term program into that of a few participants in a long-term, semester program, allowing CNU, QNU, and Tamkang to send more students and scholars to Cortland.

Beyond achieving parity, the aim of these short-term programs will be not only immediate learning about these cultures, but also promoting study abroad for longer periods as exchange students. Past success with a China Arts and History course led by a SUNY Cortland faculty member follows national U.S. trends in study abroad, where, according to the Institute of International Education, 62 percent of students studying abroad do so through programs of eight weeks or less, up from 56.6 percent in 2009–2010 (Farrugia & Bhandari, 2016). These courses provide students with a closely facilitated and monitored experience and open up access to study abroad to students whose degree programs or personal situations allow for less flexibility to study abroad for longer periods, for example, in teacher education programs requiring block course registration and practica.

The program is designed to achieve several learning objectives. First, students will obtain firsthand knowledge about rising Asia, and China in particular, by seeing and experiencing the vitality of China's and Taiwan's economic and political development and how it is changing the landscape of the world's power. Second, students will be given the opportunity to understand why and how the two different sociopolitical systems have emerged and developed, and a will have a comparative but balanced perspective on development on the two sides of the Strait. Third, in the area of Chinese culture and history, students will have the opportunity to learn knowledge about China's past and present by visiting many historical and cultural sites, and speaking with Asian students in the universities, organizations, and companies they visit. Finally, students will develop an appreciation for Chinese culture and tradition. These experiences may enhance students' ability to adapt to a dynamic world under the heavy influence of globalization.

In this program, SUNY Cortland will collaborate with four host institutions in four major cities in China and Taiwan: Capital Normal University (CNU) in Beijing, Qufu Normal University (QNU) in the Confucius' hometown, and Tamkang University (TKU) and National Kaohsiung First Technology University (NCTU) in Taiwan. Each host institution will provide learning and lodging facilities and their professors will participate in teaching. Class instruction will include a variety of interactive and reflective exercises. For example, at each place of the learning journey, we will work with the host institution to organize dialogues between American students and their Chinese counterparts to further mutual understanding and interactions between students from different sociocultural backgrounds. SUNY Cortland students will better understand the difference in beliefs and perspectives between the youth of mainland China and those of Taiwan.

4.2   *Supporting International Students on Partner Campuses*
Essential to the success of SUNY Cortland's exchange partnerships with its Chinese partners has been a shared commitment to supporting the

international students who participate in these mobility programs. Each partner commits to extending all services and curricula offered to domestic students, with added services to support the unique needs of international students. Each institution has dedicated offices and staff to provide support to incoming international students and scholars, offering services such as immigration advising, orientation and cultural adjustment advising, referrals to other campus and community resources, cultural events and programming, and peer mentoring and ambassador programs. In addition, each partner provides special academic support services such as language and culture courses, tutoring, and writing assistance.

4.3 *Collaborative Online International Learning (COIL) Projects and Technology Challenges*

In 2008, a SUNY Cortland faculty member in the English Department and her counterpart at CNU met during the visit to China by a SUNY Cortland faculty delegation, which was followed by a one-year stay by the CNU faculty member at SUNY Cortland as an exchange visitor. The two had shared interests in enhancing their students' writing through intercultural exchange. As a result, the two colleagues established a collaborative online international learning (COIL) project to design courses in which the Cortland and CNU students would work together on assignments, edit one another's writing, and participate in joint discussions and lectures. COIL provides students across disciplines with intercultural opportunities to enhance their learning, understand different perspectives, and develop communication and other skills when working with colleagues from diverse backgrounds. COIL courses expand access to international education opportunities by offering college students, only 10 percent of whom study abroad, with opportunities for intercultural exchange on their own campus.

Although these experiences have been enriching for the two instructors and their students have reported deriving benefits from engaging with their counterparts, technology has created a challenge. The two faculty have needed to adopt and adapt a series of learning management platforms that meet the technological capacity of both institutions and allow access in light of government rules and restrictions. They have moved from using simple email exchanges, to early wiki software, to Schoology – a free online system – to Blackboard.

4.4 *Intercultural Engagement in the Internationalization Context*

One of the most important elements underlying the collaborations between SUNY Cortland and the Chinese and Taiwanese partner universities described above is the need to foster intercultural understanding and clear communication. For SUNY Cortland and its Chinese partners, the key to successful interactions and negotiations has been the close involvement of several faculty originally from the region and connected to the partner institutions. These faculty have served as cultural interpreters and guides as we engage with our colleagues at CNU, QNU, and Tamkang, who also have strong intercultural skills and familiarity with U.S. culture and styles of communication, and even with SUNY Cortland itself. They have been integral to the careful negotiation of agreements to find common ground, particularly around financial arrangements, and they have lent their native expertise of the softer skills required for open and clear communication and relationship building. In one particularly fortunate case, as a four-person delegation led by SUNY Cortland's president prepared to travel to Beijing and Shandong Province to visit with partners, one of the participating SUNY Cortland faculty members, a native of Shandong, advised the U.S.-born members of the group that the gifts of clocks they were intending to give partners would have a negative cultural connotation to the Chinese partners. For some Chinese (perhaps not all), giving a clock can be seen as a curse because the Chinese word for clock is a homophone of the word for funeral (送钟 ＝送终). This small example highlights the importance of relationships and relying on faculty ambassadors within institutions to support ongoing relationships.

5 Conclusion

SUNY Cortland was one of the first U.S. higher education institutions to establish an exchange partnership with a Chinese university, CNU, after Deng Xiaoping opened the door for educational exchange in 1978. Since then, CNU and SUNY Cortland faculty and international programs staff have worked diligently to identify the needs and interests of their students and faculty related to participating in exchange. They have worked to establish win-win exchange protocols that meet their university's academic, personal, and professional interests while overcoming barriers to students, such as cost and U.S. student concerns about committing to longer-term study with less language proficiency. That this partnership has been successful for so many years, despite periods where the flow of exchange has been lower or uneven, can be attributed to the spirit of cooperation, similar academic programs, and parallel histories of development from normal schools to comprehensive institutions.

SUNY Cortland faculty and administrators have drawn from this experience to approach developing its newer partnerships with QNU in Qufu, Shandong, and with Tamkang University in Taiwan. In both cases, the partners started exploring potential partnership by looking at areas of common academic interest, considering possible student and faculty interests and needs, and forging flexible agreements that allow for a broad range of educational and cultural exchange activities. Undergirding these efforts has been the active engagement of a cadre of highly engaged faculty, some of whom are themselves exchange program alumni, who promote exchange to students, orient them to their host culture, and provide critical assistance in negotiating and communicating with the partner institutions. Time will tell how successful the two new partnerships will be, but by adopting the strategies developed through 35 years of collaborating with CNU, SUNY Cortland and its partners have built a great deal of trust, excitement, and goodwill through the program development process.

References

Belyavina, R. (2013). *U.S. students in China: Meeting the goals of the 100,000 strong initiative.* New York, NY: Institute of International Education.

Chan, D., & Lo, W. (2008). University restructuring in East Asia: Trends, challenges and prospects. *Policy Futures in Education, 6*(5), 641–652.

Farrugia, C. A., & Bhandari, R. (2016). *Open doors 2015: Report on international educational exchange.* New York, NY: Institute of International Education.

George, E. S. (2006). Positioning higher education for the knowledge based economy. *Higher Education, 52*(4), 589–610.

Goodman, A. E. (2011). U.S.-China student exchange. In Institute of International Education (Ed.), *IIEPASSPORT study abroad in China* (p. 4). New York, NY: Institute of International Education.

Laughlin, S. (2008). *Educational exchange between the United States and China: An IIE briefing paper.* New York, NY: Institute of International Education. Retrieved from http://www.iie.org/~/media/Files/Corporate/Membership/Articles-and-Presentations/US-China-Exchange-An-IIE-Briefing-Paper-2008.ashx

McGiffert, C. (2011). 100,000 strong: Building strategic trust in U.S.-China relations through education. In Institute of International Education (Ed.), *IIEPASSPORT study abroad in China* (pp. 5–6). New York, NY: Institute of International Education.

National Association of College Admissions Counselors (NACAC). (n.d.). *Admissions professionals: International.* Retrieved from http://www.nacacnet.org/International/InternationalInitiatives/Pages/Admissions-Professionals-International.aspx

Wang, R. J. (2003). From elitism to mass higher education in Taiwan: The problems faced. *Higher Education, 46*(3), 261–287.

About the Authors

Mary Schlarb is director of international programs at SUNY Cortland, overseeing the College's international partnerships, education abroad, dual diploma programs, international student and scholar services, and international visitor relations. She is a doctoral candidate in Comparative International Development Education at the University of Minnesota, and holds degrees from Cornell University and Stanford University.

Shufang Strause is an associate professor in Childhood/Early Childhood Education Department at State University of New York at Cortland (SUNY Cortland). She is prolific in publications and presentations in her field of instructional technology. She has a background in linguistics and TESOL. She initiated the partnership between SUNY Cortland and Qufu Normal University, her Alma Mater, in China.

Dennis Lu-Chung Weng is an Assistant Professor of Political Science at Sam Houston State University in Texas. Dr. Weng's research focuses on comparative politics and international relations, with an emphasis on the effect of the political institution in the decision-making process at both domestic and international levels. His research has been published in academic journals and featured in several Asian news media. Dr. Weng was faculty director of SUNY Cortland's partnership with Tamkang University in Taiwan.

CHAPTER 8

An Exploratory Journey of NYU Shanghai: Reflections from a University Chancellor[1]

Yu Lizhong

Abstract

This chapter chronicles the historic development of New York University Shanghai. Yu Lizhong, the university's Chancellor, describes how the branch campus of New York University in China provides a unique setting for students that draws upon traditions in higher education from both China and the United States.

1 Introduction: Why Was NYU Shanghai Founded?

1.1 The Development of Chinese Higher Education Demands Quality and Character

The development of Chinese higher education has gone through a long history with some successes along the way. Now we are at a critical moment when we need to pay close attention to reform and explorations of new ideas. In our opinion (NYU Shanghai), the development of Chinese higher education is no longer about creating more schools and getting more students. The true meaning of quality higher education in China requires new types of universities with unique characteristics, which prepare young generations to meet challenges in an advanced modern society and to contribute to the development of mankind. It requires ambition, vision, and encouragement (NYU Shanghai, n.d.).

1.2 Understanding Meanings of Quality University and Finding Pathways to Build One

There are many pathways to reach the goal. We have been searching the meaning of the quality university and pathways to approach it. The NYU Shanghai model was explored and researched during the process. It was built upon our strong belief that new types of universities like this represent the reformed and high-quality Chinese universities in a contemporary period. The idea of creating a school that is operated cooperatively with institutions in foreign countries is supported and regulated by the Chinese Ministry of Education guidelines. Through cooperative educational institutions, we should be able to introduce educational ideas from world-class universities, reference their instructional models, share their educational resources, and create a learning environment in the context of globalization. We grasped the opportunity and sought direct connections with world first-class universities to start the journey in higher education reform.

2   The Marriage between the New York University (NYU) and the East China Normal University (ECNU): Shared Vision and Perfect Match

2.1   *About the New York University (NYU)*
NYU is often mis-identified with other universities in the New York City. For example, the State University of New York (SUNY) and the City University of New York (CUNY) are two different university systems from NYU. Dr. C.N. Yang, a Nobel Laurate in physics was a professor in the Stoney Brook campus of SUNY that is a public university system of the New York State. There also has a large city system university in the New York City (CUNY).

NYU is a private school ranked higher than SUNY and CUNY campuses. According to university rankings by the Shanghai Jiaotong University (SJTU) in 2013, NYU was ranked the 20th among American Universities, and 27th worldwide in 2013. The Times ranked NYU at 16th in the United States and 27th in the world. For the past ten years, rankings for the New York University have moved upward continuously.

2.2   *The New York University Idea*
For the past 10 years, the development of NYU has been remarkable. NYU grew from a locally influential private school, mainly in the north east region of the United States to become one of the top ranking universities favored by American students. The rapid development can be attributed to the university educational idea and the development a premiere campus within New York City.

We have followed the growth of NYU for some time and believed that NYU is an ideal partner in pursuing our aspiring goal. Investigations on various aspects of teaching and learning in NYU, including resources, have been conducted. Among several indicators, the one with NYU faculty ranking has earned the highest score. World-class professors including Nobel Prize Laureates choose to live and work in the New York City, the world's most famous cosmopolitan city where NYU is located. While the university has made tremendous efforts to recruit and retain renowned scholars, positive changes in city life in New York play an important role. It is also worth noting that in the past ten years, eight NYU faculty members won Nobel Prize, with three in economics.

We (East China Normal University) were mostly attracted to the concept and the connotation of Global Network University proposed by NYU. Just as the president of NYU has consistently emphasized, universities in an increasingly globalized world should not be built upon one single culture and limited by the boundary of one single country. Universities should be created with multi-cultural dimensions to allow students to study worldwide. For more than a decade, NYU has had Study Away Sites in many big international cities including London, Paris, Berlin, Madrid, Florence, Tel Aviv, Sydney, and Buenos Aries. The Study Away program offers students opportunities to get exposed to different cultural and social events all over the world. Students and teachers integrate classroom studies with cultural, social and research experiences in these overseas campuses in six continents. In their four-year undergraduate education, students have the chance to live in the same dormitory and study in the same classrooms with peers who grow up in completely different environments and bring in different views and perspectives about the world. The enriched experiences are likely to promote understanding, communication, appreciation and cooperation across different cultures.

2.3   *Recounting an Inspiring Collaborative Journey. The City of Shanghai and the East China Normal University (ECNU): An Ideal Partner in an Ideal Location for NYU*

China is a natural candidate for establishing Global Network University. Shanghai, the largest and most developed city in China is undoubtedly preferred for an overseas education site because of its significant role in China's economic reform and China's open-door policy. The city, with its fast pace and colorful lifestyle has illustrated admirable and remarkable progress. As the largest internationalized city in China, Shanghai was an ideal site for NYU Study Away. In 2006, the NYU delegation visited Shanghai seeking partners. Later that year, they sent several groups to Shanghai for onsite visits to gain more and detailed information about the prospective partnership. After carefully assessing teaching, learning, and living conditions, they decided to establish a partnership with ECNU and chose to found the NYU Shanghai Center at the ECNU North Zhongshan Road campus. After ECNU and NYU signed an official agreement in 2006, the cooperation between these two campuses began, which promoted mutual understanding and strengthened the relationship immediately. In the fall of 2006, the first group of 18 NYU undergraduate students arrived at ECNU. The student number grew and quickly exceeded 100 in the third semester.

From then on, between 200–300 NYU students studied in Shanghai each year. While embracing the early success, both ECNU and NYU recognized the limitation of the center's capacity. The need for expansion and further collaboration was apparent. Plans for a joint and cooperative university started to surface in both universities.

2.4   *Establishing Partnership: Nourishing Collaborations between ECNU and NYU*

Building a university that is jointly operated with a foreign country was unprecedented in China. Preparation processes presented challenges. The collaboration required courage, creativity, and true vision for Chinese higher education in the new century. Discussion and negotiation with NYU were tough in general and very challenging sometimes. It demanded on aligned interest and mutual understanding. Regardless of all these difficulties, the project was supported by the Chinese Ministry of Education and the Shanghai municipal government from the beginning. Feedback from the public was also positive. Media provided positive energy that helped open up the path for this innovative approach in Chinese higher education. The end result was agreeable and deliverable.

In January 2011, the official letter from the Ministry of Education arrived. It approved the preparatory work for the NYU Shanghai campus after thorough and rigorous evaluations conducted by educational experts. The Shanghai municipal government prioritized the work and placed it as an important case study of experimental significance for the national comprehensive education reform. For two consecutive years, Mr. Han Zheng, the mayor of Shanghai, cited the construction work of the NYU Shanghai in his State of the Union speech illustrating high expectations and determinations from the government. In March 2011, the Shanghai Education Committee, the Pudong district, ECNU, and NYU signed a four-party agreement.

In May 2012, the Chinese Ministry of Education conducted a second-round on-site evaluation. On September 22nd 2012, the official approval letter of the cooperative venture between ECNU and NYU was finalized. The opening ceremony of NYU Shanghai was held on October 15th, 2012. On August 11, 2013, the inaugural class reported to the school in its temporary location at the ECNU North Zhongshan Road campus. Convocation was held the next day. In August 2014, the Pudong campus was ready for use. The 15-floor university building appears to be the lowest in the forest of towers on the Century Avenue in Pudong, but represents a strong institution in the city. The timeline of activities is outlined in Table 8.1.

TABLE 8.1   *Timeline*

January 2011	NYU Shanghai preparatory plan approved by the Chinese Ministry of Education
March 2011	The four-party agreement was signed
May 2012	Chinese Ministry of Education conduced the second round of on-site inspection
September 2012	NYU Shanghai was officially approved
October 2012	NYU Shanghai opening ceremony
August 2013	Inaugural class arrived at ECNU North Zhongshan Road campus
August 2014	NYU Shanghai Pudong campus opened

2.5   *Influences of NYU Shanghai*

The strong and timely support from the Chinese State Counsel and the Ministry of Education highlights the impact of NYU Shanghai that represents a new kind of higher-education model for the modern-day China. Ms. Liu Yandong, the Vice-Premier of the State Counsel of China emphasized the exploratory and experimental nature of NYU Shanghai when she met the NYU president. In the meeting, Mr. Yuan Guiren, the head of the Ministry of Education also said that NYU Shanghai should become a role model for international cooperation in higher education and a pioneer of Chinese Higher Education reform. We understood that we were taking an unprecedented journey in uncovering paths for higher education reform while creating a world-class university. The assessment of NYU Shanghai thus is placed on goals and core values of the university. Assessments would examine what innovative ideas have been introduced to curriculum design, school management, and student services. Further, the partners would investigate what approaches have been applied to teaching and learning. Finally, partners worked together to examine how to assess learning outcome. The collaborative work in NYU Shanghai was the first joint venture between China and U.S. in higher education.

3   Discovering: Direction for Higher Education Reform

What kind of school is NYU Shanghai? This a question many people raised at the time of its opening. Miss Tang Wenshen, the director of the Foundation of Madam Song Qinlin, used to work in the Ministry of Chinese Foreign Affairs and asked me the same question. After talking to her for about 15 minutes, she did not seem to be satisfied and kept raising more questions. I had to tell her that it would be impossible to provide answers to all her questions unless she came to visit the university. She eventually visited, and learned more about the guiding principles below.

3.1   Direction: Co-Founding of a Global University by the Two Top-Tier Universities from China and the United States

It is not easy to fully understand the concept and the nature of NYU Shanghai without full participations in the process. NYU Shanghai was co-founded by two world-class universities from China and the United States of America. As a member of the Global Network University at the New York University, the NYU Shanghai is a joint venture of degree-granting international universities. However, it has independent legal status. Three guiding principles are listed below.

1   Dual identities

    The status of NYU Shanghai is unprecedented. On the one hand, NYU Shanghai is an international university approved by the Chinese government and has Chinese independent legal status. That means the university legal person has Chinese nationality. On the other hand, NYU Shanghai is the third degree-granting campus of the Global Network University of the New York University. NYU is accountable for teaching quality, school ranking and reputation, etc. In his communications to faculty, deans, and department heads, the NYU president stressed their responsibilities.

2   Ultimate goal of a university operated jointly with a foreign partner

    The ultimate goal was not described in any official documents. Why is this concept important? For a long time, we have been envisioning a co-founded university with a foreign partner. In order to introduce and make good use of excellent educational resources from foreign countries, we have to generate interest and provide incentive. We need to attract our partner who will be willing to share their resources. How do we make our partners accountable for quality instruction? How do we reference foreign educational experience? How can we make the partnership beneficial to Chinese education reform? All these point toward the issue of the shared responsibility. Solutions to these questions are described in the agreement signed by ECNU and NYU. Under the agreement, neither university should seek financial return. NYU is responsible in providing high quality instruction and in granting a bachelor degree from NYU. The shared vision for excellence in higher education for the new century aspired to by the two universities is built on exploratory new models in a global context. Together, ECNU and NYU began a new joint journey in making history of Chinese contemporary higher education.

    There are misconceptions concerning co-founding a university with foreign partners. Forming a joint venture of high quality institution is not about the school name that includes the well-known NYU brand. It is not about a degree granted by NYU either. It is about the process of applying educational experience and expertise, in which we transform Chinese higher education with innovative approaches. The dual identities of the NYU Shanghai provide such opportunity. Being a member of the NYU global network, NYU Shanghai is entitled to share all resources including teachers, curriculum, books, instruction and laboratory equipment. Our students are also able to use all online resources of NYU and borrow books from libraries in NYU through the internet. One student, for example, got four books she requested through internet four days later through the NYU Shanghai library. The NYU Shanghai student ID card can be used in ECNU campus, NYU, and other 14 NYU campuses in six continents. So, the dual identities of NYU Shanghai are critical in ensuring our students who are entitled to all resources of both ECNU and NYU.

3 Open communication and mutual understanding between two universities from China and the United States pave the foundation of this joint journey.

Currently, NYU Shanghai adopted a liberal arts curriculum with English as the language of instruction. It is poised to become a world-class research university with multiple cultural dimensions and complex curricula. The ECNU-NYU agreement provides several measures to ensure operations of the university are conducted with integrity and rigor. For example, NYU sets academic standards and nominates the university executive vice chancellor who is in charge of putting these standards in effect.

As the university chancellor, I have been working closely with Dr. Jeff Lehman who serves as the vice chancellor. We have developed a very good relationship, working as one person but with two heads, as I have told the news media. Before coming to Shanghai, Dr. Lehman worked in several administrative positions in higher education. He was the president of the Cornell University. Before that, he was the Dean of the Law School at the University of Michigan. He was appointed as the Dean of the International Law School at the Beijing University. Table 8.2 lists the members of the university leader circle.

4 Operations of a Quality University

Three issues are atop the university operational plan: (i) Maintaining the first-class faculty is the core for a quality university; (ii) Recruiting and retaining the best students to minimize faculty turnover; (iii) Developing innovative instructional models and world-class curriculum to maximize student

TABLE 8.2   *NYU Shanghai leadership (shanghai.nyu.edu)*

Yu Lizhong	Chancellor
Jeffrey S. Lehman	Vice Chancellor
Joanna Waley-Cohen	Provost and Julius Silver professor of History
Eitan Zemel	Associate Vice Chancellor for Strategy
Xiao-Jing Wang	Associate Vice Chancellor for Research
Hongxia Liu	Associate Vice Chancellor for Government and Community Relations
Maria Montoya	Dean of Arts and Science at NYU Shanghai
Yuxin Chen	Dean of Business
Keith Ross	Dean of Engineering and Computer Science
Charlene Visconti	Dean of Students
Nicholas Geacintov	Vice Dean of Science in Arts and Science
Zhongjian Zhao	Associate Dean for Arts and Science

learning potential and to help students develop knowledge, skills, academics, and cultural competence.

4.1   *Our Faculty – How to Recruit and Retain First-Class Teachers?*

According to the bilateral agreement, 40% of NYU Shanghai Faculty are appointed jointly by NYU and NYU Shanghai. These faculty members spend some of their time teaching in Shanghai. Another 40% are recruited from other foreign countries over the world. The hiring process is assisted by other institutions to ensure the quality of hiring. These professors are held with the same standard as that of NYU's hiring of Tenue Track faculty. The remaining 20% are from high ranking universities in China. Some of these Chinese professors are adjunct professors, while others having the title of "Chair Professor". These faculty members present seminars and lectures. Some come from ECNU.

More than 200 NYU faculty members have expressed their interests in teaching in Shanghai. This is a group of highly qualified and experienced faculty members, including seven science and art academy members from the U.S. Among them was a well-known economist who was nominated for the Nobel Prize in economics. In the inauguration semester of 2013, five U.S. science and art academy members taught here. Several instructors in science courses are respectable fellows of the mathematics, physics, and chemistry societies of the United States. It is hard to find a strong instruction team like this for freshmen class in any university. I particularly want to mention two professors from

Israel who came in the first semester. One taught economics, and the other taught statistics. The statistics professor is the President of the Israeli Statistics Society. Both were excellent instructors and impressed students with their expertise in content knowledge and effective teaching as well. In the following semester, two professors from Paris University in France joined us.

Faculty from universities in China not only teach Chinese language, but also teach courses of Chinese culture and history in English. Faculty from ECNU instructed several courses. For example, the course of Chinese Traditional Wisdom and its Contemporary Transformation taught by Professor Yu Zhenhua, the head of the Philosophy Department, was well received by students. Professor Wu Guanjun who returned from the U.S. recently taught the course of Chinese Thinking and Political Ideas. He is a faculty member in the Political Science Department. Professor Mao Jian taught the course of Chinese Literature of the 21st Century. Faculty from other Chinese universities joined us as well. Among faculty members who have long-term of appointment in NYU Shanghai, there is a group of overseas talented instructors who are hired under "the Recruitment Program of Global Experts" (known as "the Thousand Talents Plan").

4.2 *Our Students: How to Recruit High Quality Students?*
NYU Shanghai's recruitment is divided into two groups: half are international students and the other half are Chinese students. International students are recruited by NYU. These students can choose to apply for one of the three NYU campuses: New York, Abu Dhabi, and Shanghai. So, NYU Shanghai has similar processes of international student admissions as those of NYU. The 2013 NYU Shanghai incoming students in fact had higher average SAT score than that of going to the New York campus. It is more selective because of its smaller class size. Some demographic details of the international students were: 2/3 were from U.S. (88 students), and the other 1/3 from 34 different countries. The total number of the native languages of the group is 36. Some students were awarded with the Bill Gates and other outstanding scholarships. Several students chose NYU Shanghai over other world-ranking universities.

Chinese students are recruited by NYU Shanghai. The process is complicated. Because of the dual identities of NYU Shanghai, Chinese students have to go through application processes of both U.S. and Chinese universities. However, the effort is paid off by earning degrees from both NYU Shanghai and NYU. The three steps in the application process are described in the following paragraphs.

4.2.1 Screening
Students apply and submit to a common application portal online to begin the process. At the same time, applicants send required information including

high school course grades, SAT and other exam scores, recommendation letter from the principal, etc. After the initial screen by a committee appointed by the both NYU and NYU Shanghai, between 400–500 students are selected from a group of a few thousand applicants.

4.2.2   Campus Day Visit

Activities on Campus Day are an important part in comprehensive evaluations. During the one-day campus visit, applicants are observed and interviewed by faculty members and members of the Admissions Committee. Then, the Admissions Committee has open and thorough discussions based on on-site evaluations and assign some applicants to "Group A" of conditional acceptance. If these students earn their Chinese college entrance exam grade that is above the cutoff for the first-tier Chinese universities, they are automatically admitted. Some applicants are assigned to "Group B" of waiting list. These students also need to pass the cutoff entrance exam grade for the first-tier Chinese. In addition, they will resubmit their high school course grades and go through another round of evaluation. Some of them will be admitted. Students who are not assigned to either Group A or Group B after Campus Day Visit are rejected.

The comprehensive evaluation for Chinese applications departs from the tradition of solely relying on the entrance exam score. The admission process considers other important traits, such as students' attitude and perceptions towards life and society, their abilities in learning, their desire to learn, their engagement in various social and cultural activities both inside and outside classrooms, etc.

We have found that some media reports are misleading. People often think that U.S. institutions do not pay attention to academic performance, which is not true. Even though they emphasize the comprehensive quality of applicants, U.S. universities always first make sure applicants have good grades and good course performance in high school. They then evaluate students' other abilities. To ensure that we get the best from a big pool of quality applications, we need to appreciate their achievement in other areas, for example, community services, and participations in extra curricular activities such as sport, art, math and science competitions, leadership, etc.

The comprehensive evaluation is complex and multi-faceted. The emphasis of the comprehensive quality evaluation is heavily weighted on students' goals, pursuits, and value, necessary in assessing students' learning potential. Students should be inspired and motivated by their aspirations and responsibilities. During Campus Day Visit, students participate in virtual classroom activities, team projects, and engage in writing. They have scheduled interviews as well. Through these activities, students' desire to learn, their curiosity in exploring new knowledge, their cognitive abilities, their communication skills, their ability to adapt to an unfamiliar environment, teamwork skills, behaviors, etc. are revealed. English is the language used in these activities. English proficiency is assessed during the process. Applicants are divided into groups. Each group has between 70 to 80 students with 20–30 faculty and staff members. Evaluations contain not only scores but also detailed comments. At the end of the event, members of the admission committee share observations and evaluations for each applicant and make a final decision.

Campus visit is a very important step in the admission process. It provides a two-way channel that allows both students and the university to make selections. It is an opportunity for students to reveal their true ability and identity, which allows faculty to have objective evaluations and make sure that applicants fit into the educational model of NYU Shanghai. The additional information is important and cannot be assessed based on high school academic performance reports that show applicants' basic learning abilities.

4.2.3   Participating in National Matriculation Examination and Early
         Admission Procedure

Applicants who participate in the National Matriculation Examination or National College Entrance Examination (NCEE commonly known as "Higher Education Exam") and pass the local (province) admission scores for the first-tier Chinese universities are automatically admitted by NYU Shanghai if they are placed in Group A. They can turn down our offer. To those who are placed in Group B they will be informed by the university through early admission procedure. The admission decision will be informed before the process of the first-tier Chinese universities. The 3-step admission procedure is critical to the independent recruitment that breaks traditional approaches that rely solely on academic performance and grades.

5   Core Ideas: Selecting Excellent and Suitable Students

NYU Shanghai applies two criteria to admission: (i) Excellence; (ii) Suitability. We emphasize the suitability. NYU Shanghai students come from various cultural backgrounds and have diverse and unique traits and personalities. In order to maximize their potential, the university needs to make sure that students are prepared to share educational visions, goals, and approaches. It is important that students feel they fit into the campus.

One of the important educational goals for NYU Shanghai is to prepare our students to have visions of globalization and to be creative and competent in working on the international stage. Adopting a liberal arts curriculum, NYU Shanghai emphasizes active learning and expects students to take ownership of their learning. It expects students to develop ambitious learning goals, have strong desire to learn new knowledge and explore new ideas, to go beyond excellent performance in academics. The university encourages students to develop critical thinking skills and take non-traditional approaches in trying new things. Students should be motivated to take the opportunity to broaden their views, enrich their life, and create their unique pathways to success. We expect our students to appreciate the platform and take the advantage of the NYU global network and help strengthen relationships between China and the world.

6   Results: Successful Recruitment and Admission

I participated in campus visit activities for the past two semesters, but was only an observer, not an evaluator. Students who enrolled in the university were outstanding. Many faculty members share my view, saying they can recognize the NYU Shanghai student group who don't only look good on paper.

6.1   Our Curriculum: How do We Design and Create First-Class Instructional Models and Curriculum?

Educational goals: NYU Shanghai prepares students to become the driving force and leaders in work places for a globalized world in the new century. As world citizens, they understand and appreciate culture from different parts of the world. They will be able to communicate with people with different backgrounds. They will also be able to work in multi-disciplinary and multi-cultural teams. How do we approach these goals? I draw upon the twelve-element model for undergraduate education in U.S. (source unknown), and noticed similarities and differences of the model applied in our campus. What are our emphases?

1 Scientific perspectives and curiosity
   Broad views in science and strong curiosity will motivate learners to take on unlimited journeys. Our job is to help students broaden their views and be open to scientific ideas. We also need to stimulate learning interests and curiosity.
2 Interest oriented active learning
   Even though the university makes efforts to provide students learning opportunities, student motivation and learning interest is the key for the purposeful engagement. We need to help students uncover their learning interest and ability to inspire active and authentic learning.
3 Exploratory learning spirit in practices

In-class learning is only part of the instructional approach in NY Shanghai. Students are encouraged to get out of classrooms and learn from observations of and investigative work on cultural and societal issues in a variety of engaged activities outside the classroom. Students need to make inquiries, research on their interested subject topics, and solve problems in their daily life and in communities through practical and hands-on experiences.

4 Humanism

Humanities education is an important part of the liberal art curriculum. It not only teaches students humanism and broadens their knowledge base, but also enhances student reading skills, critical thinking skills, communication skills, analytical skills, etc.

5 Critical thinking ability

Students need to learn to think critically. They should know how to use judgement to confront misconceptions in their previous learning, to face challenges from authorities, to embrace different viewpoints, to conduct self-evaluations, etc. All these are foundations for the development of creativity.

6 Interdisciplinary learning and development

With the rapid development in science and technology, expertise in a certain field is often narrowly defined. However, real-world problems are complex and multi-dimensional. Students need to understand that solutions to these problems often demand a team that includes experts across several fields and diverse paths. To effectively help students develop problem-solving skills to meet these challenges, the curriculum design has to take into account the need for interdisciplinary learning and development.

7 Global visions

To educate a new generation of world citizens for a globalized information and technology era, we emphasize our educational goal of broadened views of the world. We teach our students to be responsible to humankind and the world, to embrace different cultures, to be inclusive, to make efforts to mend gaps caused by misunderstanding, and to promote exchange and cooperation, and to advance the society.

7   Curriculum, Instruction, and Student Support

NYU Shanghai applies a liberal arts curriculum. It asks students to spend the first two years on core liberal arts courses and select a few courses related to their likely major. Students do not to need to claim a major when they first enter the school, but need to choose an academic specialization for deeper exploration and research before they finish the second year. They can choose one major with or without a minor. The university does not have a quota for each major. The major selection is students' decision, based solely on their interest. Each student has an assigned academic adviser who provides guidance in course selection. The adviser works closely with the student, and helps individually design a roadmap for the four-year study. When graduating from NYU Shanghai, each student will earn two bachelor degree diplomas, one from NYU of the United States of America, and one from NYU Shanghai of China.

All course instructions are in English. Pedagogies of small group and interactive learning are applied to all classes. In-classroom learning is always collaborative and interactive. Students are engaged in group discussions. Sometimes these discussions go with cheers and laughs. Other times, these become heated augments. During their undergraduate studies, students will have the opportunity to spend one to three semesters studying abroad as part of the University's efforts to create a cross-cultural learning environment that will help students become global citizens. One can imagine, for example, taking a course of Renaissance or a course of European history in medieval period in three different cities: Florence, Italy, New York City and Shanghai. Even with the same instructor and same textbook, different learning environments influence learning in significant ways. Situated cognition undoubtedly promotes authentic learning in a culture that creates knowledge. In the same argument, learning a course regarding social and economic development in China for the past 30 years under the reform should generate the best learning outcomes when it is offered in China. That's the main reason we emphasize learning processes that are along all directions with multiple paths. The university has combined intercultural awareness, societal observations, and research practices into a comprehensive platform to promote learning abilities and to expand students' knowledge base.

As compared to the accustomed traditional instructional approaches, the model in NYU Shanghai has the following features:

1 *Active learning.* Teaching and learning are student centered. Students need to do a lot of self-directed learning before coming to the classroom. In class, they are engaged in and contribute to discussions. In the process, they share their views and provide feedback to their peers through critically reviewing others' opinions and reflecting on their own learning. Many NYU Shanghai students still keep their class notes that record these learning situations.
2 *All English instructions.* Because half of the NYU Shanghai students are international students, English is the instructional language. International students can choose Chinese class to earn credits.

3 *The core courses of a liberal arts curriculum.* The core courses of the curriculum entail five groups of knowledge and four key words. Knowledge groups consist of: Foundations of society and culture; Foundations of science; Writing; Mathematics; Language. Key words include: Views of globalization; Multi-dimensional culture; Interdisciplinary content knowledge; Chinese element. Under each knowledge group, a few are required courses, for example, the course of Society under Globalization Views and the course of Art under Globalization Views. Many are elective courses. Writing is a very important part of the core courses. It is not designed as a single course, but is an integral part of several other courses that heavily require writing. In these courses, faculty members who teach writing provide instructions in writing sessions. Emphases of writing instructions are placed on trainings of reading, critical thinking, and communications. Mathematics education also stresses applications in various fields and problem solving.

4 *Providing time for major selection.* Students are not required to claim their major when first enrolled in the school, and can make their decision at the end of their second year. They are provided with time and experiences in choosing their major based on their interest.

5 *Interdisciplinary learning.* Students are trained in an environment that highlights the interdisciplinary nature of their future job and working environment.

6 *NYU Global Network.* The NYU International education system provides students with learning opportunities to develop leadership in their career in a globalized work place.

7.1   *Classroom Instruction*

Many in-class teaching and learning activities in NYU Shanghai are based on original scholar's work. Students are required to read these works, and participate in free and elaborated discussions, and complete related writing assignments. These activities are to enhance their abilities in reading (of original books and papers), critical thinking, and communications. Some students told me that they thought their reading assignment for the first year already exceeded the reading assignment of four years in other universities. These works by renowned Chinese and world-famous scholars and philosophers, including Confucius, Mencius, Laozi, Deng Xiaoping, Karl Marx, etc. engage them in meaningful in-class discussions and critical writing in which they learned how to effectively express their view points. Each writing assignment usually undergoes 4–5 revisions. Many times, each revision requires new and advanced ideas, and is like a new assignment.

In-class instructional methods vary. Several methods can be applied to a single course: lectures, recitations, laboratory classes, and writing classes. For example, the course of Foundations of Science has four 75-min lectures every week. Every week, it also has two 75-min recitations, and one 90-minute lab. The course of Society under Views of Globalization has one lecture, two recitations, and one writing session every week. The course is co-taught by Dr. Jeffery Lehman, the vice chancellor from U.S., and Professor Paul Roman. The two course instructors have different backgrounds, one in economics and the other is in law. They apply different perspectives that help students use different lenses in understanding different views and phenomena. The integrated teaching methods aligns teaching and learning, which provide students with time to engage in deep learning.

7.2   *Academic Resource Center*

NYU Shanghai has hired several teaching assistants (TAs) who provide teaching support to professors. Some of these teaching assistants have doctoral and master's degrees, others have bachelor's degrees. They provide students with one-on-one help in writing, mathematics, and science course through face-to-face meetings. Students go online to request tutoring help, and meet teaching assistants in the Academic Resource Center. Students highly appreciate tutoring help from TAs, who play an important role in student improved learning. Undergraduate students gave TAs good remarks for their knowledge and for their excellent teaching skills. NYU Shanghai does not pay TAs regular instructor salary, but an allowance.

I have suggested to ECNU President Chen Qun that NYU Shanghai can hire graduate students who are in master and doctoral programs. ECNU has offered them various types of scholarships. This is a pool with many talents. If they are hired as a TA with defined teaching responsibilities and higher salaries (than the scholarship), it will be beneficial to both undergraduate students and graduate students. Faculty members have limited meeting times with students. Hiring more TAs will provide students with more individual tutoring help. These teaching practices in turn will promote TAs' professional development.

7.3   *Assessment*

Assessment in NYU Shanghai focuses on three procedures. First, making the process dynamic. Each course instructor can have his/her own ways of assessment consistently throughout the semester. It is important that the instructor explains the policy to students on the first day. Many instructors use the average of all midterm grades as the course grade. Grading methods like this give student incentive to keep working hard. Second, emphasizing discipline norms. In the course of Science Foundation of the first semester, students were assigned a team research project. Students used posters to report their results. They had guidelines and made changes following the feedback from the instructor. These posters are similar to those submitted to international conferences of several professional societies. One student told me another example regarding citations in writing research paper. She did not properly quote other people's work. The instructor took it seriously, and required her to write a statement concerning plagiarism. Though she learned it the hard way, she believed she would not forget the experience. A lack of instruction in research paper writing including proper citations draws our attention to the assessment of research projects. Students need to know what a discipline's norm is and should learn how to be responsible to such norms. Feedback from the instructor's assessment prepares students for their future job and research. Third, the emphasis of hands-on skills. For example, the final project for the course of Interactive Media Technology is an exhibition of students' own product. The course integrates technology with arts, which stimulates students' creativity. The course also helps students develop skills in using technology. The course requires substantial funds in building infrastructures, expanding curriculum, and providing financial aids to students. In general, tuition in NYU Shanghai is high, but adequate resources turn most ideas into impressive products.

7.4   *Choosing a Major*

At the end of the second year, students have to choose a specific field. NYU Shanghai offers twelve majors, approved by the Chinese Ministry of Education. Two majors are in social science, one in humanities, and nine in science, technology, engineering, and mathematics (STEM). Table 8.3 shows the current majors in NYU Shanghai.

7.4.1   Student Services

Student services reflect the visions and goals of NYU Shanghai, and contribute to university culture in significant ways. The university has established a professional team to assist students. To facilitate cultural awareness, student dorm arrangement purposefully mixes Chinese and international students, which helps students better understand and communicate with people who grow up in a different country with different background. Students are encouraged to create organizations for various goals: public service, volunteer work, sports, art, music, performance, etc. Student services help students get out of the classroom and enrich their learning experiences by engaging in a

TABLE 8.3   *Majors in NYU Shanghai (current)*

Social Sciences (4)	Business and Finance; Business and Marketing; Economics; Social Science
Humanities (3)	Humanities; Global China Studies; Interactive Media Arts
Science (4)	Physics; Chemistry; Biology; Neural science
Mathematics (2)	Honors Mathematics; Mathematics
Computer Science and Computer Engineering (4)	Computer Science; Data Science; Computer Engineering Systems; Electrical Engineering Systems
Self-Designed Honors Major	

SOURCE: NYU SHANGHAI UNDERGRADUATE BULLETIN (2016–2017)

broad range of activities that are not only beneficial to the society but also to their own personal and professional development.

The career center is an important part of students services. The center has developed a four-year plan for students:

- *1st year:* Introduction to career development.
- *2nd year:* Explorations of career development directions – finding a fit and path.
- *3rd year:* Enhancing traits and skills for the career.
- *4th year:* Preparing to transition from a university student to a real-world worker.

In order to help students get their foot on career development as early as in their first year in the university, NYU Shanghai holds the "Career Fairs Month" every year. In 2013, the university and a career development company jointly held the activity and provided workshops, presentations, and "afternoon tea hours" with company recruiters. These activities offered students excellent opportunities to meet with company recruiters. Some of these one-on-one and face-to-face meetings helped students learn how to introduce and present themselves to companies and future employers while networking with representatives of various companies and research institutions. Students also learned how to perform in job interviews. Students learned what specific qualities and skills that companies look for, and how to find a fit that mutually benefits the employer and employee. We are very pleased to learn that many companies think highly of NYU Shanghai students.

8   Summary and Conclusion: Working Hard to Reach Goals

NYU Shanghai is now going into its third year. We continue to explore ways and new models for higher education reform in modern China, and work very hard to reach our ambitious goal. Among many challenges we have encountered was to sustain funding needed in providing financial aid and scholarship, updating libraries, establishing Chair Professorship, etc. In 2013, NYU Foundation assisted with fund raising. The starting funds from the city of Shanghai were very helpful. Yet, the high standard for education excellence of NYU Shanghai is in demand. Our students are from middle class families, and some of them demand financial support. The university has the responsibility to help all students succeed regardless of their family financial status. We offered scholarships as well as financial aid to 2013 incoming students. Supported by Shanghai Municipal Government, the NYU Shanghai Education Foundation was incorporated. The foundation plays a critical role to get donations from society.

There is also progress in building research infrastructure. Jointly, ECNU and NYU have established four research centers: Mathematics, Neural Science, Computational Chemistry, and Society Development. Several other joint research centers, including data science, city planning, financing, and physics are under planning and construction. These research centers will support and promote research and graduate student training. They will also enrich undergraduate students' research experiences. ECNU and NYU Shanghai have also established mechanisms that promote and support sharing recourses, which include higher levels of coordination, joint research center planning and construction, human resources, budget and finance management, student services, faculty and staff benefits, safety and security issues, news media, etc. The agreement allows both ECNU and NYU Shanghai students to share and take the advantage of resources that are available to them.

Note

1   Translated by Jia-Ling Lin, University of Minnesota.

Reference

NYU Shanghai. (n.d.). *In Wikipedia.* Retrieved from https://zh.wikipedia.org/wiki/
上海纽约大学

About the Authors

Yu Lizhong is the first Chancellor of New York University Shanghai, having held this position since 2012. He joined NYU Shanghai from East China Normal University (ECNU), where he served as president from 2006–2012. Prior to his time at ECNU, he also served as president of Shanghai Normal University. Yu Lizhong holds a PhD in Geography from University of Liverpool and honorary doctorates from École Normale Supérieure and University of Liverpool.

Jia-Ling Lin (jllin@umn.edu) graduated with a BS in physics from Shanghai Jiaotong University, MS in physics from the University of Wisconsin-Madison, and PhD in condensed matter physics from the University of Illinois at Urbana-Champaign. Dr. Lin was a scientist specializing nanotechnology and surface science at the University of Wisconsin-Madison. She later served as the director of the Undergraduate Learning Center in the College of Engineering at the University of Wisconsin-Madison before moving to Minnesota. Currently, Dr. Lin is a research scientist in the STEM Education Center at the University of Minnesota. Her research focuses on two distinct but correlated areas: innovative instructional model development and its impact on undergraduate engineering and science learning. Jia-Ling was awarded the title of Distinguished Overseas Professor for Collaborative Innovation Center for National Education Policy-making, CICNEP, East China Normal University in 2014. Dr. Lin has numerous peer- reviewed publications in physics and in engineering education.

CHAPTER 9

China Champion Program

Chi Jian and Li Li Ji

Abstract

The China Champion Program (CCP) is a special graduate program of the Beijing Sport University. It provides a select group of China's elite athletes with one year of time to study in a major university in the United States focusing on English language training, science, education, social-culture events, and professional skills pursuant to their own fields. Since the inaugural class of 2010, six classes of CCP have graduated from the University of Wisconsin-Madison and the University of Minnesota-Twin Cities. The major financial source of the program comes from the China Scholarship Council, providing international travel and living cost, whereas the hosting universities and local communities has offered generous support for their language training, courses and social interactions. The athletes and coaches graduated from the CCP have expressed overwhelmingly positive feedback and appreciation. Many of the graduates have achieved their career goals and attributed their accomplishments to the experiences gained from the CCP. Although the CCP has provided China's top athletes with an opportunity for their post-competitive professional development, the population who received this benefit is still small and limited to the top tier. This unique model of supplementary education for China's athletes may reflect some interesting characteristics of the Chinese educational system and the contribution an American university can made in this collaboration.

1 Introduction

Since China returned to the international Olympic Games in 1984, there have been astonishing achievements made by the Chinese teams in a broad spectrum of sports. Hundreds of accomplished athletes have received Olympic medals and champion titles in various sports. With the exception of a very small number of athletes who have continued to compete, the vast majority has retired from the field. Most of the retired athletes have elected to study in higher education at home and some have gone abroad. According to the record of 2008, 82% of the Olympic medalists held a Bachelor's degree, while 28% held a Master's degree (China Alumni Network, 2008). Because of the academic reputation and enrollment capacity, Beijing Sport University (BSU) became their number one choice for study, followed by Shanghai Jiao Tong University, Qing Hua University, Beijing University and Chinese People University (China Alumni Network, 2008).

Founded in 1953, BSU is the largest and oldest Sport University in China. It has played an important role in producing China's top athletes, as well as providing their post-competition reeducation. The BSU Champion Graduate Program, established in 2003, was intended to offer these athletes (and coaches) an opportunity to return to the university and earn a Master's degree through a curriculum tailored to suit their professional needs and work schedules. With the slogan, "Driven to Discover," the program adopted a number of innovative ways to teach in accordance with the students' background and needs, such as setting practicum stations within the national sport teams, academic quality control through mid-term examination, blind review of theses, and establishment of an educational foundation. Furthermore, the program promoted transformation of intellectual outcomes, international exchanges and collaborations with partner universities at home and abroad. From 2003 to 2016, the program graduated 322 champion students including 82 Olympic medalists, 182 world champions and 58 coaches who trained champion athletes (China Sport, 2008). The successful operation of the Champion Graduate Program has, to a certain extent, helped resolve a major challenge for the Chinese government to provide reeducation and job placement for elite athletes following their competitive career. "The top athletes and coaches are the treasure of our country," said BSU President Chi Jian, "how to reeducate them and bring their personal potential to full potential is both a social program and practical issue in order to make China's competitive sports sustainable and strong."

During a visit to China by a delegation formed by Kinesiology deans and chairs of eleven CIC (Central Institutional Consortium) universities in 2009, the then BSU Vice-president Chi Jian asked Li Li Ji, Chair of Kinesiology Department at University of Wisconsin-Madison, whether it was feasible for some of the champion athletes to have an overseas experience during their study. This inquiry launched a new era of the BSU Champion Graduate Program, eventually named "China Champion Program" (CCP). Within the last eight years, six classes of CCP went to UW-Madison and the University of Minnesota Twin Cities (UMTC) to spend 8–10 months studying language, culture, science and education at the host institutions and communities. The participants of the CCP brought back advanced knowledge, educational philosophy, and professional experience to BSU and their home institutions.

Many of them have developed into successful teachers, coaches, government officers, community leaders and businesspersons. The story of CCP is one of the most inspiring episodes of China's Reform and Openness course in sports over the past decade. In 2012, when the U.S. and China celebrated the 40th year of diplomatic relations, a photo of the CCP appeared in the centerfold of the Brochure of Memory, highlighting the significance of the program (Fig 9.2). The main purpose of this chapter is to provide the readers with an overview of the origin, progress, achievements and perspective of the CCP from the eyes of the authors who have developed and overseen the program.

1.1   *Demand to Provide Post-Career Education for China's Top Athletes*
After the successful return of China to the world's sport arena, China developed a Gold Medal Strategy to improve athletic performance in as many events as possible. The "production line" of elite athletes was based on a three-level training network, namely local amateur youth sport schools, competitive central sport schools at major cities and provinces, and national teams. In these levels of institutions, athletic training was the priority and encompassed most of the athletes' daily schedules, whereas cultural education had been compromised due to lack of systematic supervision and effective enforcement. As a result, many of China's top athletes and coaches, after a successful career in sports, lacked sufficient education and professional experience outside his/her sport event and thus faced difficulty in reeducation and job replacement [3]. This problem not only affected the athletes' individual post-competition career, but also hindered the sustainability of China's competitive sports as a whole and created social pressure. In 2005, Liu Peng, the then Director of the National Sport Bureau pointed out during a visit to BSU: "we must deeply recognize the challenge and seriously investigate the challenge of integrating education and sport training."

Three levels of deficiencies were identified among the top athletes: (1) Many athletes did not complete a 12-year public education due to early enrollment in certain sport schools. This placed sport training above general education; (2) During their enrollment period at BSU and other colleges, some athletes missed a considerable portion of their curricula due to conflicts with sport games, competitions, and training schedules; and (3) Even within the athletes' own specialties, there was insufficient scientific knowledge about the theory and practice of the sport due to the limitation of their coaches' background and training. Thus, the demand foreseen in the reeducation of these athletes and coaches were two-fold: (1) to elevate their educational quality and (2) to provide them with professional skills and ability to adapt to the current and prospective jobs.

The founding of a special program called the Champion Class at BSU in November 2003 was regarded as a turning point and a step in the right direction. The program admitted 54 of the Olympic medalists, world champions and medal coaches enrolled in the BSU graduate school. Because these students were retired from competition and given adequate time to take courses, conduct research, and write theses, their systematic knowledge and practical capacity were enriched and elevated to a new level. A challenge to run the Champion Class was that virtually all students were full-time employees at government offices, for national teams, training centers and other professional posts. To overcome scheduling dilemmas, most of the courses were conducted during the off-season (the break period of training such as the middle to end of November), with three and half hours of class in the morning and afternoon. Some students could not leave their training sites due to the demands of their training schedules. So some courses were taught at their respective home bases. The courses required for the Champion Class are found in Table 9.1.

By July 2008, five years after the inauguration of the Champion Class, three students completed their doctoral program and 21 Master's students passed their defenses. Their theses and dissertations provided new insights into the theory and practice of the various sports in which they participated, and they received positive feedback from the various positions they served. Eleven Champion Class students were elected to be members of the National People's Congress, or the 17th Party Congress or National Political Consultation Committee. For example, Li Linwei, regarded as the Queen of Badminton in China, was one of the three doctoral students in the Champion Class. She received her doctoral degree with the dissertation topic "Evolution and perspective of the Summer Olympic Games," which attracted attention from the IOC. In 2007, she was appointed by IOC President Rouge to be a member of the IOC Event Subcommittee.

1.2   *From the Champion Class to the China Champion Program*

The year 2008 was a turning point in China's course of competitive sports, when the Beijing Olympic Games produced a record of Olympic medalists and coaches in a wide range of events. Meanwhile, the successful organization and operation of the Olympic Games attracted delegations and visitors from all over the world to Beijing and China's major cities. The CIC Chairs and Deans in Kinesiology was an alliance that convened every year to share issues of common interests, including its globalization efforts. A year earlier, a decision was made to form a CIC delegation that would visit major sport universities, as well as Kinesiology departments of comprehensive universities. The eleven-member delegation who were dispatched in Fall of 2008 was the largest group of such in the Sino-U.S. history. Learning how China educated its huge

TABLE 9.1   *Sample curriculum of the champion class*

Course title	Credit Hr.	Instruction Hr.	Meeting Hr.
Natural Dietetics	2	32	16
Foreign Language	8	64	32
Specialty Theory	8	32	16
Theoretic Basis of Sport Training	2	32	16
Functional Monitoring and Assessment of Athletes	1	16	8
Analysis and Dynastic of Athletic Techniques	2	32	16
Nutritional Supplementation and Athletic Ability	1	16	8
Nutrition for Athletes	1	16	8
Strength Training	2	32	16
Psychology of Training	2	32	16
Medical Supervision of Sport Training	1	16	8
Prevention of Athletic Injury	1	16	8
Effect of Hypoxia Training on Athletic Function	1	16	8
Detection and Control of Doping	1	16	8
Management and Education of Athletes	1	16	8
Theory of Sport Competition	1	16	8
Statistics and Measurement of Sports	2	32	16
Athletic Skills	2	32	16
Computer Application	2	32	16
Research Methods of Sports	1	16	8
Seminars	6	64	32

number of elite athletes and coaches after they retired from their competitive careers was a topic of great interest to the delegation. During the visit to BSU, Chi Jian, who was a visiting scholar at the University of Michigan in 1998, was candid about the challenges facing the Chinese government and universities to provide post-career education and training. Knowing well that in the U.S., competitive athletes are housed mainly in universities and colleges as "student athletes" who receive academic preparations and sport training at the same time, he asked whether CIC institutions would accept a small number of athletes in BSU's Champion Class to study for a short period of time. Chi

Jian then invited Li Li Ji, the leader of the delegation to meet with a group of Champion Class athletes in a classroom. Ji is a U.S.-educated professor but has kept close contact with China over the years and was well aware of the Chinese challenges. He rationalized that due to their limited English levels, Chinese athletes would not succeed if they were dispatched individually to scattered American Universities. Instead, he suggested the formation of a cohort of Chinese champion athletes to be enrolled in a select U.S. institution with a special program. This suggestion was praised by the BSU leadership, but two main questions remained: (1) where would the funding come from for this ambitious study abroad mission; and (2) which American university would accept this group of "special students" with little English preparation? Obviously. Some special initiatives were required to manifest this idea.

Bitty Martin, the then Chancellor of the University of Wisconsin-Madison, played a critical role in the history of CCP that would not be forgotten. During her college years, she was a varsity basketball player, and her brother was a college basketball coach. In January 2010, Li Li Ji asked Vice President Vince Sweeny, with whom he became acquainted while serving on the UW Athletic Board, if it would be possible to host the Chinese champion athletes at the UW campus. Chancellor Martin called Li Li to her office the following day. "What? A group of Olympic athletes from China?" Her eyes lit up, "Let's do it!"

Meanwhile, Chi Jian was exercising all of his influences to convince the China Scholarship Council, the only funding agency under the Ministry of Education, to provide China's visiting scholars and doctoral students with financial support to study abroad, to set up a special quota for funding select Champion Class athletes. The news that UW-Madison would accept the athletes accelerated the review process. By late February, the Vice Minister of Education, the President of CSC, Hao Ping, approved the special program termed the China Champion Program. All the ingredients were in the pot waiting to be cooked.

On March 18, 2010, a motorcade was dispatched from the BSU campus to the Beijing Shangri-La hotel to pick up a UW-Madison delegation led by Chancellor Bitty Martin. The delegation was greeted with the warmest ceremony reserved for a state guest at the BSU National Team Training Complex. An announcement was made to the news media that a historical China Champion Program (CCP) would be launched and hosted at UW-Madison, on the opposite side of the globe. Chancellor Martin became an instant national name in China, while overwhelming public support flourished in newspapers, TV and radio stations in the capital. Two months later, an office MOU (Memorandum of Understanding) was signed in Beijing by UW-Madison, BSU and CSC leaders, which institutionalized the CCP. Fifteen of China's most decorated athletes, including women's Gold Medal swimmer Luo Xuejuan, Gold Medal Table

Tennis player Liu Guozheng, Captain of the China women's Olympic curling team Wang Bingyu, and Olympic Taekwondo coach Lu Xiudong, were enrolled in the Chinese Language University for three months of English language training.

July 1, 2010 was a hot Madison summer night. Hundreds of Chinese students and community members, along with dozens of UW faculty members having close ties with China, gathered in front of the Memorial Union. The Badger Marching Band was dispatched to Madison airport to welcome the arriving China Champion athletes, while Chancellor Martin was on her way to the airport. Unfortunately, a flight delay at the Chicago O'Hare airport caused the athletes to miss their connecting flight and they had to take a bus to Madison. The final arrival of the bus at almost midnight stirred a wave of applause as the first wave of CCP stepped off the bus. The next day, Chancellor Martin held a reception at her UW Presidential Residence on their behalf, attended by hundreds of China enthusiasts, completed with a marching band and Bucky Badger. Since that historical day, six classes of the CCP have studied in the U.S., three at UW-Madison and three at the University of Minnesota Twin Cities.

1.3   *A Unique Program*

Now that a class of nine athletes and coaches had been on the UW-Madison campus for a year, and the program had been broadcasted both in China and on American news media, phone calls and interview requests from the city, State of Wisconsin and China flooded UW's public relation office and Li Li Ji's office. One of the most asked questions was, "What occupies the Champions' daily schedules and what would they gain from the one-year study?" These questions circulated around Ji's mind. The first challenge was the athletes' English level. Except for one individual, most of the athletes had virtually no foreign language skills, which made it impossible for them to attend regular academic courses on campus. It was imperative that a special curriculum be designed to accommodate their special background and needs. Secondly, the athletes and coaches came from different sports, which required different scientific knowledge, practical training and management skills. Finally, there needed to be a group of competent instructors who were willing to teach this special class of highly accomplished athletes. Under the support of the Office of the Chancellor, a steering committee was formed to guide the curricular design, instructor recruitment, and supervision of the progress.

The English requirement was fulfilled at different levels. The formal classes were offered by the English as a Second Language (ESL) division on campus. Three instructors with ample experience were hired to teach listening comprehension, reading and vocabulary. This daily language training and practice were aimed to enable the athletes to gain basic grammatical

TABLE 9.2   *Fall course schedules for 2011 Chinese champion program*

Time	Monday	Tuesday	Wednesday	Thursday	Friday	Saturday	Sunday
8:30–11:30	ESL	ESL	ESL	ESL	ESL		
12:05–12:55		Ballroom Dance		Ballroom Dance	Seminar in Pedagogy		
1:20–2:10	Aquatic Conditioning Ren, Luo Modern Dance Sui, Xu Wt. Training 1 Liu, Fu, Xie, Wang		Aquatic Conditioning Ren, Luo, Xu Modern Dance Sui, Xu Wt. Training 1 Liu, Fu, Xie, Wang				
2:25–3:15	*Wt. Training 2* *Xie, Lu* Ballet II *Sui, Xu*	Sports training & Conditioning	*Wt. Training 2* *Xie, Lu* Ballet II *Sui, Xu*	Sports training & Condition			
3:45–4:35	Sport Nutrition Organization of Sport		Sport Nutrition Organization of Sport				
4:00–5:15		Amer. History		Amer. History			
6:00–8:00	Meeting with English tutors		Meeting with English tutors				Sport Events

background, engage in simple communication, and reading comprehension. Additional opportunities of learning and practice were provided by tutors in East Asia Language Department, School of Engineering and local communities such as churches, student organizations and sport clubs. Enthusiasts were delighted to make friends with China's top athletes to learn about Chinese culture, traditional Chinese sports, China's Olympic course and Chinese language. During a recent trip to Shanghai, Li Li came across a young business man at the airport who was an engineering student tutor of the CCP. He recalled with fond memory the experience of interacting with the Champion athletes, which he claimed played an important role in his decision to come to China and manage a factory.

Besides English classes, the athletes took academic courses taught by English speaking instructors with the support of a translator. The course contents were often adjusted to fit the athletes' background and language skills. Over the years the CCP created a list of 8-week short courses called "modules" to meet the specific needs of the athletes. These modules such as Exercise Physiology, Motor Control, Nutrition, Physical Education and Training, and Sport Management, provided scientific knowledge useful for the athletes for future career preparation. Furthermore, Li Li reached out to several department chairs on campus to permit champion athletes to audit courses offered in their respective departments, such as American History, Classical Music, Ballroom Dance and Ballet. These courses enriched the athletes' cultural experience and their appreciation of campus life. An example of the CCP course offerings in Fall 2010 is found in Table 9.2.

In 2014, after three successful classes of the CCP graduated, the program was translocated to the University of Minnesota Twin Cities, where Li Li Ji served as the Director of the School of Kinesiology. UMTC has a long-standing collaboration with China and enjoys widespread support from the campus, the community from Minneapolis-St. Paul, and the State. With an award-winning China Center, the infrastructure of exchanges with China is top-notch. A unique feature of the CCP curriculum at UMTC is its high quality instructors. For example, the course titled "Organization of Sport Events" is taught by former Gopher Athletic Director, Joe Maturi, and "Sport Law and Legal issues of Sport" was lectured by Michael Freeman, the Hannepin Country District Antony. UM Recreation and Wellness Center Director, James Turman, led a special facility tour for the athletes, when he delivered the lecture on sport facility management. Sometimes, classes taught by a graduate student offered just as much excitement and stimulus as the above-mentioned stars, as they provided casual discussion and hands-on opportunities. "Courses here in the U.S. are so different from Beijing Sport University," said Coach Lu, "This is why we came here."

Other than the regularly scheduled courses, athletes were involved in a wide spectrum of sport, social, cultural and business events. The athletes participated in these extracurricular activities to gain knowledge and experience not available within the classrooms. The university's varsity sports are the closest source of information for the champion athletes. To find that some of the best sports and athletes are housed not in the national training center, as in their home country, but on a university campus, was fascinating to them. They were not only the regular spectators of the Badger and Gopher games, but also appeared in training fields and ice arenas to observe practice routines of the varsity teams. By NCAA rules, foreign athletes and coaches are not permitted to be engaged in skill or technical exchanges with local university teams, yet the athletes gained valuable insights into the American systems, which were grossly different from their own experience at home. Athletic department leaders and university coaches treated them with great respect and support. Not only did they frequently receive tickets to spectate games and competitions, they were but also sometimes treated to the VIP suite and box rooms.

Another area attractive to the Chinese athletes and coaches is America's professional sports industry. The CCP organizers have made every effort to provide the athletes with opportunities to visit local professional sport teams and speak with the business leaders. Fortunately, the Twin Cities is the home of seven professional sport teams including the Minnesota Vikings, the Timberwolves, Minnesota United, the Wild, the Twins and the Lynx. They were treated with great respect and hospitality wherever they went. During a Milwaukee Brewers baseball game, the first CCP class was introduced to the entire audience during a break, stirring loud applause. At the Minnesota Timberwolves basketball headquarters, CEO Tim White personally guided the 4th class of the CCP with a tour of the facilities and the trophy room. With China's initiative to make sport a growing economic engine, these experiences are invaluable to the athletes' future endeavors and success.

The Chinese athletes did not just learn about American sport culture by attending sporting events. They also visited schools, clubs, local industry and private homes. Both the 1st and 2nd CCP classes were invited to the Mueller Sport Medicine Company and its President Brett Mueller's home as guests. They listened to the story of how a gum-selling hut grew into one of the largest supply chains of sport protection gear, which was a true success story of the American dream. In Chicago, the CCP students visited the home of UW Board of Trustee Bob Fitz, a Goldman-Sachs partner, and a downtown fitness club owned by UW alumnus Jasen Conviser. At the 3M Company headquarters, the 4th class visited the laboratory and showroom of new products, from reflective highway sign paint to the film attached to an iPhone. They also visited the largest medical equipment enterprise, Medtronic, in Minneapolis, and viewed a video about the company's own Olympic Games that it held for its employees.

While visiting political figures is probably the last activity you would think these athletes would participate in, with the support of UW and UMTC alumni and friends, the CCP has been able to integrate this unique experience into the athletes' program. In 2015, Minnesota Governor Mark Dayton invited the 4th CCP class to his Residence for a casual lunch, where he recalled with fond memory his numerous visits to China. The athletes learned that the Dayton family was one of the largest collectors of Chinese art crafts in the United States, and the family has donated most of them to the Minnesota Institute of Art. The following year, former Vice-President Walter Mondale received the 6th CCP class in his residence where he gave an emotional conversation about the role of sports in Sino-U.S. relations. Everyone was greatly moved when the Vice-President recalled how he went to Beijing in 1979 with President Jimmy Carter and had multiple meetings with Deng Xiaoping, who opened China's door to the West. The same year, China and the United States established formal diplomatic relations, eight years after the ice-breaking journal of President Richard Nixon in 1972. "That was the Ping-Pong diplomacy," the Vice-President commented with a glow in his eyes.

FIGURE 9.1. *The signing ceremony attended by Vice-President of Beijing Sport University Chi Jian (left), University of Wisconsin-Madison Chancellor Bitty Martin (middle), China Scholarship Council Secretary General Li (right) and Vice-Minister of Education Hao Ping (middle back)*

FIGURE 9.2.   *The 2010 CCP class were greeted during the University of Wisconsin-Madison homecoming football game. From the left: Lu Xiudong, Xie Yong, Fu Tianyu, Liu Guozheng, Xu Yaping, Ren Jie, Luo Xuejuan, Chancellor Bitty Martin, Wang Bingyu and Sui Jianshuang*

1.4   *It Has Changed the Champion Athletes' Life*

Six CCP classed have graduated since the program was inaugurated in 2010. According to the BSU archives, a total of 68 athletes and coaches have gone through the program. Other than three who studied at the Bilgen University in Norway, four who studied at Indiana University, and two who studied at the University of North Carolina at Chapel Hill as individual students (i.e., not as a class), most were enrolled in the University of Wisconsin-Madison and the University of Minnesota Twin Cities. A question may be asked: "What have the athletes accomplished, and what are they doing now after graduation?"

Providing an accurate and reliable answer to this question requires some careful investigation and analysis, which is beyond the purpose of this report. However, one thing is clear: the CCP has changed the life path of each individual even though the program only lasted less than one year. The authors have kept in contact with many of the former CCP members who consistently say with one voice: the program completely changed their perspectives of career and life. Because most of athletes started their training at a very young age, the exposure to the outside world has been quite limited. Although they have had numerous opportunities to attend international competitions and games, the experiences were restricted to sport arenas, fields and hotels. Besides becoming a coach, there was little inspiration and vision which they could acquired through their competitive career. Through contact with many post-competition athletes and coaches in the U.S., such as business owners, politicians, academic professionals, and teachers, they realized that only the sky is the limit for a successful athlete. "In the U.S., sport experience can be a useful knocking brick of new windows of life," they said. China is currently in the transition from an exclusively government-owned and -operated sport enterprise to a newer model which combines state, industry, social organization and private ownership. This transition has provided, and will provide, more opportunities for retired athletes to pursue their individual goals and inspirations, as long as they have the vision, courage, education and skills.

FIGURE 9.3.   The 2010 CCP members at the graduation ceremony of the University of Wisconsin-Madison. From the left: Ren Jie, Wang Binyu, Xu Yaping, Sui Jinashuang, Lu Xiudong, Luo Xuejuan, Fu Tianyu, Liu Guozheng, and Xie Yong

Several success stories of former CCP members may help enhance the above point of view. Xu Yaping, the former world champion of kayaking, chose to take a teaching position in the Physical Education Activity program at Zhejiang University. After the initial struggle of balancing work, family and raising a child, she gained inspiration and momentum for establishing an aquatic club to enrich student spare time and promote physical activity. Her persistence and relentless effort has paid off. Now she oversees a program with more than

100 watercrafts and more than 600 club members. With annual participants numbering over 3,000, it is one of the most successful student sport teams of such on Chinese campuses. Her work has expanded to other Zhejiang university campuses and around the country. "My dream is to return to UMTC to gain a doctoral degree so that I can promote China's aquatic sports more effectively," she recently told the authors.

FIGURE 9.4.   *The 2014 CCP class with the University of Minnesota and Twin Cities community members at an alumnus' home. Athletes in uniforms: front from left, Xu Qing, Ma Yibo, Gao Lihua, Li Ting, Zhang Hui, Zhang Shuo, Yang Senlian; Send row: Lu Chunlong; 3rd row: Li Bingwei, 4th from left, Zhao Delin*

Many CCP athletes were inspired to become teachers and they returned to BSU or other universities to teach either their specialty sport, or the "common physical education" classes for all students. Sui Jianshuang and Zhang Shuo, the two Olympic Rhythmic Gymnastics athletes, both continued their careers at BSU by teaching and training the next-generation of gymnasts. Last year, Sui was the choreographer for a performance show "Flying Snow Flakes," which debuted on CCTV for National New Year Eve Celebration. This is not surprising to the authors because a 12-minute video clip Sui made and showed at the graduation ceremony of the 1st CCP class in 2010 was so well-done that it moved numerous viewers to tears.

Many of the most celebrated athletes who graduated from the CCP continued their coaching or even competitive careers. For them, the experience in an American university was more subtle and probably more academic than technical. Liu Guozheng, the household name of China's table tennis, returned to his beloved sport and currently coaches the Chinese National Youth team in Beijing after graduating from the 1st CCP. His coaching schedule has been so busy that almost any time one tries to reach him, he is either in the training arena or on the road traveling. Wang Bingyu, the captain of the four "Curling Girls" who won a bronze medal at the Vancouver Winter Olympic Games and was member of the 1st CCP class, recently gave birth to a child. Last year, she was called back to lead a new national curling team for competing at the coming 2018 Winter Olympic Games in South Korea. Another winter sport athlete, Gold Medal winner of Olympic short-track ice skating Zhang Hui, has stated a skating school to train children and youths in her home town of Harbin. During her visit to the UMTC campus, she gained invaluable experience by routine involvement in local skating activities at public schools and clubs. "The Twin Cities is a paradise for winter sports," she said to Li Li Ji during his visit to Harbin in January 2016. "I really miss my friends and want to revisit with them in the near future," said Zhang. With China's successful bidding for the 2022 Winter Olympics, great emphasis has been placed on training athletes and coaches in winter sports. The CCP expects to host an increasing number of Champions in the years to come.

FIGURE 9.5. *The CCP class of 2014 at the Minnesota Governor Mark Dayton's residence. Front from left: Gao Lihua, Li Bingwei, Xu Qing, Governor Tayton, Zhang Shuo, Li Li Ji, Minnesota Higher Education Commissioner Larry Griffiths; Second from left: Yang Chunli, Ma Yibo, Sandy Wang (student), Lu Chunlong, Yang Senlian; back left: Li Ting, Zhang Hui*

One of the biggest achievements for the CCP athletes and coaches is the improvement of their English skills and capacity. Although most athletes found it challenging to keep up with English proficiency when they returned to China due to limited practice opportunities, there have been exceptions. World swimming champion, Zhou Yafei, was one of the hardest working athletes during her study at UW-Madison, without knowing when the language she diligently practiced would be put to use. However, opportunity knocked, when in 2012, one year after she returned to China, the World Swimming Championship was held in Shanghai and she was appointed as one of the commentators. Her knowledge of the sport and her English ability impressed both spectators and the television audience. Since then, Yafei has been the first choice of commentators for all major swimming competitions whether they are domestic or international.

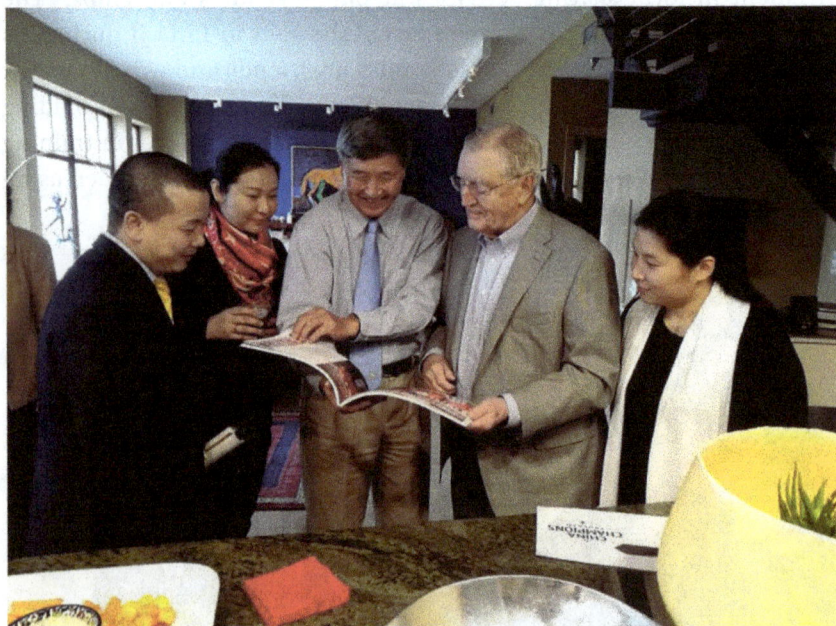

FIGURE 9.6.   *Former Vice-President Walter Mondale listened to the introduction of the CCP*
              with members of the 2015 CCP class at his residence in Minneapolis. From the left:
              Lu Xiudong, Wang Chunlu, Li Li Ji, VP Walter Mondale and Liu Haixia

One of the important goals for the CCP curriculum is to broaden the vision of the champion athletes. They are encouraged to contact people from a wide range of background in the hosting campus and city. The rationale for this approach is that the CCP members are not only champion athletes, but also have the potential to become leaders of their respective specialty, or even leaders of public offices. "The CCP provided us with numerous opportunities to learn about American society, including politics, education, history, and culture," said coach Lu Xiudong, who trained Chen Zhong, the first and most well-known Taekwondo Olympic Gold Medalist. After returning to BSU as a professor, he was appointed to the deputy director of the Competition Department. "The CCP can prepare us to take on any responsibilities as long as we have a vision," he said. Luo Xuejuan, China's Queen of the Breast Stroke, who received two gold medals at the Barcelona Olympic Games, is also an example. She was named as the Assistant to the Director of China's Aquatic Center, which oversees all training and competition of aquatic events in China. Wang Chunlu, the current Secretary General of Chinese Winter Sports, is enrolled in the 6th CCP class at UMTC. Her inspiration is very clear: to acquire administrative skills to serve as a qualified and visionary government official. She even has a dream of serving on the IOC some day and is working diligently to improve her English level. Lu Chunlong, the Gold Medal winner in Trampoline at the London Olympic Games and a member of the 5th CCP class, was named the deputy director of the Gymnastics Center at Jiangsu Province. During a recent reunion with him, the author heard a confident voice from him with a smile: "The experience during the CCP often inspires me to do better at my current job."

2   Summary

The CCP is a unique program in which top Chinese champion athletes spend up to a year of their Master's degree study in an American university as a visiting scholar. The program has filled some of the athletes' academic deficiencies during their competitive lives, enriched their social and professional skills and provided unprecedented experience for their future endeavors. The program has received overwhelming positive feedback from the athletes and coaches and gained high recognition from Chinese authorities.

However, even though the program has run for eight years, the CCP remains a pioneer program and has several limitations which require attention. First, it is a relatively small program accepting only a select group of top athletes. At present, the program cannot be expanded to a larger population of retired athletes after their competitive career. China still faces the challenge of reeducating the majority of its athletes with a domestic program that can benefit more and cost less. Second, the English proficiency of the athletes poses a major limiting factor for the quality of the program. Currently, most of the athletes' time and a significant amount of resource are spent on learning English as a second language, which could have been prepared before they left for the United States. Future programs should focus more on academic and professional preparations, while adequate language skills are required as a prerequisite.

Third, because the athletes enrolled in the CCP are from a wide range of sports, the needs for education and training may also vary widely. Thus, aside from general programmatic offerings, specific courses and activities need to be developed to meet their group or individual needs. Finally, the financial status of the program is still uncertain. Although the CSC provides the transportation and living expenses for the students, there is currently no established source for institutional education cost in the U.S. The authors appreciate the generous support received so far from the American university leaders, local communities, American Chinese community, industries and friends, and appeal for more investment and support to make the program sustainable and strong.

In the long run, the success and limitation of the CCP reflect a deep-rooted dilemma of the China's competitive sports: to produce a large number of highly successful athletes requires early recruitment and intense training, usually accomplished within a highly specialized sport school system. However, this isolated sport-first, academics-second formula compromises the athletes' public education quality and sets the stage for their struggle to succeed or even survive later in their professional lives. It is imperative that the system undergo reforms so that athletes can gain enough education and learning during, instead of after, their competitive career. The CCP has highlighted the urgency of this reform.

References

China Alumni Network. (2008). *Alumni.* Retrieved from http://www.sina.com.cn
China Sport. (2008). *Education made gold medals shine.* August 8.
Chinese Communist Party Central Committee and the State Council. (2002). *Guidelines to strengthen and improve matters related to sports in the new era* (Zhong Fa document No. 8).

About the Authors

Chi Jian is the President of Beijing Sport University (BSU). Prior to this post he served as Vice President, Vice Chairman of the University Council and Receiver of the Special Government Allowances of the State Council, Dean of Graduate School, and Director of Academic Research for BSU. In addition to his roles at his university, Jian has served as Chairman of the Sport Management Association of China Sport Science Society and as Vice Chairman of the Chinese Gymnastics, Swimming, Judo, and Karate Associations.

Li Li Ji is Professor and Director of the School of Kinesiology at UMTC since 2011. He graduated from East China Normal University in 1976, received his MS in 1982 and PhD in 1985 from the University of Wisconsin-Madison, and continued as a postdoctoral researcher at the Institute of Enzyme Research. He was an Assistant and Associate Professor at University of Illinois at Urbana-Champaign during 1987–1993. He returned to UW-Madison and was promoted to Full Professor in 1997. During 1997–2010 Dr. Ji served as Chair of the Department of Kinesiology for 10 years. Dr. Ji's research focuses on cellular and molecular exercise physiology, especially the role of free radicals and antioxidants in cellular function, adaptation, pathogenesis, and aging. He has published widely in his field, given numerous invited lectures, and served on multiple editorial boards and study sections. He is a member of the National Academy of Kinesiology and holds several guest professorships in China.

CHAPTER 10

Sino-Global Higher Education Partnerships: Student Mobility Programs

Jing Tian, Jiansheng Ma, and Juan Cai

Abstract

China sends the largest proportion of international students to U.S. higher education institutions, acts as the country which contributes the largest population of international students globally, and is increasingly attracting global students in the 21st century. Accompanied by students' bi-directional international mobility, Chinese higher education institutions have established a wide ranging global network. Although Chinese student mobility can be traced back to the late Qing dynasty, only after China adopted the reform and opening-up policy in 1978 did the Sino-global partnerships based on student mobility become a nationwide phenomenon in China. In addition to China's policies related to higher education mobility, massification of the higher education sector in the late 1990s and accession to the WTO in 2001 have dramatically influenced Chinese students' mobility prospects. In response to these rapid social changes and distinct characteristics, the popularization of studying abroad in Sino-global higher education partnerships was shaped. This chapter will present a student mobility scenario for Chinese students from historical, economic, political and educational perspectives in Chinese higher education institutions.

1 Introduction

Higher education partnerships are formal agreements spelling out collaborations on mutual goals between two higher education institutions (Morgan, 2014). Partnerships are often transnational, with activities that aim to produce new forms of scientific research or develop student capacity through mobility programs (Huang & Feng, 2012). International partnerships may also focus on joint business ventures, teacher exchange, mutual recognition of academic credentials and degrees, participation in, and holding of, international academic conferences, and technical assistance (Marginson & Sawir, 2005).

© KONINKLIJKE BRILL NV, LEIDEN, 2018 | DOI 10.1163/9789004368361_010

According to the British Council, student mobility can be divided into outbound mobility and inbound mobility (British Council, 2014). These classifications are widely accepted by the U.S., EU member countries, and other international organizations such as OECD and UNESCO. The American Council on Education indicates that student mobility, which refers to the outward flow of domestic students and engagement in an education abroad experience on one hand, and the inward flow of international students to study at U.S. campuses, on the other hand, is often a core focus of internationalization efforts in the U.S. (ACE, 2016). Such mobility is often characterized as either regional mobility and global mobility. Regional mobility describes mobility on different continents within a broad region (e.g., Asia and Oceania) or within countries themselves, while global mobility is often considered as mobility that crosses different regions of the world (Munz & Reiner, 1988).

In the internationalization era, China's higher education system is undergoing continuous reforms driven by economic, political, and educational considerations. The overall enrollment in Chinese higher education institutions is the highest in the world (Xie, Hou, & Li, 2011). At the same time, Chinese students represent the largest portion of international students in the world (Wang, 2012). The sheer number of students enrolled in or seeking opportunities in higher education creates possibilities for Sino-global partnerships that allow for focused flows of students from China to other countries and vice versa. This chapter seeks to analyze the processes of Chinese international higher education partnerships based on international student mobility programs from a historical perspective. It explores the motivations, effectiveness, problems, and characteristics of Sino-global higher education partnerships. The chapter then probes how and to what extent China's social-economic and political development and large-scale education reforms have influenced student mobility.

2 History

Student mobility programs can be traced back to the late Qing dynasty in China. The Qing regime was disastrously defeated in the First and Second Opium War (1840–1860), and the subsequent disillusion of China's Celestial Empire stimulated the Qing regime to look outward for learning opportunities. Post-defeat, the Qing region focused on gaining science and technology information from the Western world as a strategy to make China strong again. The strategy, characterized as "learning from the barbarians and warding off the barbarians," had been part of the Chinese salvation movement (Guo & Guo, 2016). Sending students to study in the West was a direct way to accomplish this goal. The government selected 120 young boys to study in the U.S. for a duration of 15 years beginning in 1871 (Zhongshan Overseas Chinese Affairs, 2013). Students were selected to acquire specialized skills such as shipping, mining, transportation, and medical science. The main destinations of these students were European countries and Japan. At this early stage, the scale of the study abroad plan remained very small (Feng, 1993). As the program evolved, China established new connections in the U.S. and Russia and began to leverage student mobility for informing science and politics successively until the middle of the 20th century.

Modern China has experienced fundamental changes in the last four decades, following the implementation of the reform and opening-up policy in the late 1970s. Comprehensive reforms focused on increasing economic prosperity for Chinese citizens and fostering the emergence of opened markets. Economic reforms trickled down to the education sector, whereby institutions experienced new opportunities to engage globally. Consistent reforms have continued since 1978 and have led to further development of the higher education system in China, which include the massification efforts that began in the late 1990s. China's reforms have facilitated a new era of education internationalization, which will likely remain a priority of education administration departments from central to local government (Li, 2012). Among various internationalization approaches, student mobility has become a cornerstone of China's higher education sector.

3   Motivations

There are various rationales for internationalization and student mobility, including economic growth, national competitiveness, regional development and responsiveness to political initiatives. These rationales can best be explained through a push-pull model that several scholars have used to characterize internationalization efforts in higher education (Altbach, 1998; Mei & Mark, 2007; García & Villarreal, 2014).

3.1   *Push and Pull Factors*
Push factors in student international mobility are more often related to domestic higher education and overseas higher education (Fang & Wang, 2014). Some students are "pushed" to study abroad because of a disadvantageous situation in the home higher education sector or economic challenges that exist in the home country (Altbach, 1998). The booming massification of higher education in the late 1990s has exacerbated the severe shortage of higher education institutions in China. High-quality higher education resources, especially for graduate education, are relatively scarce. Studying abroad can bring abundant benefits for the students, including priority and competitiveness in the job market after receiving

a diploma abroad and returning home. Educational benefit considerations, economic considerations, and the opportunity structure for graduates are all influential factors that push Chinese students to seek international mobility (Netz, 2015). Pull factors are those that attract students to an international destination. For example, students may be pulled by the outstanding quality of a higher education sector abroad (Altbach, 1998) or may be attracted to experiencing an exotic culture, boosting intercultural capacity, broadening horizons, educational travel, or even for immigration (Duffield & Kerzman, 2013). For China, economic prosperity, the improvement of the nation's competitiveness in the higher education sector, and student mobility are all linked (Xie, Huo, & Li, 2011). Cooperating with and learning from other pioneering higher education institutions around the world is a key approach for the academic development of Chinese higher education. Therefore, the most powerful national factor influencing Sino-global higher education partnerships based on student mobility is a policy aim to improve higher education quality and economic opportunities for Chinese citizens. Although there are many push and pull factors that influence students on an individual level, student mobility through institutional partnerships is driven by a desire for specific sectoral and institutional outcomes, including: integrating international education resources for higher education improvement; pursuing the development of scale, structure, quality and effectiveness in relation to higher education; improving higher education institutions' international influence; cultivating the talents of students with global competence, optimizing human resources, and increasing global dialogue (Julius, 2014).

3.2   *Global Neoliberalism and Student Mobility*

Finally, an overarching rationale and driver of how student mobility is framed is neoliberalism. Higher education institutions in developed and developing countries have undergone dramatic reform under the influence of neoliberalism since the late 20th century. Neoliberal aspects such as loosening of economic regulations, free trade competition, and consumer sovereignty have influenced how student mobility is framed in China and around the world (Chang, 2015). Higher education neoliberalism reform molds the student mobility landscape. Beyond push-pull rationales, mobility is often characterized as a tradable service and the knowledge gained through exchanges as a commodity. Higher education institutions enjoy more autonomy and tend to attract more international students, and such attraction may have profit motives. Over the past decade, the world has seen an unprecedented increase in student mobility to Western countries in conjunction with the deepening of neoliberal reform in higher education institutions. The current era of high-volume, neoliberal-driven student mobility is informing the push-pull factors that exist for Chinese higher education institutions.

4   Sino-U.S. Partnerships and Student Mobility

As one of the most economically and culturally powerful countries in the world, China is playing a key role in the web of higher education global partnerships (Hou, 2014). The Chinese higher education system is constantly being reshaped by global partnerships and student mobility. The following sections outline contemporary Chinese policy and initiatives aimed at improving the quantity (numbers served) and quality (outcomes reached) of student mobility.

4.1   *Contemporary Policy and Sino-Global Partnerships*
With an increasing number of outbound international students, the Chinese government has proposed multiple policies to attract inbound international students since the early 2000s. For instance, the Chinese Ministry of Education launched the *Study in China Project* in 2010, which aimed to enlarge the scale of foreign students to 500,000 by 2020, making China the most popular receiving country of international students in Asia. The project also focused on improving educational quality overall by promoting higher education global partnerships through student mobility (MOE, 2010). The number of foreign students studying in China in 2014 was nearly 380,000 (EOL, 2014). Student mobility was stimulated by a portfolio of approaches, including student joint supervision, short-term visiting, international internships, cooperative scientific research, credit transfer, and international academic conferences.

4.2   *Global Competency, Soft Diplomacy, and Political Influence*
A central aim of student international mobility is to develop students' global and intercultural competencies (Yang, 2015). A second core aim is to develop deeper content knowledge through exposure to different instructors and cultural understanding of topics. These aims, along with the diplomatic and political goals of strengthening the friendship and understanding between people from different countries, and further promoting world peace and socialist modernization, led the Chinese government to establish scholarship programs to attract students from all around the world, and for select native students to study abroad since the late 1990s (China Scholarship Council, 2016). These scholarship programs serve to reinforce intercultural engagement and global competence in an immediate and intensive way. By studying abroad, Chinese students can disseminate distinctive cultural heritage to the world, while their exchange partners bring valuable cultural communication opportunities to China at the same time. Likewise, China's diplomatic and economic partner nations have launched similar programs for their students to study in China. For example, the British Council launched *Generation UK – China* in 2013. This program aims to help 80,000 UK students develop a global

mindset through study and work experience in China by 2020 (British Council, 2013).

4.3   Higher Education Reform

Student mobility is a core feature of recent Chinese higher education reforms focused on the creation of world-class universities. The China State Council issued the *Overall Plan for Promoting World-Class Universities and First-Class Discipline Construction* in 2015. Part of the pathway to world-class status was believed to be through the internationalization of higher education institutions and strengthening partnerships with other world-class higher education institutions (China State Council, 2015). As a result, Chinese higher education institutions have developed abundant mobility programs with an emphasis on institutional internationalization, and the forum of Sino-global partnerships have rolled out a wide range of projects. For instance, Tsinghua University (one of the top universities in China) developed *Excellent Freshman Overseas Visit Study Program*, providing opportunities for freshmen to experience the cultures of different countries and strengthen their global intelligence (Liu, 2011). Faculty mobility, curriculum internationalization, credit transfer systems, English courses, and trans-cultural education are additional initiatives designed to deepen higher education institution internationalization.

4.4   Rapid Development of Regional Higher Education Partnerships

Although not the topic of this book, there has also been a strong rise in regional international partnerships among Chinese higher education institutions (Yang, 2012). China is an active member of many regional cooperation organizations, such as the Asia-Pacific Economic Cooperation (APEC) and Association of Southeast Asian Nations (ASEAN). The common aim of these regional organizations is to promote member countries' economic prosperity and social stability through regional engagement with the help of locational advantages (Parton, 2011). The formation of stable regional higher education relationships can facilitate sharing cultural traditions, project-oriented goals and language development, and enhance the connection of higher education to regional communities (Goddard & Puukka, 2008). Apart from these advantages, the convenience of transportation and the relatively low cost of regional travel promote mobility in certain regional hubs. Although evidence suggests that the U.S. is still the destination of choice for Chinese international students, regional alliances may influence inbound and outbound student mobility.

Further reaching regionalism and strategic regional partnerships are found in the national initiative of building the Silk Road Economic Belt and the 21st Century Maritime Silk Road (or One Belt and One Road, for short). In 2013, the One Belt and One Road strategy assisted the development of higher education partnerships of 73 countries, ranging from South Asia to Middle Asia and South Europe (Maritime Silk Road, 2016). The Chinese government encourages students to study and intern in the partner countries and welcomes students from those countries studying in China by providing scholarship support to One Belt and One Road students (Zhou & Yue, 2014).

5   Problems

Although student mobility in the Chinese higher education sector has brought significant benefits for both the sector and its international partners, several problems still exist. For example, China has an international student deficit (meaning that more students leave China for international study than international students choose China). Second, although China is seeking world-class status for its universities, there are still gaps in internationally recognized quality indicators and oversight. Finally, when China sends its best and brightest students to study overseas, there is a danger that the students won't return, thus adding to other nations' economic prosperity.

5.1   The Imbalance between Inbound and Outbound Mobility
For China, the imbalance between inbound and outbound mobility is a key issue. In 2014, there were about 377,000 international students from 203 countries studying in 775 higher education institutions in China (MOE, 2014). China has become an emerging host country of international students. However, the most distinctive characteristic of China's higher education student mobility equation is that China has the largest number of higher education students and is the greatest international student sender country in the 21st century (IIE, 2015). IIE reports that the number of Chinese students studying abroad was almost 1,260,000 and took up almost a quarter of the world's total international students (IIE, 2015). In contrast, the number of international students studying in China was 397,600 by the end of 2015 (Blue Book of Global Talents, 2015). The phenomenon of "high output and low input" describes the student mobility deficit in China (Guo & Guo, 2016), and has been described as an education service trade deficit from the perspective of the national economy. New initiatives to balance mobility numbers are underway, but at the time of this book China still experiences a mobility deficit.

5.2   Lack of an Internationally Recognized Higher Education Quality
           Assurance System
The establishment of quality assurance agencies is a priority in many countries (Knight & CBIE, 2000). China developed its higher education quality assurance

system in the early twenty-first century. However, ensuring that the quality of international higher education meets both local and international standards has become a challenge in China (Hou, 2014). Specifically, student mobility between countries in search of higher education opportunities requires a more complicated quality assurance system.

At the same time, Chinese institutions may struggle to control the actions of their partners. Driven by economic interest, foreign higher education institutions recruit Chinese students based on their desire to study abroad, and negative consequences sometimes arise in higher education partnerships. Global and Chinese news outlets have reported a variety of problems encountered by Chinese students abroad. For example, an article in 2010 *University World News* described a situation at one university in Australia that had allegedly been encouraging international students to cheat on their examinations (Altbach & Welch, 2010). Describing similar difficulties for foreign students studying in China, another story reported that students in Ukraine who could not gain entrance into Chinese universities fell prey to gambling, truancy, and failure of subjects (Li, 2007). Lacking a quality assurance system has created challenges for international partnerships.

5.3   *Brain Drain*

Brain Drain is defined as the loss of highly skilled professionals from a source country to a recipient country (Odhiambo, 2012). It intensifies sender countries' scarcity of talent, enlarges academic and scientific research gaps, and solidifies sender countries' disadvantageous position in international competition. Western countries often possess advantages that attract and retain talented students from China. Statistics show that almost half of Peking University's undergraduates choose to pursue further study in foreign countries. The number of students who returned to China was less than 12% after finishing study in the U.S. in 2005 (Welch & Zhen, 2008). The Chinese Ministry of Education study found that 229,300 students studied abroad in 2009 and found that only 108,300 returned to China (MOE, 2010).

In order to convert brain drain into "brain bridging" (Mok & Han, 2016), "brain circulation" (Larsen, 2016) or even "brain gain" (Shen, Wang, & Jin, 2016) (three terms used to describe global flows of intellectual talent and ideas even when citizens leave their home country), the Chinese government has introduced efforts to reverse the exodus, especially for the most accomplished students. The Chinese government unveiled *The Recruitment Program of Global Experts* in 2008. This program was designed to recruit overseas top scholars. In 2015, the Chinese Ministry of Education issued the *Program of Introducing Talents of Discipline to Universities*, also known as Program 111. Program 111 sets a goal of recruiting 1,000 scholars from the world's top 100 universities and building

100 world-class disciplines within China in hopes of attracting back Chinese students as well as attracting global talent from other countries (MOE, 2015).

While Chinese policy makers grapple with unequal mobility numbers and brain drain, critical scholars have characterized the brain drain process as one of neocolonialism or academic imperialism. Efforts to reverse brain drain and equalize mobility numbers may be seen as an approach to reducing academic imperialism. For example, Niu and Yin (2010) note that highly resourced Western institutions, operating in neoliberal environments, have a strong "pull" effect with little to curtail their recruitment of the most talented students. This may leave institutions in less resourced countries in a subordinate state in international higher education partnerships. In this case, powerful nations act as talent harvesters, providing a scenario where the most talented leave home for the best opportunities (Liu, 2008). Preliminary evidence in the current era of student mobility shows trends of brain drain away from China.

6   Student Mobility in China: An Emergent Trend

Despite concerns about brain drain and the development of world-class universities in China, outward mobility of Chinese students is as popular as ever. The popularity may be partially explained by China's economic successes and partially by a liberalized policy environment. As China moves toward a more open economy and policy environment, most of the student mobility barriers in China have been removed. Chinese students have more autonomy when deciding to study abroad than ever before. This freedom is most frequently exercised by self-paying students. The number of self-funded students overwhelmingly outweighed the number of government-sponsored students, with the ratio of government-sponsored to self-funded overseas students being 1:21 in 2009 (MOE, 2009). The Chinese government, seeking to both support student freedoms to study abroad but diminish brain drain, issued the policy *Decision on Educational System Reform* in 1985. This policy introduced the principle of student mobility through "*supporting studying abroad, encouraging them to return home by promising freedom of movement*" (Wang, 2014). Following this policy, individual students are granted the autonomy needed for mobility.

Although the majority of Chinese students studying internationally are now self-funded (Yang, 2012), the Chinese government continues to play a leading role in student mobility through international higher education partnerships. Chinese higher education partnerships have emerged in the form of Chinese-foreign co-run schools, credit transfer schemes, joint venture cultivation, and professional academic conferences (Altbach, 2013), all of which feature opportunities for short-term student mobility. Co-run institutions, which allow for controlled student flows and predictable participant numbers, occur in every category of institution from research universities to two-year vocational colleges in China. In 2013, the number of Sino-global co-run institutions and programs was 3,958, with as many as 550,000 participants around the world (China News Web, 2013). These partnerships tend to combine Chinese and foreign institutional resources to provide opportunities for Chinese and foreign students who are enrolled in home-country institutions.

6.1　　*Upward Trends*

As China's economy booms and the middle class grows, the costs of study abroad are well within reach for many in China. Studying abroad is becoming a common phenomenon for self-paying and Chinese-university exchange students alike. Figure 10.1 demonstrates the growing trend of Chinese students studying abroad. The total number of Chinese students studying abroad has greatly increased from 1978 to 2015. Historically, studying abroad has been a privilege of the social elites in China, with only 5% of students participating. Nowadays, more Chinese families from a wider range of incomes are willing to support their children to study abroad.

With the help of considerable student mobility scholarship programs sponsored by the central government, institutions, and other non-government organizations, studying abroad has shifted away from being only a privilege of the wealthy population. A recent survey found that 36% of Chinese international students' annual household incomes were less than $19,000 U.S. dollars. Moreover, 19% of respondents' annual household

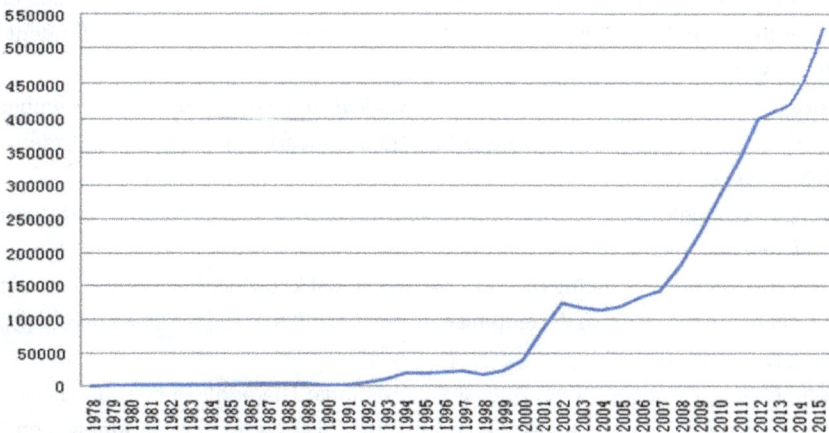

FIGURE 10.1　*Total number of Chinese students studying abroad from 1978 to 2015*

SOURCE: 2016 CHINESE STUDY ABROAD TREND REPORT.

incomes were between 19,000 and 36,000 U.S. dollars (China News, 2013). The data indicate that a combination of family and government resources may be supporting student mobility. The popularization of studying abroad is clear at individual, institutional, and governmental levels in China, and is more common now than ever in the past.

7   Summary

In summary, student mobility has long been a part of China's history. The role and purpose of mobility remains similar today to what it was centuries ago, with primary goals of learning about other cultures and skills that would serve the nation. In modern times, Chinese higher education institutions are highly engaged in international mobility programs and leverage partnerships with countries around the world in order to create mobility opportunities for students and in order to internationalize campuses. Sino-global higher education partnership initiatives based on student mobility utilize academic cooperation to enhance broader relations between China and other countries and fill the gap for Chinese students wishing to study abroad who do not wish (or cannot) commit to an exclusively self-funded foreign degree.

References

American Council on Education. (2010). *Student mobility.* Retrieved December 30, 2016, from http://www.acenet.edu/higher-education/topics/Pages/Student-Mobility.aspx

American Council on Education. (2016). *Student mobility.* Retrieved November 15, 2016, from http://www.acenet.edu/higher-education/topics/Pages/Student-Mobility.aspx

Altbach, P. G. (1998). *Comparative higher education: Knowledge, the university, and development.* Greenwich, CT: Ablex Pub. Corp.

Altbach, P. G. (2013). Advancing the national and global knowledge economy: The role of research universities in developing countries. *Studies in Higher Education, 38*(3), 316–330.

Altbach, P. G., & Welch, A. (2010, August 22). Australia: The perils of commercialism. *University World News.* Retrieved from http://www.universityworldnews.com/article.php?story=20100820152350449

Bennett, J. M. (2008). Transformative training: Designing programs for culture learning. In M. A. Moodian (Ed.), *Contemporary leadership and intercultural competence:*

Understanding and utilizing cultural diversity to build successful organizations. Thousand Oaks, CA: Sage Publications.

Blue Book of Global Talents. (2015). *Annual report on the development of Chinese students studying abroad 2015 No. 4.* Retrieved November 18, 2016, from http://www.cssn.cn/dybg/dybg_jy/201511/t20151126_2714983.shtml

British Council. (2013). *Generation UK-China.* Retrieved December 27, 2016, from https://www.britishcouncil.cn/en/programmes/education/generation-uk

British Council. (n.d.). *Postgraduate student mobility trends to 2024.* Retrieved January 20, 2016, from http://www.britishcouncil.org/sites/default/files/postgraduate_mobility_trends_2024-october–14.pdf

Chang, D. F. (2015). Implementing internationalization policy in higher education explained by regulatory control in neoliberal times. *Asia Pacific Education Review, 16*(4), 603–612.

China News Web. (2013). *China approved Chinese-foreign cooperatively-run schools are nearly 2000 project.* Retrieved October 12, 2016, from http://www.chinanews.com/edu/2013/0905/5250624.shtml (in Chinese)

China News. (2013). *Almost half Chinese students in Australia are regards as low-income, annual household no more than 25000 dollars.* Retrieved October 28, 2016, from http://www.chinanews.com/lxsh/2013/11–28/5557001.shtml

China Scholarship Council. (2016). *China scholarship council.* Retrieved December 27, 2016, from http://en.csc.edu.cn/ (in Chinese)

China State Council. (2015). *China state council's notice about overall plan for promoting world-class universities and first-class discipline construction.* Retrieved November 5, 2015, from http://www.gov.cn/zhengce/content/05/content_10269.htm (in Chinese)

Chinese Study Abroad Trend Report. (2014). *2014 report on the trend of overseas study.* Retrieved August 6, 2016, from http://www.eol.cn/html/lx/2014baogao/content.html (in Chinese)

Duffield, S., Olson, A., & Kerzman, R. (2013). Crossing borders, breaking boundaries: Collaboration among higher education institutions. *Innovative Higher Education, 38*(3), 237–250.

EOL. (2014). *2014 study abroad report.* Retrieved August 26, 2016, from http://www.eol.cn/html/lx/2014baogao/content.html.(in Chinese)

Fang, W., & Wang, S. (2014). Chinese students' choice of transnational higher education in a globalized higher education market: A case study of W University. *Journal of Studies in International Education, 18*(5), 475–494.

Feng, K. (1993). On study abroad policy in late Qing dynasty. *Modern Chinese History Studies, 93*(5), 125–148.

García, H. A., & Villarreal, M. L. (2014). The "redirecting" of international Students: American higher education policy hindrances and implications. *Journal of International Students, 4*(2), 126–136.

Goddard, J., & Puukka, J. (2008). The engagement of higher educational institutions in regional development: An overview of the opportunities and challenges. *Higher Education Management And Policy*, 20(2), 3–33.

Guo, S., & Guo, Y. (2016). *Spotlight on China: Chinese education in the globalized world*. Rotterdam, The Netherlands: Sense Publishers.

Hou, A. Y. (2014). Quality in cross-border higher education and challenges for the internationalization of national quality assurance agencies in the Asia-Pacific region: The Taiwanese experience. *Studies in Higher Education*, 39(1), 135–152.

Knight, J., & Canadian Bureau for International Education (CBIE). (2000). *Taking the Pulse: Monitoring the quality and progress of internationalization, including tracking measures* (CBIE Research Millennium Series No. 2). Ottawa: Canadian Bureau for International Education (CBIE).

Larsen, M. A. (2016). *Internationalization of higher education: An analysis through spatial, network, and mobilities theories*. New York, NY: Palgrave Macmillan.

Li, F. (2016). The internationalization of higher education in China: The role of government. *Journal Off International Education Research*, 12(1), 47–52.

Li, H., & Xiangdong, F. (2012). Exploration of higher education partnership from the perspective of knowledge flow. *China Higher Education*, 12(22), 55–57.

Li, J. (2012). The student experience in China's revolutionary move to mass higher education: Institutional challenges and policy implications. *Higher Education Policy*, 25(4), 453–475.

Li, M., & Bray, M. (2007). Cross-border flows of students for higher education: Push-pull factors and motivations of mainland Chinese students in Hong Kong and Macau. *Higher Education: The International Journal of Higher Education and Educational Planning*, 53(6), 791–818.

Li, S. (2007). Brief talk of China-Ukraine higher education partnership and communication. *Journal of National Academy of Education Administration*, 7(2), 86–87.

Liu, J. (2008). On dependence development and academic colonization of higher education. *Journal of Higher Education*, 8(12), 8–11.

Liu, Q. (2011). Education for global competence and its implementation approach: Case study of Tsinghua University. *World Education Formation*, 11(4), 44–47.

Julius, D. J., & Leventhal, M. (2014). *Sino-American joint partnerships: Why some succeed and others fail* (Research & Occasional Paper Series CSHE.1.14). Berkeley, CA: Center For Studies in Higher Education.

Maritime Silk Road. (2016). *Quanzhou's Development Plan for the Maritime Silk Road*. Retrieved from http://www.hssczl.net/#section1 (in Chinese).

Marginson, S., & Sawir, E. (2005). Interrogating global flows in higher education. *Globalisation, Societies and Education*, 3(3), 281–309.

MOE. (1993). *Notice of China state education commission issue the self-finance study abroad*. Retrieved September 5, 2016, from http://www.moe.gov.cn/s78/A20/gjs_left/moe_851/tnull_4373.html (in Chinese)

MOE. (2010). *Guidelines of the national program for medium- and long-term educational reform and development.* Retrieved September 6, 2016, from http://www.moe.edu.cn/publicfiles/business/htmlfiles/moe/moe_838/201008/93704.html (in Chinese)

MOE. (2010). *Statistic of study abroad in 2009.* Retrieved September 9, 2016, from http://www.moe.gov.cn/s78/A20/gjs_left/moe_851/201006/t20100628_90108.html (in Chinese)

MOE. (2010). *The notice of launching study in China of Ministry of Education.* Retrieved September 6, 2016, from http://www.moe.edu.cn/publicfiles/business/htmlfiles/moe/moe_850/201009/xxgk_108815.html (in Chinese)

MOE. (2014). *The statue quo of Chinese students study abroad in 2013.* Retrieved February 12, 2016, from http://www.moe.gov.cn/s78/A20/gjs_left/moe_851/tnull_4373.html (in Chinese)

MOE. (2015). *The notice of program of introducing talents of discipline to universities.* Retrieved December 16, 2016, from http://www.moe.edu.cn/srcsite/A16/kjs_gjhz/201511/t20151130_221899.html (in Chinese)

Mok, K. H., & Han, X. (2016). From "brain drain" to "brain bridging": Transnational higher education development and graduate employment in China. *Journal of Higher Education Policy and Management, 38*(3), 369–389.

Morgan, S. L. C. (2014). *The role of an international higher education partnership to improve gender equality and empower women* (Ph.D. dissertation). Retrieved from ProQuest Dissertations and Theses database. (UMI No. 3620144)

Munz, M., & Reiner, R. (1988). Ranking regression analysis of the global mobility. In W. Weidlich & G. Haag (Eds.), *Interregional migration.* Berlin: Springer.

Niu, C. S., & Min, Y. (2010). The review of U.S. and Africa higher education partnerships. *Comparative Education Review, 10*(11), 15–19.

Netz, N. (2015). What deters students from studying abroad? Evidence from four European countries and its implications for higher education policy. *Higher Education Policy, 28*(2), 151–174.

Odhiambo, G. (2012). *Brain drain in higher education: Lost hope or opportunity?* Bulgarian Comparative Education Society (BCES) 10th Annual Conference, 2012 – International Perspectives on Education, Sofia, Bulgaria.

Institute of International Education (IIE). (2015). *International students: Leading places of origin 2015.* Retrieved August 9, 2016, from http://www.iie.org/Research-and-Publications/Open-Doors/Data/International-Students/Leading-Places-of-Origin#.WBaEevmEClU

Parton, B. T. (2011). Stability for development, development for stability: The relationship between regional organizations and social cohesion through the lens of the EU and MERCOSUR. *Peabody Journal of Education, 86*(2), 129–143.

Shen, W., Wang, C., & Jin, W. (2016). International mobility of PhD students since the 1990s and its effect on china: A cross-national analysis. *Journal of Higher Education Policy and Management, 38*(3), 333–353.

Wang, H. Y. (2012). *Annual report on the development of China's study abroad.* Beijing: Social Sciences Academic Press.

Wang, L. (2014). Internationalization with Chinese characteristics: The changing discourse of internationalization in China. *Chinese Education and Society, 47*(1), 7–26.

Welch, A. R., & Zhen, Z. (2008). Higher education and global talent flows: Brain drain, overseas Chinese intellectuals, and diasporic knowledge networks. *Higher Education Policy, 21*(4), 519–537.

Xie, L., Hou, T., & Li, Z. (2011). Strategic alliance: Competitiveness of Sino-foreign cooperative school running operation. *International Education Studies, 4*(1), 51–54.

Yang, P. (2015). Enhancing intercultural communication and understanding: Team translation project as a student engagement learning approach. *International Education Studies, 8*(8), 67–80.

Yang, R. (2012). Internationalization, regionalization, and soft power: China's relations with ASEAN member countries in higher education. *Frontiers of Education in China, 7*(4), 486–507.

Zhongshan Overseas Chinese Affairs. (Eds.). (2013). *Annals of Zhongshan Overseas Chinese Affairs.* Guangzhou: Guangdong Renmin Press.

Zhou, G., & Yue, K. (2014). The talents supporting and educational solutions to the "belt and road initiative". *Educational Research, 2014*(10), 1–9.

About the Authors

Jing Tian is a lecturer from Hangzhou Dianzi University, and was a visiting international PhD at University of Wisconsin-Madison from Sept. 2016 to Sept. 2017. Jing Tian's research areas are comparative education and higher education internationalization.

Jiansheng Ma is a Professor from Institute of International and Comparative Education at Beijing Normal University in Comparative Higher Education, Educational Leadership, and Development. More information about Jiansheng Ma is available at the faculty and staff website at the Institute of International and Comparative Education, Beijing Normal University. http://www.compe.cn/english/facultyandstaff/facultyandstaff/102356.html.

Juan Cai is a Doctoral Student from Institute of International and Comparative Education at Beijing Normal University with a research focus on higher education internationalization.

CHAPTER 11

The Effect of Culture and Acculturation on the Mental Health of International Students: Implications for U.S. and Chinese Universities

Merritt Huang

Abstract

As instructors at U.S. universities see large percentages of Chinese students in their classes, it is becoming increasingly important for them to understand U.S.-China cultural differences and the strategies employed by Chinese students to acculturate to their new learning and living environments. Whether due to the coping challenges of students or inflexible environments that are organized for U.S. learner needs, some Chinese undergraduate students have faced difficult adjustments to U.S. schools. This chapter explores how Chinese students' cultural identities and common acculturation strategies may may contribute to the overall mental health of an individual student in the United States as well as emergent theory on mental health needs for U.S. students studying in China through an acculturation lens.

1   Introduction

Chinese students have been enrolling in colleges and universities in the United States for over 100 years. In the 1870s, the Qing government began sponsoring travel to the United States for cohorts of young men for this purpose, but exchange slowed to a trickle under the leadership of Chairman Mao Zedong after the Communists were victorious in the Chinese civil war.

In 1978, the Chinese Communist Party (CCP), led by Deng Xiaoping, initiated a series of economic reforms known as "Reform and Opening Up" (*gaige kaifang* 改革开放) which introduced market principles based on the capitalist system in the West, but which also contained what the CCP referred to as "Chinese characteristics" (Deng, 1984). This series of reforms, which resulted in economic growth of an average of 9.5% each year between 1978 and 2013 (Brandt & Rawski, 2008), lifted an estimated 500 million people out of poverty (World Bank, 2015).

The unprecedented metamorphosis of millions from poor to middle class has created both economic and social transformation. In terms of the economy, a 2013 McKinsey & Company report indicates that more than 75 percent of China's urban consumers are expected to earn 60,000 to 229,000 RMB ($9,000 to $34,000) per year. According to McKinsey & Company (2013), this range is between the average income of Brazilians and Italians in purchasing-parity-power terms. Just four percent of urban Chinese households were within this range in the year 2000, but 68 percent were in 2012 (ibid). A potential connection between the increase in purchasing power of the middle class and social change is evident in the manner in which students first go abroad. Where previously many students may have first pursued their undergraduate studies in China prior to going abroad for graduate studies or research exchange, the current trend seems to be for students to enroll at the undergraduate or even secondary level in western countries to begin their overseas education (Fischer, 2014). According to an annual report by the Institute of International Education (IIE), in the 2014–2015 academic year a total of 304,040 Chinese students were enrolled in U.S. colleges and universities, while Chinese students at the undergraduate level in the U.S. numbered 110,500 (ICEF Monitor, 2015). For those students who choose to study abroad and are admitted to universities, their experience abroad may be not only their first experience abroad but also their first encounter with higher education in general (Heins, 2015).

2   Recent Trends and Reasons for the Expansion in Younger Chinese
       Student Enrollment

Ten years ago, more than 80 percent of Chinese international students in the United States were studying at the graduate or post-graduate level. Today, the undergraduate/graduate split is nearly 50–50 (Fischer, 2014). One reason for this may be the growing dissatisfaction of parents and students with China's test-centric curriculum (ICEF Monitor, 2015). Hours spent memorizing information simply to pass a test designed to ascertain students' abilities to memorize is no longer sufficient for the Chinese labor market today. The lessening of Chinese state control has allowed private industry to flourish, and it is those companies who are searching for innovative young talent with critical thinking skills (McKinsey China, 2013). Cosmopolitan areas of China, such as Beijing, Shanghai, and Guangzhou, boast high-quality universities that are now recognized as such on global ranking scales. However, the opportunities for Chinese students to pursue interests in the English language, political science, and other fields in the humanities are fewer at Chinese universities than those in the United States or other western countries (Haynie, 2013). Additionally, the willingness of many U.S. universities to allow students to change their majors at any point in their studies is an attractive option for many Chinese college students (Dong, 2015).

3   John Berry's Model of Acculturation

Whether due to the coping challenges of students or inflexible environments that are organized for U.S. learner needs, some Chinese undergraduates have faced difficult adjustments to U.S. schools. The influx of Chinese adolescents at universities and colleges around the United States has created a need for culturally relevant coping approaches to be provided to an abundant population of young Chinese students undergoing the process of acculturation. Acculturation, as defined by Stella Ting-Toomey (1999, p. 254), is "a multidimensional, multifaceted process that involves both systems-level and individual-level change processes." John Berry (1997) describes an acculturation framework in which international students appraise the new situations they encounter upon entering a different culture as either positive experiences or negative stressors. In order to respond to these new experiences, international students use coping strategies, such as engaging with members of the host culture, which either effectively reduces their level of stress or contributes to it. Over the long term, students will either become accustomed to the host culture, or will become increasingly resistant to it (Berry, 1997). Berry (2005) suggests that there are often two types of responses when faced with exposure to a new culture. The first response is behavioral, affecting the manner in which an individual conducts themself in such aspects as speech patterns, food choices, and even the way in which they view themself (identity). The second response is psychological. These are the emotional responses that an individual has to acculturative stress, which sometimes culminates in depression or anxiety. The intersection of the host and home cultures may create inner conflict within an individual as they struggle to determine which aspects of each culture to incorporate in daily life and which to let go. This inner struggle can also lead to anxiety and psychological distress (Berry, 2005).

There has been considerable research conducted that explores the acculturation experiences, strategies, and outcomes of international students, and Chinese international students in particular (see Du & Wei, 2015; Heins, 2015; Huang & Brown, 2009; Roy, 2013; Stevens, 2012; Wang, Heppner, Fu, Zhao, Li, & Chuang, 2012; Yan & Berliner, 2013). Research has already been conducted in several key areas, including exploration of the various strategies Chinese international students employ to cope with stress, the U.S. university resources currently available to help international students cope with the adjustment and acculturation process, and the various ways in which Chinese students are uniquely affected by adjustment to the U.S. host culture as compared to other international student populations. To this point, one study indicates that Asian international students report greater acculturative stress as compared to European international students because European countries share more common cultural values with the United States than do Asian countries (Poyrazli, Kavanaugh, Baker, & Al-Timimi, 2004). One key intersection of research beginning to be explored is how Chinese students' cultural identities and common acculturation strategies may contribute to the overall mental health of an individual student studying in the U.S.

4   Academic Challenges Chinese International Students Face at U.S. Universities

As instructors at U.S. universities encounter increasingly large percentages of Chinese students in their classes, it is becoming ever more important for them to understand U.S.-China cultural differences and the strategies employed by Chinese students to acculturate to their new learning and living environments. The most daunting barrier faced by many Chinese students when they come to the United States for study is the language barrier (Roy, 2013). Many students may be proficient readers and writers in English, but some are unable to communicate their thoughts and concerns in a manner in which their professors can understand (ibid). As non-native English speakers, Chinese students may experience difficulty understanding their professors' lectures, jokes, colloquialisms, and idioms, as well as the long and complex sentences used by some professors. A native speaker of any language is subconsciously inclined to utilize pragmatic reductions of the language; this may contribute additional barriers to Chinese student comprehension in class (Huang & Rinaldo, 2009; Huang, 2004).

In addition to the barriers caused by language, Chinese international students may also face learning obstacles in U.S. universities due to the more informal teaching styles of their professors in the U.S. as compared to China (Huang, 2004). Huang and Rinaldo (2009) conducted a study on factors affecting Chinese graduate students' cross-cultural learning experiences in the United States. They found that some U.S. professors do not list key points of the lecture on the blackboard, for example, nor do they use discourse markers in their speech (i.e. next, then, after, and so on). The lack of such markers may make it difficult for Chinese students to differentiate one key point from another during a lecture in their second language (Cox & Yamaguchi, 2010; Huang & Brown, 2009; Lee & Carrasquillo, 2006). The informal style of U.S. higher education teaching styles, in some cases, may also prompt some professors to go off on tangents or not follow the textbook very closely. This tendency is very confusing to Chinese students who are accustomed to learning, literally, by the book. Additionally, some Chinese students may experience challenges when asked to work in teams and small groups, a hallmark of most U.S. higher education classrooms, and an activity that, until recently, was rare in Chinese university classrooms (Cox & Yamaguchi, 2010; Huang & Brown, 2009; Lee & Carrasquillo, 2006). Finally, Chinese students may be uncomfortable with open-ended class discussions, a pedagogical technique that is common in U.S. classrooms and that is still relatively foreign to Chinese students who may be accustomed to taking copious notes while a professor is lecturing in front of the class. Chinese students may be unwilling to voluntarily participate in such class discussions due to the fear of losing face, and may be summarily penalized for their lack of participation by uncomprehending U.S. professors who value outgoing and participatory personalities (Huang & Rinaldo, 2009).

U.S. universities could ameliorate some of this stress in several ways, such as by offering tuition-free or fee-reduced non-credit English classes during a student's first year on campus. By helping Chinese students raise their English proficiency levels and understanding of colloquial American speaking patterns and cultures, they may feel more comfortable attending and participating in university courses. This may, in turn, encourage increased interaction between Chinese international students and their U.S. peers, thus contributing to internationalization efforts on campus. Alternatively, universities could offer English language workshops periodically throughout the school year or promote language exchange collaboration between Chinese international students and U.S. students studying Chinese. Chinese students comprise the majority of international students at many U.S. universities and comprise the largest international student group from any one country in the United States. When a portion of the student body is struggling with issues of identity or with feeling accepted by their peers and instructors in the classroom, the entire campus is affected. As such, incoming Chinese undergraduate students could be required to take a short seminar on U.S. culture prior to beginning their formal studies. This would provide the students, at minimum, with a general overview and starting point about life in the United States, as well as an introduction to the expectations of the U.S. university classroom. Concurrently, instructors (and students) would likely benefit from a wide variety of instructional strategies being utilized in the classroom. Yan and Berliner (2009) suggest that Chinese students who have extremely high expectations about what life will be like for them in the U.S. tend to experience greater levels of stress and anxiety when their expectations don't match reality. By obtaining culturally relevant knowledge and skills, Chinese students might be able to alleviate part of their acculturative stress and perhaps shorten the amount of time they require for cross-cultural adjustment. At the same time, as faculty become more culturally aware, they may be more empathetic to the challenges international students may face.

5   Acculturative Challenges Chinese International Students Face at U.S. Universities

Beginning in the late 1970s, the Chinese government began encouraging Chinese students to study abroad in order to gain knowledge of nascent western technology practices (Yan & Berliner, 2009). For the host universities, the presence of these students provides additional diversity and may help to fulfill internationalization goals. However, these students may also be confronted with the challenge of adapting to a new culture and society. In particular, challenges may include adjusting to a new educational system, language, culture, campus climate, food, housing, social norms, and increased concern about finances (Wei et al., 2007).

When facing the reality of adapting to these new experiences, Chinese international students must go through a process of adjustment. Adapting to a new environment may be stressful for many of these students who are experiencing pressure to adjust to a new language both in the classroom and in their personal lives, new cultural values, and new social norms. This type of pressure may significantly increase students' feelings of stress or anxiety (Sullivan & Kashubeck-West, 2015). The students' feelings of anxiety stem from the differences between their home culture and that of the host culture and are what are commonly referred to as acculturative stress (Berry, 2005). If students are unable to find a release for this type of accumulated stress, it may begin to exert an undesirable effect on their psychological wellbeing. Depression is chief among the psychosomatic presenting symptoms of international students dealing with high levels of acculturative stress (Yi, Lin, & Yuko, 2003).

Chinese undergraduate international students may view being a student as a major part of their identity and shoulder the burden of fulfilling the expectations of their parents for excellent academic performance. This type of academic pressure is likely one cause of acculturative stress. *Three Character Classic*, which was used for centuries to teach children about Confucian values (Wang & Gary, 2012), details the stories of people who exerted tremendous effort and made personal sacrifices in order to achieve their academic goals. Although no longer a part of the mandatory school curriculum in China, these stories are still referenced by Chinese parents and teachers to illustrate the importance of persistence and tolerance of distress in academic pursuits (Heins, 2015).

6 Chinese International Student Experiences in University Residence Hall Environments

For any new college student, the first year of undergraduate studies is critical in terms of both student development and socialization. For international students, this period of time is especially important as it may determine whether they continue to pursue their studies in the United States (Chong & Razek, 2014). Undergraduate students, in particular, are often in the U.S. without their families, are unmarried, and may not have any prior social connections at their chosen university of study (ibid). They may need to rely heavily on available university resources and support systems in order to begin forming peer relationships and expanding their social networks. For many undergraduate students, both domestic and international, residence halls may be an organic way to become engaged in social and academic life on campus.

As Chinese undergraduate students begin their first year of study on U.S. university campuses, they may be confronted with a variety of transitional challenges, including a lack of awareness of the campus resources available to them, language barriers, acculturation issues, and the challenge of making friends. It is this last challenge that can be of particular importance in aiding student personal growth and development in college, as well as how adept they may become at adapting to a new culture, academic world, and living environment (Chong & Razek, 2014). While socialization has generally been associated with academic success for U.S. students, international students tend to use social networks as a way to maintain connections to home culture and help one another through transitional challenges (Sovic, 2009). Students who experience positive peer interactions have generally fared better academically and socially, and are able to avoid negative psychological repercussions, such as loneliness and depression (ibid).

On-campus residence halls may be a key resource for Chinese undergraduate students seeking to make friends and establish a sense of community in an unfamiliar environment. However, the same environment ripe for constructive social interactions can also be a hotbed of cultural misunderstanding if international students perceive the residence hall to have a negative racial climate or if staff members have not received proper training in intercultural communication and understanding. Chinese undergraduate students may not have had much previous exposure to U.S. academic culture and so may perceive university student life staff as catering primarily to white domestic students (Chong & Razek, 2014). Similarly, cultural programming, such as homecoming or Greek Week, may be completely unfamiliar to students unversed in U.S. university life and may act as a barrier for meaningful relationship building between domestic and international student populations (ibid).

A quantitative study conducted at a private, religiously-affiliated U.S. Midwestern higher education institution in spring 2013 was rather telling. The institution enrolled approximately 7,000 undergraduate students, of whom 1,500 were international students. Ninety-eight first-year undergraduate students participated in the study, of which 88 were from China. Survey data revealed that students who considered interactions with diverse others as beneficial were more likely to perceive their on-campus living experience as a positive experience in general (Chong & Razek, 2014). They also reported that this type of interaction enabled them to better respect other races and ethnicities on campus. The survey confirmed that residence hall programming needs to be very intentional in educating students about differences in order to have meaningful results. One caveat to bear in mind when considering the survey results, however, is that as Hofstede (1980) suggests, Chinese societies are more collectivist in nature than is U.S. society. Concern for the wellbeing of the group over the individual may have prompted Chinese students to avoid negative survey evaluations for fear of upsetting authority figures in the residence halls where they live (Chong & Razek, 2014).

In line with the collectivist mentality, some Chinese students may hold onto their ethnic identities as a means of boosting a sense of group pride and self-esteem. This emotional connection may provide them with the fortitude necessary to tackle the challenges of acculturation upon arrival in the United States (Tong, 2014). As Chinese students acculturate, they may face additional stress as new identifies form that contain aspects of both the home and host cultures – a type of third culture (Walters & Auton-Cuff, 2009). Despite this, participation in university classes and interaction with U.S. students may provide Chinese undergraduates with a representation of values and beliefs of U.S. culture and enable them to observe firsthand U.S. ways of thinking and behaving. The relationship between intercultural interaction and acculturation is very important; it is this intersection that may prevent maladaptive coping strategies and other mental health challenges in Chinese students (Wei et al., 2011).

7   Social Stressors Unique to Chinese International Students

Yeh and Inose (2003) suggest that Chinese international students tend to experience high levels of adjustment difficulties due to vast differences in social and cultural norms between China and the United States. When such large differences between a student's home and host country exist, it is natural to assume that the acculturative process may be more challenging for that student than that of a student whose country of origin is more similar to the host country. Samovar and Porter (1997) noted that there are maximum sociocultural differences between Western and Asian countries, and cited the United States and China as a prime example of maximum cultural distance. Cultural distance can be defined as the extent to which the shared norms and values in one country differ from those in another (Chen & Hu, 2002). A study conducted by Zhang, Lin, Nonaka, and Beom (2005) examined 1,631 college students from China, Korea, Japan, and Taiwan. Findings showed that the students endorsed traditional Confucian values of interpersonal harmony, relational hierarchy, and traditional conservatism despite increased globalization and culture change in East Asian cultures. The study concluded that Chinese students provided the highest ratings for interpersonal harmony and relational hierarchy among the four cultures (Zhang, Lin, Nonaka, & Beom, 2005).

Students from China are generally raised in a historically collectivist culture, which focuses on the importance of maintaining social harmony and places the welfare of the group over that of the individual (Yan & Berliner, 2009). Berry (2005) says that good "sociocultural adaptation" is dependent on the group's cultural knowledge, degree of contact with local populations and positive intergroup interactions. From a Chinese student perspective, the U.S. tendency to be more individualistic and to place emphasis on the value of privacy often prevents the establishment of deep and meaningful friendships between U.S. students and Chinese international students. Although the majority of Chinese student respondents participating in a survey conducted at a large public university in the Southwestern United States revealed that they perceived U.S. domestic students to be friendly, they also felt that the friendliness was superficial and that the domestic students held different expectations of friendship than they did (Yuan, 2011).

One method that Chinese undergraduate students may utilize in order to achieve better sociocultural adaptation is to socialize with other Chinese students; that is, live within the values and beliefs of their home culture (Tong, 2014), but also gradually add to their host cultural knowledge and understanding by establishing intercultural contact with their U.S. professors and classmates. Maintaining a sense of their primary ethnic identity (that is, of being Chinese) is critical at this juncture because of the tendency of humans to gain strength from feeling like a member of a group and having a sense of belonging. When this sense of belonging is threatened, Chinese students may become anxious and experience what Berry (2005) refers to as acculturative stress. As this type of stress and sense of alienation builds, a student may feel pressured and avoid contact with their U.S. classmates, which might lead to further alienation. This type of avoidance would likely be based upon the threat the Chinese student perceives to her ethnic identity as she navigates U.S. culture and ways of life (Phinney, 2003). Ideally, Chinese students will find a way to adapt to the host culture through intercultural interactions with university professors and peers, thus redefining their personal identities as bicultural in nature. Additionally, students may elect to utilize the opportunity to use the Internet and other technological means to explore U.S. culture, history, and habits on their own terms, thereby enabling them to take control of their acculturation process and providing them with a positive experience of acculturation and adaptation to their new lives in the United States. By increasing the amount and extent of cross-cultural exchange occurring on campus, U.S. universities will be able to better facilitate successful transitions and acculturative experiences for both domestic and international student populations (Yan & Berliner, 2013).

8   Visa Stressors

Chinese international students are required to enroll full-time at U.S. colleges and universities in order to maintain their F-1student visa status (USCIS, 2016). This requirement restricts their ability to seek additional part-time work off-campus for organizations or businesses (ibid). This type of restriction may incite additional anxiety in many Chinese students due to the great uncertainties about their futures in the United States. Students may face the additional hardship of feeling unable to return to China to visit loved ones because they may fear being refused visas when they apply for new visas to return to the United States for school (Yan & Berliner, 2013). The long separation from their families and social networks in China may place a great deal of stress on students who are accustomed to having a strong support system surrounding them. Some Chinese students may desire to remain in the United States after graduation, but may face acute difficulties in changing their visa status, as there are extremely limited opportunities for international students to swap student visas for employment visas or become permanent residents of the U.S. (USCIS, 2016). For this reason alone, many students may elect to pursue studies in the STEM fields, because the U.S. government provides more leniency to those with expertise under the "technical immigrant quota system," because a majority of U.S. domestic students will choose not to enter doctoral programs in this field (Yan & Berliner, 2009).

Yan and Berliner (2013) conducted a semi-structured interview of 18 Chinese students at a large, public university in the southwestern United

States. Ten of the respondents identified financial concerns as a continuing severe problem. They further confirmed that they chose their university based on how much financial aid they could receive rather than on the academic reputation of the university. In the event that funding fell through, two-thirds of the respondents concluded that they would consider changing their majors to another where financial aid was available, regardless of the applicability of the new major to their personal research interests or background (Yan & Berliner, 2013). Universities may wish to consider the idea of providing student loans to Chinese students who demonstrate financial emergencies. These students may also be offered the opportunity to seek on- or off-campus employment to supplement their incomes. International students should be provided with better information regarding any employment restrictions placed upon them due to their visa status immediately upon arrival at their universities, or perhaps even prior to accepting admission.

9   Mental Health Challenges

Depression is one of the top presenting concerns for Chinese international student populations seeking help from university campus counseling centers in the United States (Chen, Liu, Zhao, & Yeung, 2015). Acculturative stress has been associated with incidences of presenting depressive symptoms in this population (ibid). A cross-sectional survey of 130 Chinese international undergraduate and graduate students at Yale University found that 45% exhibited symptoms of depression, while in comparison, a recent study of university students in Harbin, China found a prevalence of depressive symptoms of just 11.7% (Han, Han, Luo, Jacobs, & Jean-Baptiste, 2013). This suggests that Chinese international students face a greater burden of psychological distress than their counterparts in China (ibid). Even in incidences when Chinese students experience more acute psychological distress than other international student populations, their outward appearances may belie this distress. Chinese culture still attaches a great deal of stigma to issues of mental health and encourages reliance on family members rather than outside resources to handle any emotional problems (Zhang, 2012). Chinese international students are not likely to actively pursue or participate in on-campus resources of mental health counseling because of the Chinese cultural perception that an admission of emotional difficulties is shameful (Yan, 2008). The revelation of personal issues is regarded as an individual weakness and reflects negatively on the individual's family. The concept of "saving face" is linked so integrally to the concept of shame in Chinese society that individuals are discouraged from expressing concerns or seeking help from resources outside of family and friends (ibid).

To cope with acculturation stressors and emotional distress, many Chinese students rely on self-reflection and forbearance, two concepts that are embedded in Confucian principles (Wei, Liao, Heppner, Chao, & Ku, 2011). The concept of self-reflection requires the student to examine and critique herself in order to determine how she is responsible for the distress she is currently experiencing, with the ultimate goal of achieving inner harmony. Forbearance coping is a common strategy utilized by Chinese students that refers to the minimization or hiding of problems in order to maintain social harmony and not burden others (Yeh, Arora, & Wu, 2006; Moore & Constantine, 2005). In collectivist cultures, such as China, individuals are encouraged to put the group before the individual; consequently, Chinese students may be reluctant to share personal anguish so as not to burden others or cause others to worry about them (Yan, 2008).

The problem here is that emotional suppression may make these students more vulnerable to depression (Ying & Han, 2006). However, it is also vital to bear in mind the individual differences between members of a given cultural group and how those differences may affect the mental health of an individual. Wei et al. (2007) hypothesized that maladaptive perfectionism could be a vulnerability factor in predicting depression in Chinese international students in the United States. Maladaptive perfectionism is defined as the "failure to meet one's standards for performance" (Slaney, Rice, Mobley, Trippi, & Ashby, 2001). Wei et al. considered this aspect of personality to be of particular relevance among Chinese students because of the tendency of Chinese parents to have high expectations of an excellent academic performance once their children begin their studies at a U.S. university. However, parental expectations, together with students' self-perceptions of poor English language skills, may create undue pressure that threatens well-being and even feelings of self-worth (Yan & Berliner, 2013).

10   Subjective Well-Being

Although the concept of "subjective well-being" (SWB) has been extensively studied since the 1960s, when researchers became interested in finding the key to happiness, SWB as a component of acculturation has not received much attention to date (Du & Wei, 2015). SWB is comprised of two components: (1) cognitive, which represents students' perceptions of how satisfactory they find their lives; and (2) affective, which refers to the presence of positive affect and the absence of negative affect (ibid). Research on subjective wellbeing provides a more comprehensive view of students' physical and psychological health. SWB does not solely focus on a student's challenges, but also examines what has been working well for the student and how the student can continue to build on strengths exhibited (Wang et al., 2012). Most Chinese international students will find that their SWB is affected by their experiences studying abroad in the United States. At the same time they are going through the process of acculturation, they are also experiencing enculturation. Although acculturation and enculturation are two separate processes, they may happen simultaneously within an individual (Kang, 2006). Du and Wei's study (2014) indicated that Chinese international students with strong enculturation orientations will feel less connected to U.S. culture and society, which, in turn, would lead to feelings of less satisfaction with their lives in the U.S. Contrarily, as Chinese students are immersed in U.S. culture, their sense of identity within the culture may intensify and promote closer ties and a stronger feeling of well-being over time (Cemalcilar & Falbo, 2008). The most well-adjusted group of students had a social network that included both U.S. domestic students and other Chinese students.

11   Considerations for U.S. Universities

Chinese students preparing to come to the United States for their university years could receive a series of pre-departure orientation seminars designed to introduce the most pressing or relevant concepts of university life in the U.S. For example, the instructor of such a seminar could explain to incoming students what the expectations will be in a U.S. classroom, such as the tendency of U.S. university professors to assign small group work or presentations. Additionally, Chinese students could receive instruction in common cultural norms in the U.S., for example, the propensity of residents of the Midwest to discuss the weather when meeting in social settings such as at the bus stop or in an elevator. These seminars should be organized by the local representative office of the University in which the students will be enrolled. If such an office does not exist, alumni networks or university partnerships in China could be utilized for that purpose, assuming associated costs will not be prohibitive.

Second, university faculty could be offered the opportunity to learn more about the Chinese education system. By doing so, faculty working with Chinese students will have a better understanding of the type of academic environment in which their students built the foundation of their educations prior to coming to the United States. U.S. faculty may be challenged to devise methods through which they may introduce the concepts of formulating original arguments and utilizing critical thinking in the classroom to students who may not have had the opportunity to fully develop those skills in the Chinese education system. Additionally, U.S faculty may need to find innovative ways to share concepts of academic integrity and the importance of not plagiarizing academic works with Chinese students who may not have encountered similar academic protocol prior to attending college in the U.S.

Third, Chinese students are often very interested in meeting U.S. domestic students and becoming friends, but may lack the knowledge or applicable skills of how to do so. University student affairs offices could consider collaborating with International Student and Scholar Services offices to provide additional student programming designed to help U.S. and Chinese or other international students meet and mingle organically. Enabling Chinese students to meet their domestic peers will help them better integrate into the local university campus climate, which could help to ameliorate feelings of isolation and disconnectedness. This achievement would have the added benefit of potentially reducing Chinese student experiences with depression, loneliness, and acculturative stress.

Fourth, most U.S. universities with long histories of accepting international students to the student body have active international student affairs departments or international student and scholar service offices. However, staff working in these offices are not always knowledgeable about the particular problems Chinese students encounter after arrival in the U.S., such as the tendency of individuals in emotional distress to hide this from others to avoid shaming the family (Zhang, 2012).

U.S. university counseling services struggling to reach out to Chinese students could mitigate cultural difference in this regard by hiring Chinese personnel or U.S. staff with exceptional Chinese language skills and extensive overseas living experience in China. Having an understanding of the acculturation and enculturation levels of Chinese international students will enable university counselors to determine the best treatment plan for each student. Acculturation, as discussed earlier in this chapter, is the process of becoming cognizant of the effect U.S. culture and society is having on one's experiences in the U.S., while enculturation is defined as retention of one's ethnic or home culture. University counseling services may also play a role in supporting Chinese student populations by considering the idea of building support groups for those students who wish to increase their level of enculturation by socializing with other Chinese international students, or by encouraging Chinese students with higher levels of acculturation to join domestic student organizations in order to help the students continue to integrate with the campus culture and community.

Finally, orientation and training could be provided to faculty and staff who work with Chinese students in order to provide them with a more comprehensive understanding of Chinese culture and behavioral norms, as well as the importance of maintaining ethnic social connectedness for Chinese students. U.S. faculty could be encouraged to empathize with students who feel the need to enculturate as a way of maintaining ethnic identity while in the United States. In order to promote the psychosocial adjustment of Chinese international students, university departments and offices could offer social events and mentoring programs that encourage social connections with both domestic and international student groups. Through increased mutual understanding, Chinese and American students will both enjoy the benefits of internationalization.

12   U.S. Students Studying in China: A Comparison

As discussed earlier in this chapter, acculturation has become a well-recognized and important area of study (Berry, 1980, 2006; Tadmor, Tetlock, & Peng, 2009). John Berry (2005) suggested that exposure to a new culture often elicits two types of responses, behavioral and psychological. It is the latter emotional response that sometimes leads to acculturative stress. This occasionally culminates in depression or anxiety as an international student struggles with which aspects of the host culture to accept and which aspects of the home culture to let go (ibid).

This acculturative process is similar for U.S. students studying in China. In November 2009, President Obama announced a goal to increase to 100,000 the cumulative number of Americans studying in China over a four-year period. Known as the 100,000 Strong Initiative, it encouraged all types of educational experiences for students in U.S. high schools, colleges, and universities interested in traveling to China (Belyavina, 2013).

Over the past decade, the number of American students studying in China for academic credit has increased at an average of 18 percent per year, from 3,291 students in 2000 to 15,647 in 2010–2011 (IIE, 2012). However, in contrast to most Chinese students studying in the U.S., a large percentage of American students traveling to China go abroad on shorter, not-for-credit programs such as study tours, internships, and volunteering (Belyavina, 2013).

Between October 2011 and September 2012, the Institute of International Education (IIE) conducted a study with support from the Ford Foundation in Beijing. The study was designed to more comprehensively determine the number of U.S. students studying in China and what type of educational pursuits the students were undertaking while they were there. The study revealed that the majority of U.S. post-secondary students studying in China are undergraduates, comprising more than 76 percent of the total number of American students in China, while 21 percent were graduate students and just over three percent of students held associate degrees or were non-degree seeking students (IIE, 2012). More than 58 percent of the students were participating in study abroad activities and earning academic credit from their universities in the U.S. Those students in China pursuing not-for-credit activities were primarily immersed in educational study tours and Chinese language classes. A small number of students, estimated at about nine percent, were pursuing full degrees in China (bachelor, master, or doctoral level). This is in contrast to Chinese students in the U.S., where the number of graduate students has overtaken the number of undergraduates (Fischer, 2014).

According to China's education ministry, 21,975 American students studied in China in 2015. However, increasing the number of American students studying in China is only one part of the mandate of the 100,000 Strong Initiative. The Initiative also aims to increase the diversity of American students studying in China. The generally homogenous nature of Chinese students in the U.S. may reflect the population back home in China. However, according to U.S.-China Strong Foundation president Carola McGiffert, the typical U.S. student studying abroad is an undergraduate female student from an upper socioeconomic status, which hardly reflects the diversity of the U.S. student population. Indeed, one of the goals of the 100,000 Strong Initiative is to diversify the student population studying in China (Belyavina, 2013).

In 2014, the initial goal of seeing 100,000 American students study abroad in China was surpassed (U.S.-China Strong Foundation, 2015). Language and social adjustment challenges of international students in China are apparent (Baohua & Watkins, 2006; Liu, 2010). China, as a traditionally high-context culture, may pose many additional challenges to U.S. international students than may the low-context cultures of western countries, such as England or Australia. This and other acculturative stressors demonstrate a clear need for Chinese universities to provide resources that enable their international students from the west to be successful in their academic pursuits. Studies have indicated that factors such as linguistic competence, social support networks, understanding of the host culture, previous international experience, and managing expectations of the host culture all contribute to greater satisfaction and better acculturation while abroad (Castro, 2003).

Large-scale, long-term studies on the adjustment of American students studying at Chinese university campuses are virtually non-existent at this moment in time. Future studies are likely, given China's status as the fifth largest recipient of overseas higher education students, hosting 7% of the total number of international students in the higher education market (Organization for Economic Cooperation & Development, 2010). One study that has been published reports on the affective variables of studying Chinese in China as a second language student and the sociocultural/academic adaptation of the international students described in the study. Masgoret and Ward (2006) created a model of the intertwining relationships between target language proficiency, ability to communicate with native speakers, satisfactory intercultural interactions, and sociocultural adaptation. They found that the core components of an international student's sociocultural adaptation were language proficiency and ability to express oneself, supported by satisfactory intercultural interaction (Masgoret & Ward, 2006). Ward (2004) concluded that competence in the target language facilitated better social support and interpersonal relationships, which, in turn, help with adaptation.

Several studies have shown that sociocultural adaptation improves with time spent in the host country (Ward et al., 1998; Senyshyn, Warford, & Zhan, 2000; Yu & Watkins, 2008). Yu and Watkins (2008) conducted a study of international students studying Chinese at a Chinese university and discovered that students in their second year reported less integration and higher anxiety about language proficiency among all of the study participants, who ranged from year one to year four. Past research (Brown, 1980; Lysgaard, 1955) has indicated that acculturation in second language acquisition follows a u-curve that begins with excitement, moves into culture shock, gradually becomes a recovery, and results in either assimilation or adaptation. Based on this theory, Yu and Watkins' study seems to indicate that year 2 students would be located approximately around the stage of gradual recovery and that the longer they remain in China, the more assimilated or adapted to the culture they will become.

Yu and Watkins' study was conducted at Beijing Language and Culture University (BLCU). BLCU is considered a key university in China, as it is host to the largest number of international students majoring in Chinese. Data was collected during two sessions over a nine-month period of time. In each session, students were required to complete the same questionnaire, which had been translated into Chinese. A total of 90 students participated in the study ranging in age from 18 to 41. They came from Europe, Asia, the Middle East, and Africa. The survey consisted of questions related to age of arrival, length of residence, local friendship networks, and perceived cultural distance. Additionally, the survey requested information about affective variables, such as attitudes towards Chinese culture, attitudes toward learning Chinese, desire to learn Chinese, Chinese class anxiety, Chinese use anxiety, interest in foreign languages, instrumental orientation, integrative orientation, and motivational intensity.

Yu and Watkins' findings suggest that an individual student's integrative motivation is an important factor in the process of acculturation. This finding suggests integrative motivation is positively correlated with sociocultural adaptation because students who are integratively motivated may harbor longer desires and interests in identifying with the host country population, which likely contributes to better sociocultural adaptation in the long term. In addition, the impact of perceived cultural distance was discovered to decrease as time goes on. The researchers were surprised to learn that length of residence was negatively correlated with academic adaptation, which suggests that the longer the students in the survey had been in China, the lower the level of academic adaptation they reported at both the beginning and the end of the second year of study. Yu and Watkins hypothesized that this could be due to the following explanation. Previous studies (e.g. Senyshyn, Warford, & Zhan, 2000) revealed that Year 2 for international students in China may be a critical point in their acculturative journeys. If students who have been in China for 3–4 years are placed in a Year 2 level language course, they may become frustrated with their Chinese studies and even depressed as a result of not coping well in the language environment. In such a situation, these feelings may lead to withdrawal from their peer group and teachers (Yu & Watkins, 2008). The results of this study suggest that academic adaptation may be regarded as a contributing factor to the acculturative process. For this reason, Chinese universities may consider investing in language partner programming or other academic resources to help their international students with language proficiency.

The behavior and attitudes of international students in China (and other locales) are often misinterpreted by their universities (Andrade, 2006). Chinese university administrators should try to gain a deeper understanding of their international students' academic, sociocultural, and psychological challenges (Roberson et al., 2000). For example, Chinese administrators may underestimate the challenges a student is experiencing in sociocultural or academic situations, or may not be fully prepared to teach a student whose formative years were spent in a very different academic environment. Universities may need to develop systematic training programs to equip faculty and staff with the skills and understanding needed to help international students in China succeed in both their academic and social pursuits.

One way to aid students in sociocultural adjustment would be to pair international students with local host students, who can show their international buddy how to handle routine matters, such as going to the bank, or attend an extracurricular activity together, such as a campus variety show. Peer support networks may provide an important step in providing international students with sociocultural awareness and an increased understanding of their host institution and country.

13   Conclusion

Cross-cultural living and experiences are exciting, but also challenging. The need for constant adaptation to a series of continual changes can be stressful.

In addition to adjusting to a new physical environment, international students, whether in the United States or China, must also undergo psychological adjustments. This chapter has explored the acculturative stressors and associated impact on mental health of Chinese students studying in the U.S., as well as a brief comparison of U.S. students and their acculturative experiences in China. Based on findings in both published and unpublished studies, the author has provided some practical suggestions for educators and professional to help Chinese and U.S. international students to go through the acculturative process and to enhance the services and programs universities offer to their international students.

Although educators and researchers are gaining an increasing understanding of the effect intercultural contact and acculturation has on the mental health of international students, much remains to be further explored and monitored by research over the coming years. This is especially true for American students studying in China. Thus far, published research has provided some insights into how individual student motivation has played a role in students' adjustment to a new country and culture. However, there is a lack of multilevel studies that integrate social and individual characteristics in understanding acculturation and its effect on mental health. Ideally, such research should be both longitudinal and comparative. Only longitudinal research can provide a thorough representation of the integration between the cultural and psychological changes that occur during acculturation, while only comparative research can provide a global landscape of data from which to learn. Only when sufficient information is available in these forms will we be able to provide a comprehensive picture of the acculturation experience and its effects on mental health.

References

Andrade, M. S. (2006). International students in English-speaking universities. *Journal of Research in International Education, 5*(2), 131–154.

Barton, D., Chen, Y., & Jin, A. (2013, June). Mapping China's middle class. *McKinsey Quarterly*. Retrieved from http://www.mckinsey.com/industries/retail/our-insights/mapping-chinas-middle-class

Belyavina, R. (2013). *U.S. students in China: Meeting the goals of the 100,000 strong initiative: A pilot study on U.S. student participation in education abroad activities in China*. New York, NY: Institute of International Education (IIE). Retrieved from https://www.iie.org/Research-and-Insights/Publications/US-Students-in-China

Berry, J. W. (1980). Acculturation as varieties of adaptation. In A. M. Padilla (Ed.), *Acculturation: Theory, models and some new findings* (pp. 9–25). Boulder, CO: Westview.

Berry, J. W. (1997). Immigration, acculturation, and adaptation. *Applied Psychology: An International Review, 46*, 5–24. doi:10.1080/026999497378467

Berry, J. W. (2005). Acculturation: Living successfully in two cultures. *International Journal of Intercultural Relations, 29*, 697–712.

Berry, J. W. (2006). Contexts of acculturation. In D. L. Sam & J. W. Berry (Eds.), *The Cambridge handbook of acculturation psychology* (Cambridge handbooks in psychology) (pp. 27–42). Cambridge: Cambridge University Press.

Brandt, L., & Rawski, G. T. (2008). China's great economic transformation. In L. Brandt & G. T. Rawski (Eds.), *China's great economic transformation* (pp. 1–26). Cambridge: Cambridge University Press.

Brown, H. (1980). The optimal distance model of second language acquisition. *TESOL Quarterly, 14*(2), 157–164.

Castro, V. S. (2003). *Acculturation and psychological adaptation.* Westport, CT: Greenwood Press.

Cemalcilar, Z., & Falbo, T. (2008). A longitudinal study of the adaptation of international students in the United States. *Journal of Cross-Cultural Psychology, 39*(6), 799–804.

Chen, H., & Hu, M. Y. (2002). An analysis of determinants of entry mode and its impact on performance. *International Business Review, 11*(2), 193–210.

Chen, J., Liu, L., Zhao, X., & Yeung, A. (2015). Chinese international students: An emerging mental health crisis. *Journal of the American Academy of Child and Adolescent Psychiatry, 54*(11), 879–880.

Chong, J., & Razek, N. (2014). Feeling welcome with no "buts": Chinese student engagement in residence life. *Academy of Educational Leadership Journal, 18*(3), 137–149.

Cox, K., & Yamaguchi, S. (2010). Japanese graduate nursing students' perceptions of the teaching performance of an intercultural teacher. *Nursing Education Perspectives, 31*(3), 156–159.

Deng, X. P. (1984, June 30). Building socialism with a specifically Chinese character. *People's Daily.* Retrieved June 23, 1999, from http://english.peopledaily.com.cn/dengxp/vol3/text/c1220.html

Dong, S. (2015, September 7). Chinese students heading to U.S. for college face tough transition. *NBC News.* Retrieved from http://www.nbcnews.com/news/world/chinese-students-heading-u-s-college-face-tough-transition-n419436

Du, Y., & Wei, M. F. (2015). Acculturation, enculturation, social connectedness, and subjective well-being among Chinese international students. *The Counseling Psychologist, 43*(2), 299–325.

Fischer, K. (2014, November 30). Chinese students lead foreign surge at U.S. colleges. *The New York Times.* Retrieved from http://www.nytimes.com/2014/12/01/education/chinese-students-lead-foreign-surge-at-us-colleges.html

Han, X., Han, X., Luo, Q., Jacobs, M., & Jean-Baptiste, M. (2013). Report of a mental health survey among Chinese international students at Yale University. *Journal of American College Health, 61*, 1–8.

Haynie, D. (2013, November 11). U.S. sees record number of international college students. *U.S. News and World Report*. Retrieved from http://www.usnews.com/education/best-colleges/articles/2013/11/11/us-sees-record-number-of-international-college-students

Heins, K. (2015). *Key experiences in the adjustment of academically successful Chinese undergraduate international students at the University of Minnesota: A qualitative study* (Unpublished doctoral dissertation). University of Minnesota, Minneapolis, MN.

Huang, J. (2004). Voices from Chinese students: Professors' use of English affects academic listening. *College Student Journal, 38*(2), 212–223.

Huang, J., & Brown, K. (2009). Cultural factors affecting Chinese ESL students' academic learning. *Education, 129*(4), 643–653.

Huang, J., & Rinaldo, V. (2009). Factors affecting Chinese graduate students' cross-cultural learning. *International Journal of Applied Educational Studies, 4*(1), 1–13.

ICEF Monitor. (2015). *Chinese enrolment in the U.S. shifting increasingly to undergraduate studies* [Data file]. Retrieved October 10, 2016, from http://monitor.icef.com/2015/05/chinese-enrolment-in-the-us-shifting-increasingly-to-undergraduate-studies/

Institute of International Education (IIE). (2012). *Open doors 2012: Report on international educational exchange*. New York, NY: Institute of International Education.

Institute of International Education (IIE). (2014). *Open doors 2014: International students in the United States and study abroad by American students are at all-time high* [Data file]. Retrieved from http://www.iie.org/Who-We-Are/News-and-Events/Press-Center/Press-Releases/2014/2014-11-17-Open-Doors-Data

Liu, J. J. (2010). Assessing students' language proficiency: A new model of study abroad program in China. *Journal of Studies in International Education, 14*(5), 528–544.

Lysgaard, S. (1955). Adjustment in a foreign society: Norwegian fulbright grantees visiting the United States. *International Social Science Bulletin, 7*(1), 45–51.

Masgoret, A. M., & Ward, C. (2006). Culture learning approach to adaptation. In D. L. Sam & J. W. Berry (Eds.), *The Cambridge handbook of acculturation psychology* (Cambridge handbooks in psychology) (pp. 58–77). Cambridge: Cambridge University Press.

McKinsey China. (2013). *The $250 billion question: Can China close the skills gap?* [Data file]. Retrieved December 4, 2016, from http://www.mckinseychina.com/the-250-billion-question-can-china-close-the-skills-gap/

Organization for Economic Cooperation & Development (OECD). (2010). *Education at a glance 2010*. Paris: OECD Publishing.

Phinney, J. (2003). Ethnic identity and acculturation. In K. M. Chun, P. B. Organista, & G. Marin (Eds.), *Acculturation: Advances in theory, measurement, and applied research* (pp. 63–81). Washington, DC: American Psychological Association.

Poyrazli, S., Kavanaugh, P. R., Baker, A., & Al-Timimi, N. (2004). Social support and demographic correlates of acculturative stress in international students. *Journal of College Counseling, 7*, 73–82. doi:10.1002/j.2161-1882.2004.tb00261.x

Roberson, M., Line, M., Jones, S., & Thomas, S. (2000). International students, learning environments, and perceptions: A case study using the Delphi technique. *Higher Education Research & Development, 19*(1), 89–101.

Roy, S. (2013). Educating Chinese, Japanese, and Korean international students: Recommendations to American professors. *Journal of International Students, 3*(1), 10–16.

Samovar, L., & Porter, R. (1997). *Intercultural communication: A reader* (8th ed.). Belmont, CA: Wadsworth Publishing Company.

Senyshyn, R. M., Warford, M. K., & Zhan, J. (2000). Issues of adjustment to higher education: International students' perspectives. *International Education, 27*, 5–21.

Slaney, R. B., Rice, K. G., Mobley, M., Trippi, J., & Ashby, J. S. (2001). The revised almost perfect scale. *Measurement and Evaluation in Counseling and Development, 34*, 130–145.

Sovic, S. (2009). Hi-bye friends and the herd instinct: International and home students in the creative arts. *Higher Education, 58*(6), 747–761.

Stevens, S. (2012, March). Chinese students in undergraduate programs: Understanding and overcoming the challenges. *Wrap Up: A Resource for the Recruitment, Admissions, and Preparation Knowledge, 9*(1). Retrieved from http://www.nafsa.org/ .../Chinese%20Students%20 in%20Undergraduate%20Programs.pdf

Tadmor, C. T., Tetlock, P. E., & Peng, K. (2009). Acculturation strategies and integrative complexity: The cognitive implications of biculturalism. *Journal of Cross-Cultural Psychology, 40*(1), 105–139.

Ting-Toomey, S. (1999). *Communicating across cultures*. New York, NY: The Guilford Press.

Tong, V. (2014). Understanding the acculturation experience of Chinese adolescent students: Sociocultural adaptation strategies and a positive bicultural and bilingual identity. *Bilingual Research Journal: The Journal of the National Association for Bilingual Education, 37*(1), 83–100.

U.S.-China Strong Foundation. (2017). *100,000 strong*. Washington, DC: U.S.-China Strong Foundation. Retrieved from http://100kstrong.org/initiatives/100k-strong/

U.S. Citizenship and Immigration Services. (2016). *Students and employment*. Retrieved December 9, 2016, from https://www.uscis.gov/working-united-states/students-and-exchange-visitors/students-and-employment

Walters, K., & Auton-Cuff, F. (2009). A story to tell: the identity development of women growing up as third culture kids. *Mental Health, Religion & Culture, 12*(7), 755–772.

Wang, K., Heppner, P. P., Fu, C. C., Zhao, R., Li, F., & Chuang, C. C. (2012). Profiles of acculturative adjustment patterns among Chinese international students. *Journal of Counseling Psychology, 59*(3), 424–436.

Ward, C. (2004). Psychological theories of culture contact and their implications for intercultural training. In D. Landis, J. Bennet, & M. Bennet (Eds.), *Handbook of intercultural training* (3rd ed., pp. 185–216). Thousand Oaks, CA: Sage Publications.

Ward, C., Okura, Y., Kennedy, A., & Kojima, T. (1998). The U-curve on trial: A longitudinal study of psychological and sociocultural adjustment during cross-cultural transition. *International Journal of Intercultural Relations, 22*(3), 277–291.

Wei, M., Heppner, P. P., Mallen, M. J., Ku, T. Y., Liao, Y. H., & Wu, T. F. (2007). Acculturative stress, perfectionism, years in the United States, and depression among Chinese international students. *Journal of Counseling Psychology, 54*, 385–394.

Wei, M. F., Liao, K. Y. H., Heppner, P. P., Chao, R. C. L., & Ku, T. Y. (2011). Forbearance coping, identification with heritage culture, acculturative stress, and psychological distress among Chinese international students. *Journal of Counseling Psychology, 59*(1), 97–106.

World Bank. (2015). *China overview.* Washington, DC: World Bank Group. Retrieved April 24, 2015, from http://www.worldbank.org/en/country/china/overview

Yan, K. (2008). *Chinese international students' stressors and coping strategies in the United States* (Unpublished doctoral dissertation). Arizona State University, Phoenix, AZ.

Yan, K., & Berliner, D. C. (2009). Chinese international students' academic stressors in the United States. *College Student Journal, 43*, 939–960.

Yan, K., & Berliner, D. C. (2011). An examination of individual level factors in stress and coping processes: Perspectives of Chinese international students in the United States. *Journal of College Student Development, 52*(5), 523–542.

Yan, K., & Berliner, D. C. (2013). Chinese international students' personal and sociocultural stressors in the United States. *Journal of College Student Development, 54*(1), 62–84.

Yeh, C., & Inose, M. (2003). International students' reported English fluency, social support satisfaction, and social connectedness as predictors of acculturative stress. *Counselling Psychology Quarterly, 16*(1), 15–28.

Yi, J. K., Lin, G. J.-C., & Yuko, K. (2003). Utilization of counseling services by international students. *Journal of Instructional Psychology, 30*, 333–342.

Ying, Y.-W., & Han, M. (2006). The contribution of personality, acculturative stressors, and social affiliation to adjustment: A longitudinal study of Taiwanese students in the United States. *International Journal of Intercultural Relations, 30*, 623–635.

Yu, B. (2010). Learning Chinese abroad: The role of language attitudes and motivation in the adaptation of international students in China. *Journal of Multilingual and Multicultural Development, 31*(3), 301–321.

Yu, B., & Watkins, D. (2006). *Relationships among motivation, cross-cultural adaptation and Chinese language achievement: An investigation of international students studying Chinese in the universities of the PRC.* Paper presented at the Asia-Pacific Educational Research Association (APERA) conference, Hong Kong, 2006. Hong Kong: Hong Kong University.

Yu, B., & Watkins, D. (2008). Motivational and cultural correlates of second language acquisition: An investigation of international students in the universities of the people's republic of China. *Australian Review of Applied Linguistics, 31*(2), 17–22.

Yuan, W. L. (2011). Academic and cultural experiences of Chinese students at an American university: A qualitative study. *Intercultural Communication Studies,* 20(1), 141–157.

Zhang, Y. (2012). *An examination of acculturative stress, perceived social support and depression among Chinese international students* (Unpublished master's thesis). Syracuse University, Syracuse, NY.

Zhang, Y. B., Lin, M. C., Nonaka, A., & Beom, K. (2005). Harmony, hierarchy and conservatism: A cross-cultural comparison of Confucian values in China, Korea, Japan, and Taiwan. *Communication Research Report,* 22(2), 107–115. doi:10.1080/00036810500130539

About the Author

Merritt Huang is Program Manager for the Chinese Overseas Flagship Program at the American Councils for International Education. Prior to her position at ACIE, she served as the Associate Director of the Global Executive MBA program at the University of Minnesota. Previously, she managed and led professional development training programs for Chinese university administrators and government officials at the University of Minnesota's China Center. Prior to her work at the China Center, she lived and worked in Beijing, China for four years developing marketing and communications strategies for a Chinese firm and implementing nonprofit foundation and academic initiatives. During this time, she worked with the Chinese Academy of Social Sciences academic press translating white papers on legal, educational, and social development in China from Chinese to English.

Merritt earned an M.A. in Organizational Leadership and Policy Development with a specialization in Comparative and International Development Education from the University of Minnesota. She holds a B.A. in Mandarin Chinese from the University of Wisconsin-Madison.

CHAPTER 12

Conclusions and Way Forward

Christopher J. Johnstone

Drawing together the diverse chapters of this book is no small task. However, three key themes appear to be present in the book and may provide guidance for international education leaders. First, there appears to be a strong desire for continued collaboration between China and the U.S. in the area of higher education partnership. Each of the chapters identified challenges faced in creating sustainable collaboration, but also highlighted the importance of ongoing dialogue in order to find workable solutions for both partners.

Second, layers of culture appear to be at work and a core tendency of partnership. Interpersonal communication was cited in several chapters as a key factor in the development of partnerships. However, institutional culture also appeared to be an important predictor. Examples from NYU Shanghai, SUNY Cortland, University of Hawai'i and University of Minnesota demonstrate that universities that have common missions (research focus, teacher development, global education focus, sport, etc.) may have immediate starting points for forging partnerships. This book provides preliminary information on this concept, but further exploration of how similar institutions working across national boundaries collaborate will help move the field of international education forward.

Finally, the chapters in this book highlighted differences in national cultures related to higher education (Johnstone & Proctor, 2017). There is tremendous contrast between the highly centralized, party-driven higher education culture in China and the highly-decentralized, market-driven higher education culture in the U.S. Recognition of these differences and willingness to work across national higher education culture requires both skilled practitioners and informants within institutions who understand both systems well.

The way forward for international education partnerships between Chinese and U.S. higher education appears clear. As a first step, more research is needed on how to evaluate partnerships. The chapters featured in this book provided examples of partnerships that were deemed successful by authors. The qualitative reporting on how success was perceived provides researchers with clues about what outcomes indicators may be important for such variables. The field of international education, and its component feature (partnerships) may benefit from tools that evaluate partnerships on indicators developed

© KONINKLIJKE BRILL NV, LEIDEN, 2018 | DOI 10.1163/9789004368361_012

by both parties. Such practice is already in place in other fields that involve U.S. domestic higher education partnerships (such as community-based service learning) (see Clayton, Bringle, Senor, Huq, & Morrison, 2010). Further, emerging research on mutuality models for international partnerships are promising and may be used as conceptual models for better understanding partnerships (see Mwangi, 2017).

In addition to new research agendas related to evaluation of partnerships, a perusal of the chapters in this book also indicate that more information is needed on smaller, regional universities. The vast majority of partnerships examined in this book took place in large, research-driven universities. Future books in this series may feature technical institutions, more universities with regional foci, and universities in traditionally economically disadvantaged regions of the two countries. Our initial foray into the *Rise of Higher Education Partnerships* demonstrates a large-school bias, and could be followed up with additional research on more diverse institutions.

In any case, we as an editorial team would like to thank the chapter authors for their contributions as well as our editorial assistants Laura Seithers and Yilin Wei. Understanding how and why partnerships work from the perspectives of practitioners and scholars is vital in a time when partnership and cooperation is a core feature of international education plans of universities. If there is one final summative statement we can make, it is that no partnership is the same. Cultural, communicative, institutional, and governmental dynamics all play into the development and eventual outcomes of international partnerships between Chinese and U.S. institutions. These factors are experienced differently by individuals and institutions, meaning that there may never be a blueprint for success in every situation. Rather, there is a constant need in our field to tell the stories of those who have and have not succeeded (in their own eyes), and garner lessons that may transfer to other situations only after reflection upon context and culture.

References

Clayton, P. H., Bringle, R. G., Senor, B., Huq, J., & Morrison, M. (2010). Differentiating and assessing relationships in service-learning and civic engagement: Exploitative, transactional, or transformational. *Michigan Journal of Community Service Learning, 16*(2), 5–22.

Johnstone, C. J., & Proctor, D. (2017). Aligning institutional and national contexts with internationalization efforts. *Innovative Higher Education, 43*(1), 5–16.

Mwangi, C. A. G. (2017). Partner positioning: Examining international higher education partnerships through a mutuality lens. *The Review of Higher Education, 41*(1), 33–60.

About the Author

Christopher J. Johnstone is an Assistant Professor in the Department of Organizational Leadership, Policy, and Development. His research areas include internationalization of higher education and inclusive education in schools and universities. He serves as the coordinator of his department's Leadership in International and Intercultural Education PhD program and has written on international education topics such as international student integration, institutional culture as it relates to internationalization, and international partnerships. Prior to his faculty role, Johnstone served as Director of International Initiatives and Relations at the University of Minnesota's College of Education and Human Development.

www.ingramcontent.com/pod-product-compliance
Lightning Source LLC
Chambersburg PA
CBHW072120020426

42334CB00018B/1656